OpenGL Game Development By Example

Design and code your own 2D and 3D games efficiently using OpenGL and C++

Robert Madsen

Stephen Madsen

[PACKT] PUBLISHING

open source*
community experience distilled

BIRMINGHAM - MUMBAI

D1211171

OpenGL Game Development By Example

First published: March 2016

Production reference: 1010316

Published by Packt Publishing Ltd.
Livery Place
35 Livery Street
Birmingham B3 2PB, UK.

ISBN 978-1-78328-819-9

www.packtpub.com

Credits

Authors
Robert Madsen
Stephen Madsen

Reviewers
Artemis Tsouflidou
Simon W. J. Vanhauwaert
Pantelis Lekakis

Commissioning Editor
Julian Ursell

Acquisition Editor
Shaon Basu

Content Development Editor
Siddhesh Salvi

Technical Editor
Parag Topre

Copy Editor
Priyanka Ravi

Project Coordinator
Paushali Desai

Proofreader
Safis Editing

Indexer
Monica Ajmera Mehta

Graphics
Disha Haria

Production Coordinator
Nilesh Mohite

Cover Work
Nilesh Mohite

About the Authors

Robert Madsen is an accomplished game programmer, with dozens of published games to his credit. He started programming in 1979, and he has been a programmer for all of his professional life. He entered the game industry in 2004, and he founded SynapticSwitch, LLC in 2010. As studio director, he continues to code while also managing the broader needs of an independent game development studio.

Stephen Madsen completed his degree in game development from Full Sail Real World Education in 2007, beginning his first job as a game programmer in 2008. He then joined SynapticSwitch, LLC as the lead software engineer in 2012. He has developed and published many titles on the mobile, console, and personal computer platforms with OpenGL being the foundational rendering technology for most of these platforms.

About the Reviewers

Artemis Tsouflidou is a game developer based in London, and she has experience in gameplay programming. She studied computer engineering at the University of Thessaly in Greece, and she continued her studies at Goldsmiths University where she earned a master's degree in computer games. She is interested in programming and game development.

Simon W. J. Vanhauwaert is a Belgian game development programmer. He graduated in digital arts and entertainment, and he is currently professionally employed in the UK.

Pantelis Lekakis has been in the game industry for 4 years now, and he has been actively programming and developing his own projects since 2002.

His experience lies in rendering and game engines, and he has worked with various versions of Direct3D and OpenGL.

www.PacktPub.com

Support files, eBooks, discount offers, and more

For support files and downloads related to your book, please visit www.PacktPub.com.

Did you know that Packt offers eBook versions of every book published, with PDF and ePub files available? You can upgrade to the eBook version at www.PacktPub.com and as a print book customer, you are entitled to a discount on the eBook copy. Get in touch with us at service@packtpub.com for more details.

At www.PacktPub.com, you can also read a collection of free technical articles, sign up for a range of free newsletters and receive exclusive discounts and offers on Packt books and eBooks.

https://www2.packtpub.com/books/subscription/packtlib

Do you need instant solutions to your IT questions? PacktLib is Packt's online digital book library. Here, you can search, access, and read Packt's entire library of books.

Why subscribe?

- Fully searchable across every book published by Packt
- Copy and paste, print, and bookmark content
- On demand and accessible via a web browser

Free access for Packt account holders

If you have an account with Packt at www.PacktPub.com, you can use this to access PacktLib today and view 9 entirely free books. Simply use your login credentials for immediate access.

Table of Contents

Preface   **ix**

Chapter 1: Building the Foundation   **1**

Introducing the development environment   **1**

A quick look at Visual Studio   3

Start screen   3

The Solution Explorer panel   4

The Standard Toolbar panel   4

The code window   5

The output window   6

Starting your project   6

The game loop   **7**

The game structure   7

Initialization   8

The game loop   8

Shutdown   9

Creating the game structure   9

Port of access   11

The Windows message loop   11

Introducing OpenGL   **13**

What is OpenGL?   13

The other GL   14

Downloading OpenGL   14

Adding OpenGL to the project   15

Linking to the OpenGL library   15

Summary   **17**

Chapter 2: Your Point of View   **19**

Plotting your revenge   **20**

The OpenGL coordinate system   20

Making your point   21

Understanding the code   23

Running the program	26
Stretching your point	27
Getting primitive	29
A triangle by any other name	29
A primitive example	30
From triangles to models	32
Introducing textures	**33**
Using textures to fill the triangles	33
A matter of reference	35
Hanging out in the quad	36
Coding the quad	37
Rendering a texture	38
Loading the texture	38
Texture wrapping	39
Creating a textured quad	42
Putting the pieces together	**43**
Summary	**44**
Chapter 3: A Matter of Character	**45**
Spritely speaking	**45**
Sprites versus non-sprites	46
Flipbook animation	46
Framed animation	47
Creating sprites	**47**
Working with PNGs	47
Linking to the SOIL library	50
Including the SOIL header file	51
Opening an image file	51
Coding a sprite class	52
Creating sprite frames	58
Saving each frame	59
Loading a sprite from individual textures	59
Creating a sprite sheet	60
Loading a sprite sheet	61
Loading our sprites	61
Rendering	**65**
Adding a render to the game loop	65
Implementing the main Render function	66
Implementing Render in the Sprite class	67
UV mapping	69
One more detail	70
A moving example	**70**
Adding update to the game loop	71
Implementing the main Update call	71

Implementing Update in the Sprite class 72
Character movement 73
Using delta time 73
Calculating delta time 74
Flipping 75
Scrolling the background 76
Using an atlas **77**
Summary **78**
Chapter 4: Control Freak **79**
A penny for your input **79**
The keyboard input 80
Using the mouse 80
Touch 81
Other inputs 81
Someone is listening **82**
The WndProc event listener 82
Handling the message queue 84
Handling mouse and keyboard inputs 85
Creating the Input class 86
Virtual key codes 87
Querying for input 88
Implementing the Input class 89
Adding input to the game loop 90
Processing our input 91
Changes to the Sprite class 94
Graphical User Interface **95**
Creating a button 95
Enhancing the Input class 95
Adding UI elements to the list 96
Checking each UI element 97
Pushing your buttons 98
Adding our pauseButton 99
State management **100**
Creating a state manager 101
Pausing the game 101
Summary **104**
Chapter 5: Hit and Run **105**
Out of bounds! **105**
Getting anchored 106
Collision rectangles 110

Embedding	113
Fixing the background	115
Collideables	**116**
Ready to score	116
A friend indeed	117
Time to spawn	117
Circular collision detection	**120**
The Pythagorean Theorem	121
Adding the circular collision code	122
Why use circular collision detection?	124
Wiring in the collision detection	125
Rectangular collision detection	**127**
The enemy within	127
Spawning the enemy	127
Adding the rectangular collision code	130
Wiring continued	132
Summary	**132**
Chapter 6: Polishing the Silver	**133**
The state of the game	**134**
State machines	135
Why do we need a state machine?	135
Planning for state	137
Defining the new state	139
Implementing the state machine	139
Making a splash	**143**
Creating the splash screen	143
Defining the splash screen	144
Loading our resources	145
What's on the menu?	**147**
Creating the menu	147
Defining the menu buttons	148
Getting some credit	**151**
Creating the credits screen	151
Getting back to the main menu	152
Working with fonts	**154**
Creating the font	154
Drawing text	155
Wiring in the font support	156
Level up!	**157**
Displaying the score	157

Game progression	158
Defining game levels	159
Game stats	160
The next level screen	161
Continuing the game	161
Game over	**162**
The game over screen	163
Replaying the game	164
Summary	**166**
Chapter 7: Audio Adrenaline	**167**
Bits and bytes	**168**
A sound by any other name	168
Making noise	169
Revving up your engine	**171**
Accessing the FMOD .dll file	172
Linking to the library	172
Point to the include files	175
Initializing FMOD	**177**
Virtual channels	178
Channel priority	178
Bleeps and bloops	**179**
Sound effects	179
Setting up the sounds	180
Playing sounds	182
UI feedback	185
The sound of music	**187**
Cleaning up the house	**188**
Release sprites	188
Release input	189
Releasing fonts	190
Releasing audio	190
Summary	**190**
Chapter 8: Expanding Your Horizons	**191**
Into the third dimension!	**191**
Simulating 3D	192
Real 3D	193
3D Coordinate Systems	194
The camera	**196**
Remember those home movies?	196
Steady as she goes!	197

The viewport 197
Entering the matrix **199**
Vectors 199
Combining vectors 200
Identity matrix 202
Coding in 3D **202**
Creating the project 202
Retrieving OpenGL files 204
Linking projects to OpenGL libraries 204
Setting up the OpenGL window **205**
Including header files 206
Defining global variables 206
Creating a function to create the OpenGL window 207
Sizing the OpenGL window 207
Initializing the OpenGL window 209
Creating a function to remove the OpenGL window 210
Creating the OpenGL window 211
Creating the Windows event handler 215
The Game loop 216
The finale 217
Summary **218**
Chapter 9: Super Models **219**
New Space **220**
A computer in a computer **220**
Drawing your weapons **223**
Getting primitive 223
Drawing primitives 224
Making your point 226
Gl_Points 226
Getting in line 226
Gl_Lines 226
Gl_Line_Strip 226
Gl_Line_Loop 227
Triangulation 227
Gl_Triangles 228
Gl_Triangle_Strip 228
Gl_Triangle_Fan 228
Being square 229
Gl_Quads 229
Gl_Quad_Strip 229
Saving face 229
Back to Egypt 230

A modeling career **231**
Blending in 231
Blender overview 232
Building your spaceship 232
Exporting the object 235
Getting loaded 236
Summary **240**

Chapter 10: Expanding Space **241**
Creation 101 **241**
Preparing the project 242
Loading game objects 243
The Model class header 244
Implementing the Model class 246
Modifying the game code 253
Taking control **258**
Implementing input 258
Asteroid slalom **261**
Setting up collision detection 261
Turning on collision 264
Summary **265**

Chapter 11: Heads Up **267**
Mixing things up **267**
The saving state 269
Push and pop 269
Two state rendering 273
A matter of state **277**
Adding the state machine 277
Getting ready for a splash 278
Creating the user interface **280**
Defining the text system 281
Defining textures 283
Wiring in render, update, and the game loop 285
Summary **290**

Chapter 12: Conquer the Universe **291**
A fun framework **292**
Setting up the Visual Studio project 292
Setting up the Windows environment 293
Setting up the OpenGL environment 294
Setting up the game loop 294

Texture mapping   **296**
  Loading the texture   297
  Rendering the cube   298
  Mapping operations   301
Let there be light!   **302**
  Defining a light source   303
The skybox   **304**
Advanced topics   **306**
  Game physics   306
  AI   307
The future   **307**
Summary   **307**
Index   **309**

Preface

Welcome to *OpenGL Game Development Blueprints*! We are excited that you chose this book as your guide to both OpenGL and game development. This section will provide you with a brief preview of each chapter, followed by the technologies that are required to complete the work that is presented in the book. Finally, we will discuss the target audience for this book so that you will know whether this book is right for you.

What this book covers

Chapter 1, Building the Foundation, guides you through creating the code framework for the game. Games use a particular structure that is known as the *game loop*. By the end of this chapter, you will understand and have created the game loop for the game as well as initialized the required OpenGL elements.

Chapter 2, Your Point of View, introduces you to the first project in the book—creating a 2D platform game. The first step in this project will be to define the type of view that is required by OpenGL, and render the background of the game.

Chapter 3, A Matter of Character, covers the creation of sprites that move on the screen. 2D frame-based animations are the core of any 2D game, and you will learn how to create simple graphics and render them to the screen.

Chapter 4, Control Freak, teaches you how to build an input system that will allow you to control the main character and other aspects of the game. You will also create a basic user interface that allows you to start the game and navigate to various options.

Chapter 5, Hit and Run, covers collision detection. You will learn how to stop the character from falling through the ground, how to land on objects, and how to detect whether enemies have hit you or have been hit by player weapons. By the end of this chapter, you will be able to play the game for the first time.

Chapter 6, Polishing the Silver, covers the topics that make a game presentable (but are often overlooked by novice developers). You will learn how to implement a scoring system, game over and game won scenarios, and simple level progression. This chapter will conclude the 2D project of the book.

Chapter 7, Audio Adrenaline, guides you through implementing sound effects and music in the game. We will provide links to some audio files that you can use in your game.

Chapter 8, Expanding Your Horizons, will start the second project of the book—a 3D first-person space shooter. At the end of this chapter you will have created a new project, starting the framework for a 3D game.

Chapter 9, Super Models, introduces you to the concepts of 3D art and modeling, and then guides you through the process of loading 3D models into the game environment. Although you will be able try your hand at creating a 3D model, the resources that are required for the game will be provided online.

Chapter 10, Expanding Space, expands on many of the concepts that were covered in the 2D segment of the book and applies them to a 3D world. Movement and collision detection are revamped to take this new dimension into consideration. An input scheme to move in 3D space is implemented. By the end of this chapter, you will be able to control a 3D model in 3D space.

Chapter 11, Heads Up, guides you through creating a 2D user interface on top of the 3D world. You will create a menu system to start and end the game, as well as a heads-up-display (HUD) that shows the score and stats in game. By the end of this chapter, you will have created a playable 3D shooter game.

Chapter 12, Conquer the Universe, introduces you to some of the more advanced concepts that were beyond the scope of the book, and it gives you some direction to advance your skills.

What you need for this book

Each chapter in the book will have exercises that you will need to code. Each exercise is a building block toward creating your first game using OpenGL. It is vitally important that you actually write the code. In our experience, you can't learn any kind of computer programming without actually writing code. Don't just read the book, do the book!

The first chapter of the book will go through the details of setting up a development environment so that you can code the examples in the book. In general, you will need the following:

- **A Windows-based personal computer**: You could use a Mac, but the examples used in the book are based on a Windows 10 operating system.

- **A copy of Visual Studio**: We will show you how to obtain and install this for free in chapter one, or you can go to `http://www.visualstudio.com/downloads/download-visual-studio-vs` right now. Again, you could use another development tool and compiler, but you are on your own to set it up.

- **A 2D image editor program**: We recommend GIMP, which you can download for free at `http://www.gimp.org/`.

- **A 3D modeling program**: We recommend Blender, which you can download for free at `http://www.blender.org/`.

- **An Internet connection**: You could complete the exercises without this, but an Internet connection is very useful for looking up additional resources.

- Some free time and dedication!

That's it! The good news is that as long as you have a personal computer, the technology and tools that are used to create games using OpenGL are completely free!

Who this book is for

If you are reading this book, it is pretty obvious that you are interested in game development. You have either heard of OpenGL or perhaps even used it, and you want to learn more. Finally, you are already a programmer in some computer language or you want to be.

Does this sound like you? Read on!

This book assumes that you have some familiarity with computer programming in the C++ computer language. If you have programmed in some other language, such as C#, Java, JavaScript, or PHP, then you are pretty familiar with the constructs of the C++ language. Nevertheless, if have never programmed in C++ then you may need to brush up on your skills. You can try *Microsoft Visual C++ Windows Applications by Example*, also published by *Packt Publishing*. If you feel comfortable with programming in general, but have not coded in C++, you can look at the free online C++ tutorials at `http://www.cplusplus.com/doc/tutorial/`.

We don't assume that you have any knowledge of OpenGL—that is what this book is going to give you. We start by explaining the basic concepts of OpenGL and move through more advanced concepts by example. As you learn, you will also code, providing you with the opportunity to put what you have learned into practice. This book won't make you an OpenGL expert overnight, but it will give you the foundation to understand and use OpenGL. At the end of this book, we will give you some pointers to other resources that will allow you to learn even more about OpenGL.

We also don't assume that you have any experience developing games. This book is rather unique in that it provides you with a primer to learn OpenGL and a primer to learn game development. There are many books out there that teach OpenGL, but most do so within a more academic or theoretical framework. We felt that it was better to teach you OpenGL while you were using it to create an actual game. Actually, you will code two games: one in 2D, and one in 3D. Two for the price of one!

Conventions

In this book, you will find a number of text styles that distinguish between different kinds of information. Here are some examples of these styles and an explanation of their meaning.

Code words in text, database table names, folder names, filenames, file extensions, pathnames, dummy URLs, user input, and Twitter handles are shown as follows: "As usual, change the middle line in update to call drawQuad."

A block of code is set as follows:

```
void CheckCollisions()
{
  if (player->IntersectsRect(pickup))
  {
    pickup->IsVisible(false);
    pickup->IsActive(false);
    player->SetValue(player->GetValue() + pickup->GetValue());
    pickupSpawnTimer = 0.0f;
  }
}
```

When we wish to draw your attention to a particular part of a code block, the relevant lines or items are set in bold:

```
pause->Update(p_deltaTime);
  resume->Update(p_deltaTime);

  pickup->Update(p_deltaTime);
  SpawnPickup(p_deltaTime);

  CheckCollisions();
}
```

New terms and **important words** are shown in bold. Words that you see on the screen, for example, in menus or dialog boxes, appear in the text like this: "For the **Configuration** drop-down box, make sure you select **All Configurations**."

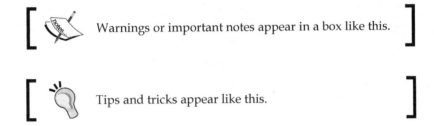

Warnings or important notes appear in a box like this.

Tips and tricks appear like this.

Reader feedback

Feedback from our readers is always welcome. Let us know what you think about this book—what you liked or disliked. Reader feedback is important for us as it helps us develop titles that you will really get the most out of.

To send us general feedback, simply e-mail feedback@packtpub.com, and mention the book's title in the subject of your message.

If there is a topic that you have expertise in and you are interested in either writing or contributing to a book, see our author guide at www.packtpub.com/authors.

Customer support

Now that you are the proud owner of a Packt book, we have a number of things to help you to get the most from your purchase.

Downloading the example code

You can download the example code files from your account at http://www.packtpub.com for all the Packt Publishing books you have purchased. If you purchased this book elsewhere, you can visit http://www.packtpub.com/support and register to have the files e-mailed directly to you.

Errata

Although we have taken every care to ensure the accuracy of our content, mistakes do happen. If you find a mistake in one of our books—maybe a mistake in the text or the code—we would be grateful if you could report this to us. By doing so, you can save other readers from frustration and help us improve subsequent versions of this book. If you find any errata, please report them by visiting http://www.packtpub.com/submit-errata, selecting your book, clicking on the **Errata Submission Form** link, and entering the details of your errata. Once your errata are verified, your submission will be accepted and the errata will be uploaded to our website or added to any list of existing errata under the Errata section of that title.

To view the previously submitted errata, go to https://www.packtpub.com/books/content/support and enter the name of the book in the search field. The required information will appear under the **Errata** section.

Piracy

Piracy of copyrighted material on the Internet is an ongoing problem across all media. At Packt, we take the protection of our copyright and licenses very seriously. If you come across any illegal copies of our works in any form on the Internet, please provide us with the location address or website name immediately so that we can pursue a remedy.

Please contact us at copyright@packtpub.com with a link to the suspected pirated material.

We appreciate your help in protecting our authors and our ability to bring you valuable content.

Questions

If you have a problem with any aspect of this book, you can contact us at questions@packtpub.com, and we will do our best to address the problem.

1
Building the Foundation

Building a game is like building a house. Except this is a crazy house with rooms sticking out everywhere, and at any time someone might decide to add another room just *here*, and remove a room over *there*. You had better have a good foundation!

This chapter will take you through the process of setting up the foundation to build your game. You will learn, how to set up a development environment using Visual Studio. Next, you will set up the game loop, which is the foundation for every game ever created. Finally, you will set up the development environment to use OpenGL as your rendering engine.

Introducing the development environment

The **development environment** is the set of tools that you use to edit, compile, and run your program. There are many development tools out there; some tools are glorified text editors, while others are entire suites of tools that are integrated into a single application. These more advanced suites are known as **Integrated Development Environments (IDEs)**.

Microsoft's Visual Studio is by far the most widely used IDE, and the good news is that you can obtain and use it for free. Go to `https://www.visualstudio.com/en-us/products/visual-studio-express-vs.aspx` and follow the links to download the latest version of **Visual Studio Community**, previously known as **Visual Studio Express**. Visual Studio Community is not a trial version and will not expire. You will probably see trial versions of Visual Studio being offered, so make sure you download the free version of Visual Studio Community.

Visual Studio offers several languages to program in. We will be using C++ throughout this book. When you first use Visual Studio, you may be asked which language you want to set up the development environment for. I recommend that you choose the C++ settings. However, you will still be able to use Visual Studio for C++ even if you choose a different default programming language.

Visual Studio Community 2013 was the current version at the time this book was written. All of the screenshots you see in the book are from that version. It is quite likely that a later version of Visual Studio will have come out by the time you get your hands on this book. The general functionality stays the same from one version to another, so this should not be a problem. If you are using a different version of Visual Studio, then the exact location of some commands may not be the same as in the screenshots in this book.

 Microsoft differentiates between programs written for Windows Desktop and those written for Windows Universal. Ensure that you download Visual Studio Community Express for Desktop.

When you first start Visual Studio, you will be asked for a few options, so I thought I'd cover them here:

- If you are asked which programming language you would like to set up as your default development environment, it really doesn't matter which language you choose. If you think you will be using C++ a lot, then pick C++. If you pick another language as your default you will still be able to code in C++.

- You will be asked to sign into your Microsoft account. If you have ever used MSN, Hotmail, or Windows Messenger, then you already have a Microsoft account. At any rate, if you don't have a Microsoft account you can use your own e-mail address to create one, and it doesn't cost anything.

- You may be asked to set up a developer license for Windows. Just click **I Agree** and it will be done. Again, no charge!

A quick look at Visual Studio

As Visual Studio can do so many things, it may be a bit intimidating the first time you use it. I have been using Visual Studio for over 20 years and there are still parts of it that I have never needed! Let's take a look at the key components, in the following screenshot, that you will use every day:

Start screen

The start screen, as shown in the preceding screenshot, allows you to quickly start a new project or open an existing project. The most recent projects that you have worked with can be quickly accessed from the list of recent projects.

The Solution Explorer panel

The **Solution Explorer** panel allows you to navigate and work with all of the code and other resources in your project. If you do not see the **Solution Explorer** window on your screen, click **View | Solution Explorer**.

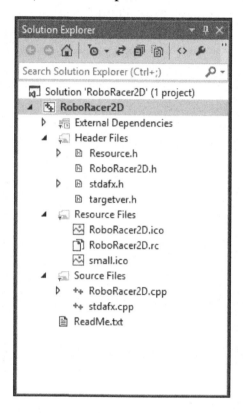

From this window you can:

- Double-click on any item to open it
- Right-click to add existing items to the project
- Right-click to add new items to the project
- Create folders to organize your code

The Standard Toolbar panel

The **Standard Toolbar** panel contains buttons for the most common tasks:

- Save the current file
- Save all modified files

- Undo and Redo
- Run the program

 There are basically two ways to run your program. You can run the program with or without debugging. Debugging mode allows you to set checkpoints that stop the program and let you view the state of variables, and perform other operations while the code is running. If you run the program without debugging, you will not be able to do these things.

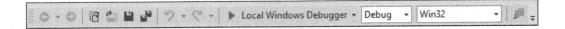

The code window

The center of the IDE is dominated by the code window. This is where you type and edit your code. You can have several code windows open at once. Each code window will add a tab across the top, allowing you to switch from one piece of code to another with a single click:

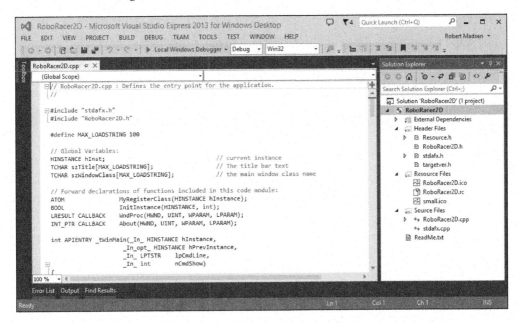

You will notice that the text is color-coded. This allows you to easily see different types of code. For example, the comments in the code in the preceding screenshot are in green, while the C++ objects are in blue. You can also zoom in and out of the code by holding down the *Ctrl* button and using the scroll wheel on the mouse.

The output window

The output window is typically at the bottom of the IDE. This window is where you will look at to see the status of the current run, and where you will find errors when you try to compile run your program.

If you see an error in the output window, you can usually double-click on it, and Visual Studio will take you to the line in code that caused the error:

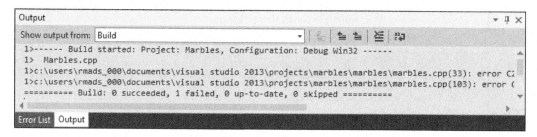

Starting your project

It's time to stop reading and start doing! We are going to use Visual Studio to start our game project.

1. Open Visual Studio and click the **New Project** link in the start window.

2. Navigate to the left-hand side panel and select **Win32** under the **Visual C++** branch of **Templates**.

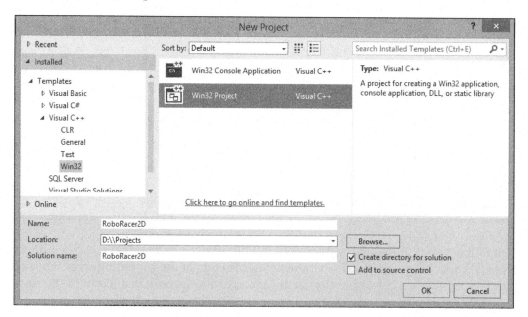

3. Select **Win32 Project** in the center area.

4. Give the project a name. The first game we will be working on is a 2D robot racing game that we'll call RoboRacer2D.

5. Choose a folder location to store the project, or just leave the default location.

6. The solution name is almost always the same as the project name, so leave that as it is.

7. Leave **Create directory for solution** checked.

8. Click **OK**.

9. On the next screen click **Finish**.

We need to tell Visual Studio how to work with Unicode characters. Right-click on the project name in the Solution Explorer panel and choose Properties. Then select General. Change the Character Set property to Not Set.

Congratulations! You have now created your Windows application and set up your development environment. It's time to move on to creating the framework for your game.

The game loop

The game loop is the primary mechanism that moves the game forward in time. Before we learn how to create this important component, let's briefly take a look at the structure of most games.

The game structure

There are three phases to most games: the initialization phase, the game loop, and the shutdown phase. The core of any game is the game loop.

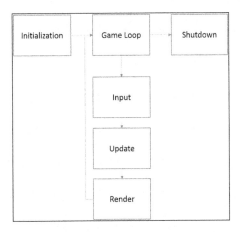

The game loop is a sequence of processes that run continuously as long as the game is running. The three main processes that occur in the game loop are input, update, and render.

The input process is how the player controls the game. This could be any combination of keyboard, mouse, or control pad. Newer technologies allow the game to be controlled via a sensing device that detects gestures, while mobile devices detect touch, acceleration, and even GPS.

The update process encompasses all of the tasks required to update the game: calculating where characters and game objects have moved, determining whether items in the game have collided, and applying physics and other forces in the game.

Once the preceding calculations have been completed, then it is time to draw results. This is known as the **render process**. OpenGL is the library of code that handles the rendering for your game.

Many people think that OpenGL is a **game engine**. This is not accurate. OpenGL – the open graphics language – is a **rendering library**. As you can see, rendering is only one process involved in the execution of a game.

Let's take a closer look at each stage of the game so that we can get a better idea of how OpenGL fits in.

Initialization

There are certain parts of the game that must be set up only once before the game can run. This typically includes initializing variables and loading resources. There are certain parts of OpenGL that must be initialized during this phase as well.

The game loop

Once the initialization is complete, the game loop takes over. The game loop is literally an endless loop that cycles until something tells it to stop. This is often the player telling the game to end.

In order to create the illusion of movement, the render phase must occur several times a second. In general, games strive to render at least 30 frames to the screen every second, and 60 frames per second (**fps**) is even better.

 It turns out that 24 fps is the threshold at which the human eye begins to see continuous motion instead of individual frames. This is why we want the slowest speed for our game to be 30 fps.

Shutdown

When the game does end, it isn't enough to just exit the program. Resources that are taking up precious computer memory must be properly released to the reclaim that memory. For example, if you have allocated memory for an image, you will want to release that memory by the end of the game. OpenGL has to be properly shut down so that it doesn't continue to control the **Graphics Processing Unit** (**GPU**). The final phase of the game is to return control to the device so that it will continue working properly in its normal, nongaming mode.

Creating the game structure

Now that we created our RoboRacer2D project in Visual Studio project, let's learn how to modify this code to create our game structure. Start Visual Studio and open the project we just created.

You should now see a window with code in it. The name of the code file should be RoboRacer2D.cpp. If you don't see this code window, then find **Solution Explorer**, navigate to RoboRacer2D.cpp, and open it up.

I'll be the first person to admit that the Windows C++ code is both ugly and intimidating! There is a lot of code created from you by Visual Studio when you choose the Windows desktop template to create your project. In fact, you can run this code right now by clicking **DEBUG** from the menu bar and then choosing **Start Debugging**. You can also press the *F5* key.

Go ahead and do it!

You will see a window telling you that the project is out of date. This simply means that Visual Studio needs to process your code and turn it into an executable—a process called building the project. For the computer science majors out there, this is where your code is compiled, linked, and then executed by the operating system.

Click **Yes** to continue.

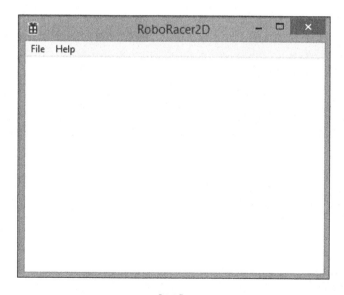

Congratulations! You have now created and run your first program in Visual Studio. It may not look like much, but there is a lot going on here:

- A fully sizeable and moveable window
- A working menu system with **File** and **Help** choices
- A title bar with **RoboRacer2D**
- Working minimize, maximize, and close buttons

Keep in mind that you haven't written a single line of code yet!

Now that you see it, feel free to use the close button to close the window and return to Visual Studio.

But wait, this doesn't look like a game!

If you are thinking the RoboRacer2D program doesn't look much like a game, you are correct! In fact, to make a game we typically strip away about everything that you now see! However, for this demonstration, we are going to keep the window just like it is, and worry more about the code than the appearance.

Port of access

Every program has a starting point, and for a Windows program the entry point is the _tWinMain function. Look for the following line of code:

```
int APIENTRY wWinMain
```

The _wWinMain function will start running and will set up everything required to run a Windows desktop program. It is beyond the scope of this book to go into everything that is going on here. We will just take it for granted that the code we are looking at sets things up to run in Windows, and we will focus on the things that we need to modify to make a game.

The Windows message loop

It turns out that _wWinMain already sets up a loop. In a similar manner to games, Windows programs actually run in an endless loop, until they receive some kind of event that tells them to stop. Here's the code:

```
// Main message loop:
while (GetMessage(&msg, nullptr, 0, 0))
{
  if (!TranslateAccelerator(msg.hwnd, hAccelTable, &msg))
  {
    TranslateMessage(&msg);
```

```
        DispatchMessage(&msg);
    }
  }
```

As you can see, these lines of code set up a while loop that will continue to run until the result of the GetMessage call is false.

Again, we won't worry about the exact details, but suffice to say that GetMessage constantly checks for messages, or events, that are sent by Windows. One particular message is the quit event, which will return a result of false, ending the while loop, exiting the _tWinMain function, and ending the program.

Our goal is to modify the Windows message loop and turn this block of code into a game loop:

```
StartGame();
//Game Loop
bool done = false;
while (!done)
{
  if (PeekMessage(&msg, NULL, 0, 0, PM_REMOVE))
  {
    if (msg.message == WM_QUIT)
    {
      done = true;
    }
    else
    {
      TranslateMessage(&msg);
      DispatchMessage(&msg);
    }
  }
  else
  {
    GameLoop();
  }
}
EndGame();
```

Study the preceding code. You will see that we have added three new functions: StartGame, GameLoop, and EndGame.

- StartGame comes before the Windows message loop, which means that everything in StartGame will run once before Windows enters its loop. We will put all of the game initialization code in the StartGame function.

- EndGame comes after the Windows message loop. This means that the code in EndGame will only execute one time after the Windows message loop has exited. This is the perfect place for us to release resources and shut the game down.

- GameLoop is interleaved in the Windows message loop. Basically, the code is saying, "*Keep running until you receive a Windows message to quit. While you are running, check to see if Windows has passed any events that need to be handled. If there are no messages to handle, then run our game.*"

 Order is important. For example, you have to declare these functions before the wWinMain function. This is because they are called by wWinMain, so they have to exist before tWinMain uses them. In general, a function has to be declared before the code that uses it.

In order for these new functions to be valid, go to the line just before the _tWinMain and enter some stubs for these three functions:

```
void StartGame()
{
}

void GameLoop()
{
}

void EndGame()
{
}
```

The idea here is to help you see how easy it is to convert the standard Windows message loop into a game loop.

Introducing OpenGL

We have spent a lot of time so far talking about game loops and Visual Studio. We are finally going to discuss the main topic of this book: **OpenGL**!

What is OpenGL?

OpenGL makes it possible to render sophisticated 2D and 3D graphics on your computer screen. In fact, OpenGL is also the technology behind most mobile devices and tablet devices.

OpenGL works in conjunction with your device's graphics device to draw graphics on the screen. Most modern computing devices have two processors: the **Central Processing Unit (CPU)** and the **Graphics Processing Unit (GPU)**.

Drawing modern 2D and 3D graphics is a very processor intensive task. In order to free the computer's main processor (the CPU) to do its job, the GPU takes on the task of rendering to the screen. OpenGL is a language that tells the GPU what to do and how to do it.

Technically, OpenGL is an API, or application programming interface. Another way to understand this is that OpenGL is a library of code that you can access once you have included the proper headers in your code. There are different versions of OpenGL. This book uses OpenGL 1.1. Although this is the very first version of OpenGL, it is included in all versions of Windows and provides the building blocks for all future versions.

The other GL

By the way, you have probably heard of the "other" graphics engine—Microsoft's DirectX. Similar to OpenGL, DirectX allows programmers to talk to the GPU. A lot of people want to know the differences between OpenGL and DirectX, and which is the best choice.

Although there are certainly going to be fans and defenders of both technologies, the only real difference between DirectX and OpenGL is the specific way that you code them. Both technologies are about the same when it comes to features and abilities.

There is one advantage that OpenGL has over DirectX. DirectX only works on Microsoft technologies, while OpenGL works on Microsoft technologies and many others, including most modern cell phones, and the Apple Mac line of computers.

Downloading OpenGL

I remember when I was first learning OpenGL. I searched in vain, looking for the link to download the OpenGL SDK. It turns out that you don't have to download the OpenGL SDK because it is already installed when you install Visual Studio.

You do want to make sure that you have the latest OpenGL driver for your video card. To do that, go to `http://www.opengl.org/wiki/Getting_started#Downloading_OpenGL` and follow the appropriate link.

Adding OpenGL to the project

In order to use OpenGL in our program, we will need to add some code. Open the `RoboRacer2D` project that we have been working on, and let's do this!

Linking to the OpenGL library

Everything that you need to use OpenGL is found in the `OpenGL32.dll` lib file. It's up to you to tell Visual Studio that you want to use the OpenGL library in your project.

Right-click on **Project | RoboRacer2D properties**.

 By the way, Visual Studio first creates a **solution**, and then puts a **project** in the solution. The solution is the top entry in the **Solution Explorer** hierarchy, and the project is the first child. In this case, make sure you right-click on the project, not the solution.

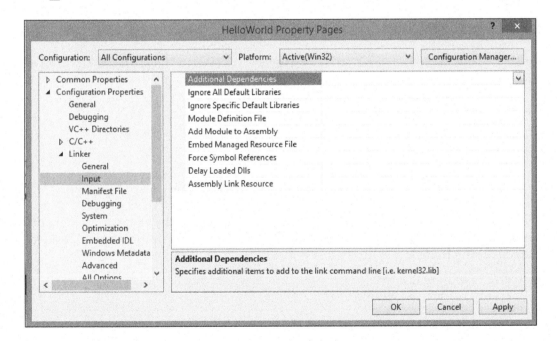

1. For the **Configuration** drop-down box, make sure you select **All Configurations**.
2. Open the **Configuration Properties** branch, then the **Linker** branch.
3. Select the **Input** option.

4. Click the dropdown for **Additional Dependencies** and choose **<Edit…>**.

5. Enter `OpenGL32.lib` into the dialog window and click **OK**.

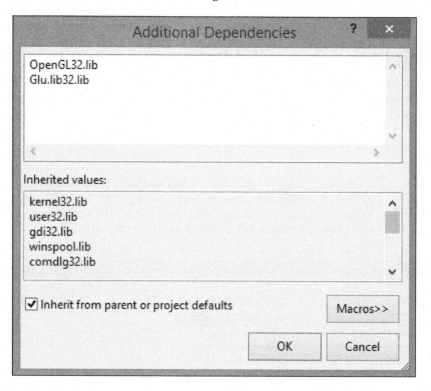

6. Close the **Property Pages** window.

Even if you are writing a 64 bit application, you will use the OpenGL 32 bit library.

Next, we need to tell Visual Studio that you want to include the OpenGL headers in your program. If you take a look at the top of your code, you will see several headers already being loaded:

```
#include "stdafx.h"
#include "RoboRacer2D.h"
```

Just below these lines, add the following:

```
#include <Windows.h>
#include <gl\GL.h>
#include <gl\GLU.h>
```

GL.h is the main header for the OpenGL library. GLU.h stands for GL Utility and is an additional library of features that make OpenGL a little easier to use. These headers correspond to the OpenGL32.lib and Glu32.lib libraries that we added to the project.

Congratulations! You have set up the development environment to use OpenGL and you are now ready to program your first game.

Summary

We covered a lot of ground in this chapter. We learned how to set up your development environment by downloading and installing Visual Studio. Next, we created a C++ Windows Desktop application.

We discussed the structure of most games and the importance of the game loop. Recall that an average game should run at 30 fps, while top-end games shoot for 60 fps to provide smooth animations.

Finally, we learned about OpenGL and how to initialize OpenGL in your project. Remember, OpenGL is the graphics engine that will be responsible for drawing every image and piece of text to your screen using the power of your GPU.

After all this work, there still isn't a lot to see. In the next chapter, we will go into all of the details of how to render your first image to the screen. Believe it or not, getting your development environment properly set up means you have already accomplished a great deal toward creating your first game using OpenGL.

2
Your Point of View

Imagine that you are making a video. You've got your cell phone out, and you point it at the area that you want to shoot and press record. You're taking a video of the Grand Canyon, so you have to pan the camera around to get the whole scene in. Suddenly, a bird flies past the field of view, and you've captured the whole scene.

The preceding scenario is pretty much how games work as well. The game has a virtual camera that can be positioned and even moved around. Similarly to the video camera on your cell phone, the game camera can only see a part of the game world, so sometimes you have to move it around. Any game objects that move in front of the camera will be seen by the player.

This chapter will explain how things are rendered in the game. Rendering is the process of actually displaying images on the screen. In order to get your get your game onto the screen, you will need to have a solid understating of the following terms:

- **Coordinate systems**: The coordinate system is the reference that allows you to position objects in the game
- **Primitives**: Primitives are the fundamental building blocks of the images that you see on screen, and OpenGL was designed to work with them
- **Textures**: Textures are image files that are used to give the objects in your game a realistic appearance

By the time you have read this chapter, you will understand how to use images to build your game world and display it on the screen.

Plotting your revenge

Okay, so you're not really plotting your revenge. But you are plotting everything in your game as if you were putting it all down on a piece of graph paper. Remember high-school geometry? You got out your graph paper, drew a couple of lines for the X and Y axis, and the plotted points on the graph. OpenGL works in pretty much the same way.

The OpenGL coordinate system

The OpenGL coordinate system is a standard X and Y axis system that you have most likely learned all your life. You can conceptualize $(0, 0)$ as being the center of the screen.

Let's say that we want to display a moving car on the screen. We could start by plotting our car at position $(5, 5)$ in the coordinate plane. If we then moved the car from $(5, 5)$ to $(6, 5)$, then $(7, 5)$, and so forth, the car would move to the right (and eventually leave the screen), as illustrated in the following figure:

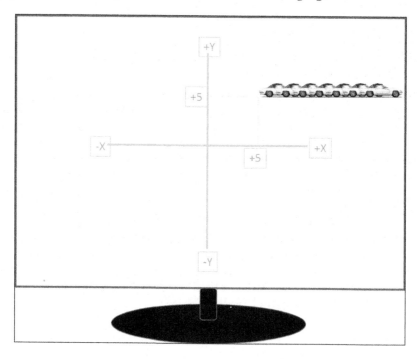

We haven't been completely honest with you. Since OpenGL is a 3D rendering engine, there is actually one more axis called the Z-axis that we haven't discussed. As this part of the book focuses on 2D game programming, we will ignore the Z axis for now.

Making your point

As we learn each concept, we will actually write code to demonstrate each point. Speaking of points, we will write code to plot points using OpenGL.

We are going to set this project up as a separate project from the actual game. We will use this project to demonstrate how to code basic OpenGL tasks. To keep this thing as simple as possible, this project will be created as a console project in Visual Studio. A console project doesn't have many of the features of a full-blown Windows project and therefore, the setup code is much smaller.

Start Visual Studio and create a new project. For the project template, choose **Win32 Console Application** from the **Visual C++** group of templates. Name the project **OpenGLFun**, and click **OK**. Click **Finish** to complete the project wizard.

 You should notice that the code is much simpler than the code that was created in the previous chapter for a full-blown Windows application. We will return to using the more complicated code as we continue building the game.

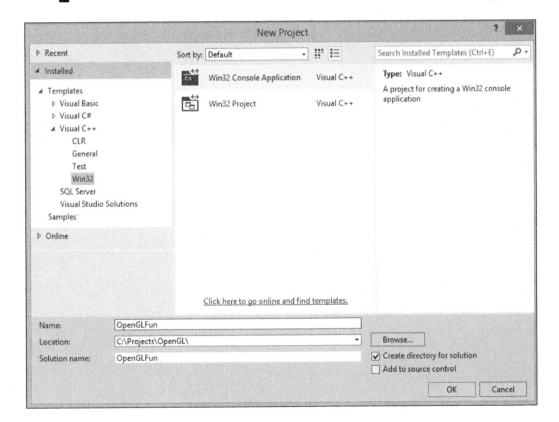

Once you have the project created, type following the code into the code window:

```
#include "stdafx.h"
#include <windows.h>
#include "glut.h"

void initGL() {
  glClearColor(0.0f, 0.0f, 0.0f, 1.0f);
}

void drawPoints()
{
  glBegin(GL_POINTS);

  glColor3f(1.0f, 1.0f, 1.0f);
  glVertex2f(0.1f, -0.6f);
  glVertex2f(0.7f, -0.6f);
  glVertex2f(0.4f, -0.1f);

  glEnd();
}

void update()
{
  glClear(GL_COLOR_BUFFER_BIT);
  drawPoints();
  glFlush();
}

int _tmain(int argc, _TCHAR* argv[])
{
  glutCreateWindow("GL Fun");
  glutInitWindowSize(320, 320);
  glutInitWindowPosition(50, 50);
  glutDisplayFunc(update);
  initGL();
  glutMainLoop();
  return 0;
}
```

Understanding the code

As we will be using the code to demonstrate the fundamentals of OpenGL, we will look at it in detail so that you understand what the code is doing.

Header files

This code uses three header files:

- `stdafx.h`: This header file loads the precompiled header that was created by Visual Studio when we created the project
- `windows.h`: This header file allows the window that renders the OpenGL content to be created
- `glut.h`: This header file allows us to use the OpenGL Utility Toolkit, which simplifies the setup and use of OpenGL

> You will need to download the GLUT files and place them in your project folder. Download the files from `http://user.xmission.com/~nate/glut/glut-3.7.6-bin.zip`. Open the zipped file and copy `glut.h`, `glut32.dll`, and `glut32.lib` into the folder that contains your source code. You may have to add glut.h to your project (right-click on `Header files` | `Add` | `Existing item`).

Initializing OpenGL

You will notice a function called `initGL`. This function currently contains a single line of code whose sole purpose is to set the background color of the screen at the start of each frame. This is often referred to as the *clear color* because it is the default that OpenGL clears the background to before it begins to render additional items:

```
glClearColor(0.0f, 0.0f, 0.0f, 1.0f);
```

The four numbers inside the parenthesis define the color, and the opacity of the color. The first three numbers represent the amount of red, green, and blue (RGB) that will be used to create the color. The fourth number represents the opacity (or seen another way, the transparency) of the color. This is also referred to as the alpha channel (RGBA). The values above create a black background that is 100 percent opaque.

All values in OpenGL have a range from 0 to 1. This means that there will be many decimal values, known in C++ as floats. Thus, the range in C++ lingo is from `0.0f` to `1.0f`.

C++ is different from many languages, which use integers or even hexadecimal numbers to express their ranges. For example, many other languages use a range of 0 to 255 for each color component. In these cases, integer 0 corresponds to `0.0f`, and integer 255 corresponds to `1.0f`.

 To convert an integer of range 0 to 255 to OpenGL's system, use the formula *(1/255) * value*, where value is the integer value you are trying to convert. Thus, to convert the number 50, you would calculate *(1/255) * 50*, which results in 0.1096.

The main entry point

Every program has to have a starting point, known as the entry point. In our program, this is the `_tmain` function. We put this at the very end because C++ expects the functions that are being used to have been defined before the function that calls them. There are various tricks around this, but we'll keep our examples simple and just always define `_tmain` as the last function in the code.

When we start the program, there are a few things that have to be done to set up the environment to render OpenGL. Here is the anatomy of the `_tmain` function:

- `glutCreateWindow("GL Fun")`: This function creates the window that will render the OpenGL content. We include the name of the program as a parameter.

- `glutInitWindowSize(320, 320)`: This function initializes the size of the window. We have specified 320 pixels by 320 pixels. Feel free to try larger (or smaller) window sizes.

- `glutInitWindowPosition(50, 50)`: This function sets the position of the window's upper-left corner in relation to the device's screen. In this case, the window will start drawing 50 pixels from the left and 50 pixels from the top of the screen. Feel free to try other positions.

- `glutDisplayFunc(update)`: Remember the previous chapter where we talked about the game loop? The game loop is the part of the program that runs over and over again (that is, every *frame*). We need to tell GLUT the name of the function that we want to run every frame. In this case, we are telling GLUT to use a function named `update` (described in the next section).

- `initGL()`: This simply calls the `initGL` function that we described earlier.

- `glutMainLoop()`: This function starts the main game loop, which in turn will call our `update` function every frame. This essentially starts our program, which will run in an infinite loop until we close the program.

- `return 0`: This line is required by the `_tmain` function. It basically tells our system that the program has exited and everything is okay. This line of code won't run until we exit the program.

The update function

The update function is called every frame. Any work that we want to do will have to be coded in this function. The update function currently has three lines of code:

- `glClear(GL_COLOR_BUFFER_BIT)`: The `glClear` function resets the *render buffer* to the color that was specified earlier by the `glClearColor` function. The render buffer is a separate location in the memory where OpenGL renders objects before they are displayed on the screen. Later, when all of the render operations are completed, the contents of the buffer are displayed on the screen in one fast transfer.

- `drawPoints()`: This is a function that we wrote to display three points on the screen. Later, we will replace this line of code to draw other objects. This function is described in the next section.

- `glFlush()`: This function flushes the OpenGL buffer, including the back buffer that currently holds our render. As a result, the rendering buffer is flushed, and all of the contents are rendered to the device screen.

 OpenGL uses two buffers to draw. One is the screen buffer, which is what the player currently sees on the computer display. The other is the back buffer, which is where we create the objects that we intend to render in the next frame. Once we are done creating the render in the back buffer, we quickly swap the contents of the back buffer onto the current screen. This occurs so quickly that the player cannot detect the swap.

Drawing the points

The `drawPoints` function does the actual work of determining what to draw, and where to draw it. Here is what each line of code does:

- `glBegin(GL_POINTS)`: The call to `glBegin` tells OpenGL to prepare to render items to the screen. We also tell OpenGL what we want to render. In our example, we are directing OpenGL to interpret the data that we send it as individual points. Later, we will learn to render other objects, such as triangles using `GL_TRIANGLES`, or rectangles using `GL_QUADS`.

- `glColor3f(1.0f, 1.0f, 1.0f)`: As the name suggests, `glColor` sets the color of the item that is going to be rendered. Remember, OpenGL uses the RGB color system, so the color will be white (0, 0, 0 specified black).

- `glVertex2f(0.1f, -0.6f)`: Each point in OpenGL is known as a *vertex*. This code tells OpenGL to render a single point at the coordinates (`0.1`, `-0.6`). In this case, zero means the center of the screen, and one means one unit from the center. The settings for the camera determine exactly how far one unit from the center actually is on the screen. There are three `glVertex` calls in our example code, one for each of the points that we want to render to the screen.

> The names of OpenGL functions give you a clue as to how to use the function. For example, `glVertex2f` means that this function takes 2 parameters and they will be of type `float`. In comparison, the `glVertex3f` function takes three parameters of type `float`.

- `glEnd()`: Just like all good things must come to an end, we have to tell OpenGL when we are done rendering. That is the purpose of the call to `glEnd`.

> You have probably noticed a lot of the use of the lower case letter f; this stands for *float*, meaning that a number that may contain a part after the decimal point (as opposed to an *integer*, which is always a whole number). So, a number, such as `0.0f`, is telling C++ to treat the number zero as a floating point number. OpenGL uses a similar naming convention for its functions. For example, the function `glVertex2f` indicates that the function requires two floating point numbers (in this case, the *x* and *y* coordinates of the point to render).

Running the program

Now that you have entered your code, it's time to see it in action. When you run the program (**Debug | Start Debugging**), here is what you will see:

You'll have to look at it closely, but if all went well, you should see three white points in the lower-right area of the screen. Congratulations! You have rendered your first OpenGL objects!

Hopefully, you have been able to follow the code. Think of _tmain as a manager that controls the program by setting everything up and then calling the main loop (just like we will do in our game). Then GLUT takes over and calls the update function every frame. The update function initializes the render buffer, draws objects to the render buffer, and then transfers the contents of the render buffer to the screen. In a game running at 60 frames per second, this entire operation will happen 60 times a second!

Stretching your point

Let's see how easy it will be to modify GLFun to draw other objects. This time we will draw two lines. Add the following function to your code just under the drawPoints function:

```
void drawLines()
{
  glBegin(GL_LINES);

  glColor3f(1.0f, 1.0f, 1.0f);
  glVertex2f(0.1f, -0.6f);
  glVertex2f(0.7f, -0.6f);
```

```
    glVertex2f(0.7f, -0.6f);
    glVertex2f(0.4f, -0.1f);

    glEnd();
}
```

Next, go to the update function and replace `drawPoints` with a call to `drawLines`. The new `update` function will look like this:

```
void update()
{
    glClear(GL_COLOR_BUFFER_BIT);
    drawLines();
    glFlush();
}
```

You will notice that there are four `glVertex` calls. Each pair of vertices sets the beginning and ending points of a line. As there are four points defined, the result is that two lines are drawn.

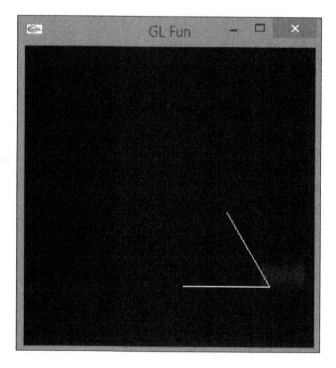

Getting primitive

Basic objects, such as points and lines, are called primitives. It would be pretty difficult to create everything out of points and lines, so OpenGL defines other primitive shapes that you can use to create more complicated objects.

In this section, we will dig a little under the hood and find out how OpenGL actually creates more realistic images on your screen. It may surprise you that a single, geometric figure is used to create everything from the simplest to the most complex graphics. So, roll up your sleeves and get ready to get a little greasy.

A triangle by any other name

Have you ever seen a geodesic dome? Although the dome appears to be spherical, it is actually built out of a combination of triangles. It turns out that triangles are very easy to put together in such a way that you can add a slight amount of curvature to the object. Each triangle can be attached at a slight angle to the others, allowing you to create a dome made out of flat triangles. Also, consider this: the smaller the triangle, the more convincing the end result!

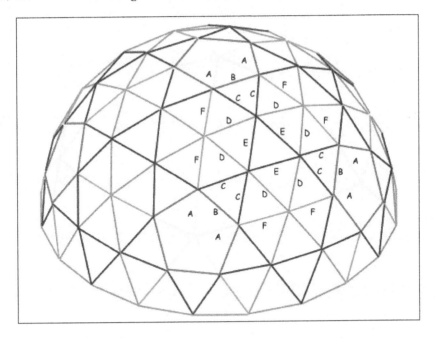

The basic unit that is used to draw all modern graphics is the humble triangle. Graphic cards have been specifically engineered to be able to draw triangles — really small triangles — really fast. A typical graphics card can draw millions of triangles every second. Higher end cards reach billions of triangles per second.

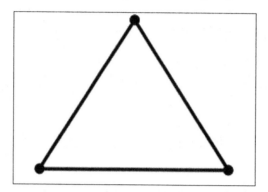

Remember when we drew points and lines earlier? Each point had one vertex, and each line had two vertices. Of course, each triangle has three vertices.

A primitive example

It's time to take a look at some code in action. Add the following code after the drawLines function in the GLFun project:

```
void drawSolidTriangle()
{
  glBegin(GL_TRIANGLES);

  glColor3f(0.0f, 0.0f, 1.0f);
  glVertex2f(0.1f, -0.6f);
  glVertex2f(0.7f, -0.6f);
  glVertex2f(0.4f, -0.1f);

  glEnd();
}
```

Then change the middle line of the update function to call drawSolidTriangle:

```
void update()
{
  glClear(GL_COLOR_BUFFER_BIT);
  drawSolidTriangle();
  glFlush();
}
```

Run the program, and you will see the following output:

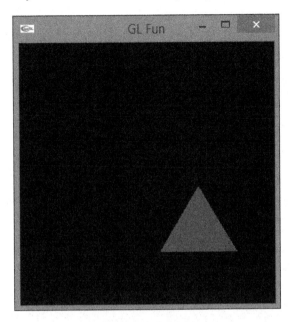

You may notice a similarity between the code for drawSolidTriangle and drawPoints. Look closely at the code, and you will see that the three glVertex functions define the same three points. However, in this case we told OpenGL to draw triangles, not points. You should also take a look at the code and make sure you understand why the triangle is rendered blue.

Let's take one more example. Add the following code below the drawSolidTriangle function:

```
void drawGradientTriangle()
{
  glBegin(GL_TRIANGLES);

  glColor3f(1.0f, 0.0f, 0.0f);
  glVertex2f(0.3f, -0.4f);

  glColor3f(0.0f, 1.0f, 0.0f);
  glVertex2f(0.9f, -0.4f);

  glColor3f(0.0f, 0.0f, 1.0f);
  glVertex2f(0.6f, -0.9f);

  glEnd();
}
```

Be sure to change the middle line in update to call `drawGradientTriangle`:

```
void update()
{
  glClear(GL_COLOR_BUFFER_BIT);
  drawGradientTriangle();
  glFlush();
}
```

Run the program, and this is what you will see:

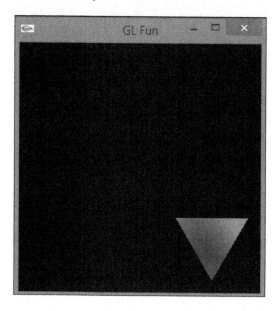

You will immediately notice that this triangle is filled with a gradient instead of a solid color. If you look closely at the code, you will see that a different color is being set for each vertex. OpenGL then takes care of interpolating the colors between each vertex.

From triangles to models

Triangles can be put together in an infinite number of ways to form almost any shape imaginable. It is important to understand that triangles are just geometry. Triangles are used to build the shape of your object. We call these shapes models.

Building a model using a single triangle at a time would be very time consuming, so 3D graphics programs, such as **Maya** and **Blender**, allow you to create models out more complex shapes (which are themselves built out of triangles). These models can then be loaded into your game and rendered by OpenGL. OpenGL literally sends a the list of points to form these triangles directly to the video card, which then creates and image out of them on the screen. We will see this process in action when we begin to deal with 3D game design.

Introducing textures

Images in games are called textures. Textures allow us to use real world images to paint our world. Think about what it would take to create a dirt road. You could either color the triangles in exactly the right way to make the overall scene look like dirt, or you could apply an actual image (that is, a texture) of dirt to the triangles. Which of these do you think would look more realistic?

Using textures to fill the triangles

Let's say that you are going to paint your bedroom. You can either use paint to color the walls, or you could buy some wallpaper and put that on your walls. Using images to add color to our triangles is pretty much like using wallpaper to color our bedroom walls. The image is applied to the triangle, giving it a more complex appearance than what could be created by color alone:

When we want to get really tricky, we use textures to fill the inside of our triangles instead of colors. A marble texture has been applied to the triangle in the preceding image. You could imagine using this technique to create a marble floor.

Remember the car we were working with before? It didn't look much like a triangle, did it? In fact, many real-world objects look more like rectangles than triangles:

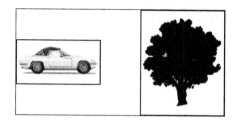

It turns out that that all the textures that we use in games are actually rectangles. Imagine that the car that we have been dealing with is actually embedded inside an invisible rectangle, depicted in the following image as light gray:

Most graphic programs use a checkerboard background to indicate the areas of the image that are transparent.

Using rectangles for all of our shapes solves one big problem that you might not have thought of earlier. If you recall, it was very important to position the car at exactly (5, 5). To do so, we decided to place the bottom-left corner of the car at point (5, 5).

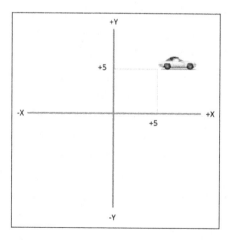

Looking at the car, it is actually a little difficult to figure out exactly where the bottom-left corner would be. Is it the lower left corner of the bumper, the tire, or somewhere else?

By embedding the car inside of a rectangle, as we just discussed, the problem is immediately solved.

A matter of reference

When working with a texture, it is very important to know what point is being used as a reference, usually known as the pivot point. In the following images, a black dot is used to represent the pivot point. The pivot point affects two critical issues. First, the pivot point determines exactly where the image will be placed on the screen. Second, the pivot point is the point on which the image will pivot when rotated.

Compare the two scenarios depicted in the following images:

The pivot point for the car in the preceding image has been set to the bottom-left corner of the image. The car has been rotated 90 degrees counter-clockwise.

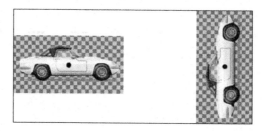

The pivot point for the car in the preceding image has been set to the center of the image. The car has been rotated 90 degrees counter-clockwise. Notice how the pivot point affects not only how the car is rotated but also its final position in relation to its original position after the rotation is completed.

Hanging out in the quad

So, are you confused yet? First, I tell you that the most basic shape used to create images is a triangle, and then I tell you that all textures are actually rectangles. Which one is it?

Just then, your high-school geometry teacher silently walks into the room, goes up to the chalkboard that just magically appeared on your wall, and draws something like the following diagram:

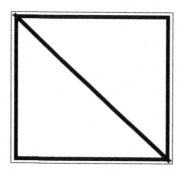

Of course! You suddenly realize that two triangles can be fit together to form a rectangle. In fact, this arrangement is so useful that we have given it a name: **quad**.

When it comes to 2D graphics, the quad is the king.

Coding the quad

It's time to take a look at some code. Add the following code beneath the drawGradientTriangle function in GLFun:

```
void drawQuad()
{
    glBegin(GL_QUADS);

    glColor3f(0.0f, 1.0f, 0.0f);
    glVertex2f(0.1f, -0.1f);
    glVertex2f(0.1f, -0.6f);
    glVertex2f(0.6f, -0.6f);
    glVertex2f(0.6f, -0.1f);

    glEnd();
}
```

As usual, change the middle line in update to call drawQuad. Run the program, and you will get a pretty green square, er quad! It's important to note that the points are defined in order starting from the upper-left corner and then moving counter-clockwise in order.

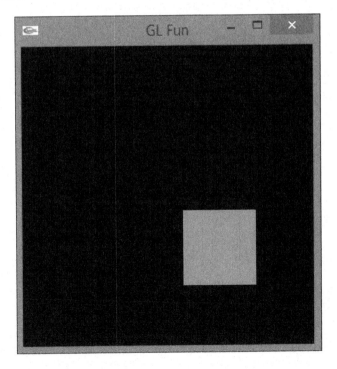

> The order that the points are defined in is known as *winding*. By default, a counter-clockwise winding tells OpenGL that the side facing out is the side that is considered the front. This helps determine, among other things, whether this face should be lit, and it becomes even more significant when we begin working in 3D. As it turns out, GLUT simplifies our life so that it doesn't matter if we use clockwise or counter-clockwise winding when using GLUT.

Rendering a texture

Rendering a texture consist of two steps: loading the image and rendering the image using an OpenGL primitive. Our final achievement in this chapter will be to modify GLFun so that it will render a texture using a quad.

Loading the texture

Our first step is to create a function to load a texture. As it turns out, this isn't all that easy. So, I'm going to give you the code for a function that loads a 24-bit BMP file, and we'll treat it like a black box that you can use in your own code.

Add this code to the top of your existing GLFun code:

```
GLuint texture;
#pragma warning(disable: 4996)
bool loadTexture(const char* filename)
{
    unsigned char header[54];
    unsigned char* data;
    int dataPos;
    int width;
    int height;
    int imageSize;

    FILE * file = fopen(filename, "rb");
    if (!file) return false;
    if (fread(header, 1, 54, file) != 54) return false;
    if (header[0] != 'B' || header[1] != 'M') return false;

    dataPos   = *(int*)&(header[0x0A]);
    imageSize = *(int*)&(header[0x22]);
    width     = *(int*)&(header[0x12]);
    height    = *(int*)&(header[0x16]);
```

```
        if (imageSize == 0) imageSize = width*height * 3;
        if (dataPos == 0) dataPos = 54;

        data = new unsigned char[imageSize];
        fread(data, 1, imageSize, file);
        fclose(file);

        glGenTextures(1, &texture);
        glBindTexture(GL_TEXTURE_2D, texture);
        glTexImage2D(GL_TEXTURE_2D, 0, GL_RGB, width, height, 0, GL_RGB,
    GL_UNSIGNED_BYTE, data);
        glTexParameteri(GL_TEXTURE_2D, GL_TEXTURE_MAG_FILTER, GL_NEAREST);
        glTexParameteri(GL_TEXTURE_2D, GL_TEXTURE_MIN_FILTER, GL_NEAREST);
        return true;
    }
```

Add these lines of code to `initGL`:

```
    glEnable(GL_TEXTURE_2D);
    glTexEnvf(GL_TEXTURE_ENV, GL_TEXTURE_ENV_MODE, GL_MODULATE);
```

We are not going to dissect this piece of code line by line. In brief, it opens the image file, extracts the first 54 bytes of the file (the bmp header data), and stores the rest of the file as image data. A few OpenGL calls are made to assign this data to an OpenGL texture and that's it.

You need to have a call that loads the texture in, so add this line of code to `_tmain` just after the call to `initGL`:

```
    loadTexture("car.bmp");
```

Of course, replace `car.bmp` with the file that you want to load in. Ensure that you have placed the appropriate graphic files in the source code folder.

Texture wrapping

In order to display a texture on the screen, OpenGL maps the texture onto another primitive. This process is known as texture wrapping. As textures are rectangular, it makes sense to map the texture onto a quad.

The following image shows a texture the way that OpenGL sees it: a rectangle with four texture coordinates:

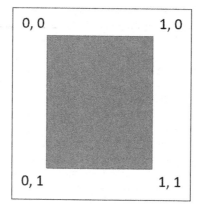

The upper-left is texture coordinate **0, 0**. The lower-right is texture coordinate **1, 1**. You should be able to identify the texture coordinates of the other corners.

 It might make it easier to conceptualize OpenGL numbers if you convert them to percentage, where 0 is zero percent and 1 is 100 percent. For example, you can think of the lower-left corner as being zero percent of the width of the texture and one-hundred percent of the height of the texture.

In order to render a texture, we overlay it (or wrap it) onto a quad. So, let's say we have the following quad defined:

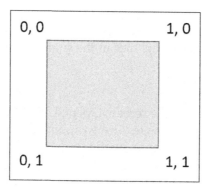

We could map the texture coordinates to the quad coordinates:

Texture Coordinate	Maps to	Quad Coordinate
0, 0		0, 0
1, 0		1, 0
1, 0		1, 0
0, 1		0, 1

The following figure shows this graphically:

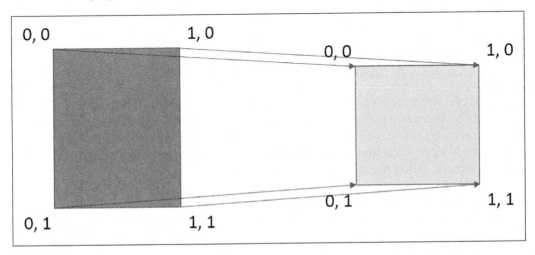

In its simplest form, texture wrapping is the process of mapping the corners of a texture to the corners of a quad.

You will see texture wrapping also referred to as *uv* wrapping. I always tried to figure out what *uv* meant! Here's the real story: *x* and *y* were already used to refer to the quad coordinates, and we had to have something else to call the texture coordinates, so some bright person said, "Let's use u and v!"

Creating a textured quad

Now, we will write the code to render a textured quad. Add the following function to the code:

```
void drawTexture()
{
  glBindTexture(GL_TEXTURE_2D, texture);
  glBegin(GL_QUADS);
  glTexCoord2d(0.0, 0.0); glVertex2d(0.0, 0.0);
  glTexCoord2d(1.0, 0.0); glVertex2d(0.5, 0.0);
  glTexCoord2d(1.0, 1.0); glVertex2d(0.5, 0.5);
  glTexCoord2d(0.0, 1.0); glVertex2d(0.0, 0.5);
  glEnd();
}
```

Here is what this code does:

- `glBindTexture(GL_TEXTURE_2D, texture)`: Even if we have thousands of textures in a game, OpenGL can only work with one texture a time. The call to `glBindTexture` tells OpenGL which texture we are working with right now. Each time a texture is created, OpenGL assigns a number to that texture, called the texture handle.

  When we loaded our bitmap, we used the `glGenTextures(1, &texture)` command, which instructed OpenGL to generate one texture and save the handle into the variable called texture. We then pass this value into the `glBindTexture` function, along with a flag that tells OpenGL that we are working with a 2D texture.

- `glTexCoord2d(0.0, 0.0); glVertex2d(0.0, 0.0)`: We put these two lines together because they work together. You should recognize the call to `glVertex2d`. This function tells OpenGL how to wrap the texture onto the quad (you should also recognize that we are drawing a quad because we set that up in the previous line of code).

- Each call to `glTexCoord2d` defines a texture coordinate. The very next line of code maps the texture coordinate to a quad coordinate. The order is essential: first define a texture coordinate, then define the corresponding quad coordinate.

By the way, don't forget to replace the middle line of code in update with the following line of code:

```
drawTexture();
```

Now, run the program!

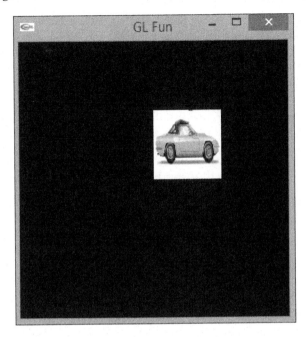

Putting the pieces together

The following image is a composite that illustrates most of the concepts we have covered so far. See if you can you identify the following:

- The transparent areas
- The triangles
- The vertices
- The pivot point
- The texture
- The quad

Summary

This chapter has covered the core concepts that are required to display images on your screen. We started by discussing the OpenGL coordinate system for a 2D game. The coordinate system allows you to place objects on the screen. This was followed by a discussion about the camera, OpenGL's way of viewing objects that appear on your screen.

Next, you learned how triangles and quads are used to create simple graphics, and how textures can be applied to these primitives to render 2D images to the screen.

You could finally see an image on your screen that has been rendered by OpenGL. As they say, a picture is worth a thousand lines of code!

In the next chapter, you will learn how to turn your still photography into moving pictures through the wonder of animation!

3
A Matter of Character

A video game wouldn't be much fun without characters, and this chapter is all about bringing your game characters to life. Games typically have two kinds of characters. First, there is the character or characters that you are playing as. These are called the player characters. The characters that are controlled by the computer are called the non-player characters or NPCs.

This chapter will explain how to create characters for your game. Along the way we will cover:

- **Sprites**: Sprites are any textures that the player interacts with in the game. This includes the player characters, NPCs, and other objects in the game.
- **Animation**: The art of making an image appear to move is called animation. You will learn how to use multiple images to make your textures move on the screen.
- **Atlases**: Images can be stored one at a time, or they can be combined into single composite texture known as a **sprite sheet** or an **atlas**.

Spritely speaking

Many years ago, a computer geek invented a cool way to render and display small images on a computer screen. These images would move around on the screen and even collide with other objects. The computer geek called these images sprites, and that name has stuck ever since.

Sprites versus non-sprites

A sprite is simply an image that represents an object on the screen. Examples of sprites include characters, NPCs, weapons, alien spaceships, and rocks. Anything that can move on the screen or be hit by another object in the game is a sprite. Objects that don't interact with other objects aren't sprites. Examples might include mountains in the background, the ground, and the sky.

Obviously, it takes both sprites and non-sprites to implement a game. Also, the distinction is a little arbitrary. Some games implement all of the images in the game as sprites because it is more convenient to treat all images in the game in a consistent manner.

Flipbook animation

Did you ever create a flipbook when you were a kid? To jog your memory, here is how it worked. First, you sketched a simple figure on a notepad. Then you went to the next page and sketched the same image, but this time something was slightly different. You continued sketching images that were slightly different from the original on successive pages. When you were done, you flipped the pages at the notebook edge and saw what appeared to be a rudimentary movie.

Another example is a movie. Movies are recorded on film as frames. The film is then run through a projector, which plays the film back one frame at a time. The key, as mentioned before, is to play frames back at least 24 frames per second to fool the eye into thinking that there is fluid motion.

Framed animation

2D sprite animation works much like a flipbook. An artist draws successive versions of an image. When the images are rendered one after another, it appears to move. Each image in an animation is called a frame. It takes at least 24 or more fps to create a convincing animation. Obviously, more frames will create a smoother animation.

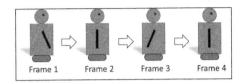

The preceding image illustrates a very simple animation using four frames. The only thing that changes is the robot's arm position. Played in sequence from **Frame 1** through **Frame 4**, the arm would appear to swing from the front to the back and then forward again. If this was combined with moving the sprite to the right, then you would get a very simple animation of a walking robot.

As the preceding example illustrates, I am not an artist! I am a coder, so the art created for this book will be very simple. It is actually common for very simple placeholder art to be used in the initial stages of a game. This allows the programmers to test features of the game while the art team is working on the real art that will be put in the game at a later stage.

Creating sprites

Professional 2D artists use programs, such as Adobe Photoshop, to create 2D assets for a game. Unfortunately, we can't take the time to teach you how to use a program as sophisticated as Photoshop.

If you want to play around with creating your own assets, then you might try the Paint program that comes installed on any Windows based computer. If you really want to dig deep into 2D art creation without digging deeply into your bank account, then you can download GIMP (http://www.gimp.org), a free, full-features 2D image manipulation program.

Working with PNGs

In the previous chapter, we loaded and rendered a bitmap file. It turns out that bitmaps aren't the best format to work with sprites because they take more file space (and therefore, more memory) than PNGs, and bitmaps do not support transparency.

Before we had image formats that allowed transparency to be directly encoded as part of the image, we used a specific background color, and then expected our image library to remove that color when it handled the image. Magenta was often used as the background because it is a color rarely used in images.

Bitmaps are larger in file size than PNGs because they are not stored in a compressed format. Compression allows an image to be stored in less space, and this can be very important on devices, such as mobile phones.

PNGs are stored using a **lossless** compression algorithm. Lossless means that the image quality is not sacrificed to achieve the compression. Other formats, such as JPEG, can be stored in a compressed format, but use a **lossy** algorithm that degrades the image quality.

PNGs also support transparency using an **alpha** channel. In addition to storing the red, green, and blue component of each pixel (RGB), PNGs also store each pixel's transparency in the alpha channel (RGBA).

You will recall from the previous chapter that all textures are represented as rectangles in a game. However, real shapes aren't rectangular. Trees, cars, and robots all have much more complex shapes.

If we used bitmaps for all of our images, then the full rectangle of the texture would be rendered blocking out everything behind the sprite. In the following image, our robot is passing in front of a pipe, and part of the pipe is occluded by the blank space in the bitmap.

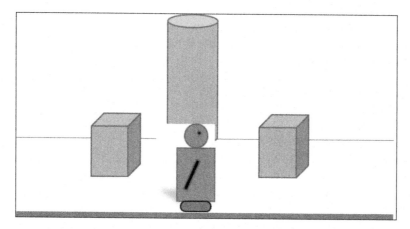

In a PNG image, we set the blank space to be transparent. In the following image, the pipe is no longer occluded by the transparent parts of the image of the robot:

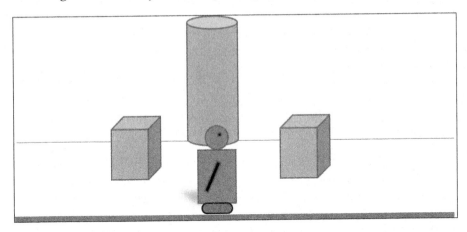

In the previous chapter, we wrote a code to load a BMP file. Normally, we would have to write different code to load a PNG file. In fact, we would have to write a loader for each different type of image we wanted to work with.

Fortunately, someone has already done all of this work and made it available in a library known as **SOIL: Simple OpenGL Image Library**. You can download your copy from http://www.lonesock.net/soil.html.

There are several advantages to using the SOIL library:

- We no longer have to worry about writing our own loader for every type of image that we want to use. SOIL supports BMP, PNG, and many other formats.
- File loading is not completely abstracted. You don't have to worry about how the code works, only that it does.
- SOIL has other features that may be useful (such as the ability to write out image files).

The download comes as a zipped folder. Once you unzip the folder, you will see a folder named Simple OpenGL Image Library. This folder contains a lot of files, but we only need soil.h.

Linking to the SOIL library

Now, it is time to add the SOIL library to our project:

1. Find the folder where you unzipped the SOIL code.
2. Open the `lib` folder and find `libSOIL.a`.
3. Copy `libSOIL.a` to the folder that contains the **RoboRacer2D** source code.
4. Open the **RoboRacer2D** project.
5. Right-click on the **RoboRacer2D** project in the **Solution Explorer** panel and choose **Properties**.
6. For the **Configuration** drop-down box, make sure that you select **All Configurations**.
7. Open the **Configuration Properties** branch, then the **Linker** branch.
8. Select the **Input** option.
9. Click the dropdown for **Additional Dependencies** and choose **<Edit...>**.
10. Enter `opengl32.lib` and `glu32.lib` on separate lines in the dialog window and click **OK**.

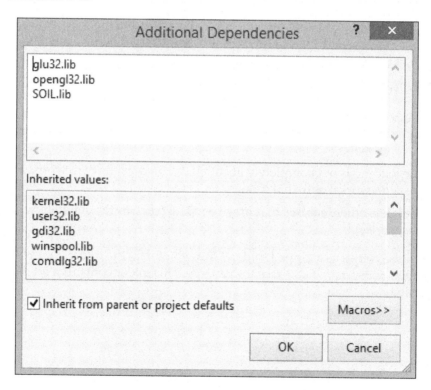

Library files for Windows usually end in .lib, while those written for UNIX end in .a. The standard SOIL distribution comes with the UNIX library; you need to use the Windows library. You can either find SOIL.lib online, use the SOIL source code to create your own Windows library file, or download SOIL.lib from the book's website.

Including the SOIL header file

Next, we need to copy the SOIL header file into our project and include it in our code:

1. Find the folder where you unzipped the SOIL code.
2. Open the src folder and find SOIL.h.
3. Copy SOIL.h to the folder that contains the **RoboRacer2D** source code.
4. Open the **RoboRacer2D** project.
5. Open RoboRacer2D.cpp.
6. Add #include "SOIL.h" to the list of includes.

You will notice that there are many other files that were unzipped as part of the SOIL package. This includes all of the original source files and several samples for how to use the library.

Opening an image file

Now, we are ready to write a function that loads an image file. We will pass in the name of the file, and the function will return an integer representing a handle on the OpenGL texture.

The following lines of code uses SOIL to load an image:

```
GLuint texture = SOIL_load_OGL_texture
(
  imageName,
  SOIL_LOAD_AUTO,
  SOIL_CREATE_NEW_ID,
  0
);
```

All of the work is done by the call to `SOIL_load_OGL_texture`. The four parameters are the most generic settings:

- The first parameter is the path and filename to the image file.
- The second parameter tells SOIL how to load the image (and in this case, we indicate that we want SOIL to figure things out automatically).
- The third parameter tells SOIL to create an OpenGL texture ID for us.
- The fourth parameter, if used, can be set to several flag bits that tell SOIL to perform some custom processing. We are not using this, so we just send a 0.

We will use code, such as this one, to load images into our `sprite` class.

> If you want to see all of the options available to you, open `SOIL.h` and read the source code comments.

Coding a sprite class

In order to easily incorporate sprites into our game, we will create a class specifically for dealing with sprites.

Let's think about the features that we want:

- An array of images.
- An index that represents the current frame.
- A variable that holds the total number of frames.
- Variables to store the current *x* and *y* position of the sprite. For this game, this will be the upper-left corner of the image.
- A variable that stores the x and y components of the current velocity of the sprite (`0` if it isn't moving).
- Variables that store the width and height of the image. Note that if the sprite has multiple images, they must all be the same size.
- A Boolean that tells us if this sprite collides with other sprites.
- A Boolean that tells us if this sprite should be rendered normal or flipped.
- A Boolean that tells us if this sprite is visible right now.
- A Boolean that tells us if this sprite is active right now.

In addition to these properties, we would also like to be able to manipulate the sprite in several ways. We may add methods to:

- Add an image to the sprite
- Update the position of the sprite
- Update the animation frame for the sprite
- Render the sprite to the screen

Open your game project, and add a new class called Sprite.cpp with a header file called Sprite.h.

 In Visual Studio, right-click on the **Header Files** filter in the Solution Explorer pane. Then choose **Add Class**. Give the class the name Sprite and click **Add**. Visual Studio will create a template header and source code files for you.

Use the following code for Sprite.h:

```
#pragma once:
#include <gl\gl.h>

class Sprite
{
  public:
struct Point
{
  GLfloat x;
  GLfloat y;
};

   struct Size
  {
  GLfloat width;
  GLfloat height;
};
struct Rect
{
  GLfloat top;
  GLfloat bottom;
  GLfloat left;
  GLfloat right;
};

  protected:
  GLuint* m_textures;
```

```
    unsigned int m_textureIndex;
    unsigned int m_currentFrame;
    unsigned int m_numberOfFrames;
    GLfloat m_animationDelay;
    GLfloat m_animationElapsed;

    Point m_position;
    Size m_size;
    GLfloat m_velocity;

    bool m_isCollideable;
    bool m_flipHorizontal;
    bool m_flipVertical;
    bool m_isVisible;
    bool m_isActive;
    bool m_useTransparency;
    bool m_isSpriteSheet;

    public:
    Sprite(const unsigned int m_pNumberOfTextures);
    ~Sprite();

    void Update(const float p_deltaTime);
    void Render();

    const bool AddTexture(const char* p_fileName, const bool p_
useTransparency = true);
      const GLuint GetCurrentFrame() {
    if (m_isSpriteSheet)
    {
     return m_textures[0];
    }
    else
    {
     return m_textures[m_currentFrame];
    }
   }

    void SetPosition(const GLfloat p_x, const GLfloat p_y) { m_
position.x = p_x; m_position.y = p_y; }
     void SetPosition(const Point p_position) { m_position = p_position;
}
   const Point GetPosition() { return m_position; }
   const Size GetSize() const { return m_size; }
```

```
void SetFrameSize(const GLfloat p_width, const GLfloat p_height) {
m_size.width = p_width; m_size.height = p_height; }
   void SetVelocity(const GLfloat p_velocity) { m_velocity = p_
velocity; }
   void SetNumberOfFrames(const unsigned int p_frames) { m_
numberOfFrames = p_frames;   }

   const bool isCollideable() const { return m_isCollideable; }
void IsCollideable(const bool p_value) { m_isCollideable = p_value;   }
   void FlipHorizontal(const bool p_value) { m_flipHorizontal = p_
value; }
   void FlipVertical(const bool p_value) { m_flipVertical = p_value; }
   void IsActive(const bool p_value) { m_isActive = p_value; }
   const bool IsActive() const { return m_isActive; }
void IsVisible(const bool p_value) { m_isVisible = p_value; }
const bool IsVisible() const { return m_isVisible; }
void UseTransparency(const bool p_value) { m_useTransparency = p_
value; }
};
```

I know, it's a lot of code! This is a typical object-oriented class, consisting of protected properties and public methods. Let's take a look at the features of this class:

- `#pragma once`: This is a C++ directive telling Visual Studio to only include files once if they are included in several source files.

> An alternative is to use header guards:
> ```
> #ifndef SPRITE_H
> #define SPRITE_H
> ...code...
> #endif
> ```
> This stops the code from being included if `SPRITE_H` has already been defined. Then the header has already been included and will not be included more than once.

- We include `gl.h` in this header file because we need access to the standard OpenGL variable types.

- Inside the class, we define two very useful structures: point and rect. We work with points and rectangles so much that it makes sense to have simple structures that hold their values.

- The member variables are as follows:

    o   `m_textures` is a `GLuint` array that will dynamically hold all of the OpenGL texture handles that make up this sprite.

- ° m_textureIndex starts at zero, and is incremented each time a texture is added to the sprite.

- ° m_currentFrame starts at zero, and is incremented each time we want to advance the frame of the animation.

- ° m_numberOfFrames stores the total number of frames that make up our animation.

- ° m_animationDelay is the number of seconds that we want to pass before the animation frame advances. This allows us to control the speed of the animation.

- ° m_animationElapsed will hold the amount of time that has elapsed since the last animation frame was changed.

- ° m_position holds the x and y positions of the sprite.

- ° m_size holds the width and height of the sprite.

- ° m_velocity holds the velocity of the sprite. Larger values will cause the sprite to move more quickly across the screen.

- ° m_isCollideable is a flag that tells us whether or not this sprite collides with other objects on the screen. When set to false, the sprite will pass through other objects on the screen.

- ° m_flipHorizontal is a flag that tells the class whether or not the sprite image should be horizontally flipped when it is rendered. This technique can be used to save texture memory by reusing a single texture for both right and left movement.

- ° m_flipVertical is a flag that tells the class whether or not the sprite image should be vertically flipped when it is rendered.

- ° m_isVisible is a flag that indicates whether the sprite is currently visible in the game. If this is set to false, then the sprite will not be rendered.

- ° m_isActive is a flag that indicates whether the sprite is currently active. If this is set to false, then the sprite animation frame and sprite position will not be updated.

- ° m_useTransparency is a flag that tells the sprite class whether or not to use the alpha channel in the sprite. As alpha checking is costly, we set this to false for images that don't have any transparency (such as the game background).

- m_isSpriteSheet is a flat that tells the sprite class if a single texture is used to hold all of the frames for this sprite. If set to true, then each frame is loaded as a separate texture.

- Next, we have the methods:

  - `Sprite` is a constructor that takes a single parameter, `p_numberOfTextures`. We have to tell the class the number of textures that will be used when the sprite is created so that the correct amount of memory can be allocated for the textures dynamic array.

  - `~Sprite` is the class destructor.

  - `Update` will be used to update the current animation frame and the current position of the sprite.

  - `Render` will be used to actually display the sprite on the screen.

  - `AddTexture` is used once the sprite is created to add the required textures.

  - `GetCurrentFrame` is used when the sprite is rendered to determine which frame of the sprite to render.

- The remaining methods are simply accessor methods that allow you to modify the class properties.

Next, let's start the class implementation. Open `Sprite.cpp` and add the following code:

```
#include "stdafx.h"
#include "Sprite.h"
#include "SOIL.h"

Sprite::Sprite(const unsigned int p_numberOfTextures)
{
  m_textures = new GLuint[p_numberOfTextures];
  m_textureIndex = 0;
  m_currentFrame = 0;
  m_numberOfFrames = 0;
  m_animationDelay = 0.25f;
  m_animationElapsed = 0.0f;
  m_position.x = 0.0f;
  m_position.y = 0.0f;
  m_size.height = 0.0f;
  m_size.width = 0.0f;
  m_velocity = 0.0f;

  m_isCollideable = true;
  m_flipHorizontal = false;
  m_flipVertical = false;
  m_isVisible = false;
  m_isActive = false;
  m_isSpriteSheet = false;
```

```
}

Sprite::~Sprite()
{
  delete[] m_textures;
}
```

Here are some details about the implementation code:

- Along with `stdafx.h` and `Sprite.h`, we include `SOIL.h` because this is the actual code block that we will use to load textures
- The `Sprite` constructor:
    - Dynamically allocates space for the `m_textures` array based on `p_numberOfTextures`.
    - Initializes all of other class properties. Note that most of the Boolean properties are set to `false`. The result is that a newly created sprite will not be active or visible until we specifically set it to be active and visible.
- The `~Sprite` destructor deallocates the memory used for the `m_textures` array

We will implement the `Update`, `Render`, and `AddTexture` methods next.

> You probably noticed that I prefix many of the variables in my code with either m_ or p_. m_ is always used to prefix the name of class properties (or member variables), and p_ is used to prefix variables used as parameters in functions. If a variable does not have a prefix, it is usually a local variable.

Creating sprite frames

We already discussed how 2D animations are created by drawing multiple frames of the image with each frame being slightly different. The key points that must be remembered are:

- Each frame must have exactly the same dimensions
- The placement of the image within the frame must be consistent
- Only the parts of the image that are supposed to move should change from frame to frame

Saving each frame

One technique to save your frames is to save each frame as its own image. As you will eventually have a lot of sprites and frames to work with, it is important to come up with a consistent naming convention for all of your images. For example, with our three frame robot animation that were illustrated previously, we might use the following filenames:

- `robot_left_00.png`
- `robot_left_01.png`
- `robot_left_02.png`
- `robot_left_03.png`
- `robot_right_00.png`
- `robot_right_01.png`
- `robot_right_02.png`
- `robot_right_03.png`

Every image in the game should use the same naming mechanism. This will save you endless headaches when coding the animation system.

 You should save all of your images in a folder named "resources" which should be created in the same folder that holds your source files.

Loading a sprite from individual textures

Let's take a look the code to load a sprite that has each frame saved as an individual file:

```
robot_right = new Sprite(4);
 robot_right->SetFrameSize(100.0f, 125.0f);
 robot_right->SetNumberOfFrames(4);
 robot_right->SetPosition(0, screen_height - 130.0f);
 robot_right->AddTexture("resources/robot_right_00.png");
 robot_right->AddTexture("resources/robot_right_01.png");
 robot_right->AddTexture("resources/robot_right_02.png");
 robot_right->AddTexture("resources/robot_right_03.png");
```

The important points to notice about the preceding code are:

- We create a new instance of our sprite class to store the information. We have to tell the sprite class to allocate space for 4 textures for this sprite.

- We first store the width and height of each frame. In this case, this happens to be the width and height of each texture that makes up this sprite. As every texture that makes up a particular sprite must have the same dimensions, we only have to make this call once.

- We then store the number of frames in this sprite. This might seem to duplicate the number of textures that we specified in the constructor. However, as you will see in the next section, the number of textures does not always equal the number of frames.

- We now add each texture to the sprite. The sprite class takes care of allocating the necessary memory for us.

Creating a sprite sheet

An alternative method to store your sprites is to use a sprite sheet. A sprite sheet holds all of the sprites for a particular animation in a single file. The sprites are often organized into a strip.

As the dimensions of each frame are identical, we can calculate the position of each frame in a particular animation as an offset from the first frame in the sprite sheet.

You can download a cool little program called **GlueIt** at http://www.varcade.com/blog/glueit-sprite-sheet-maker-download/. This small program allows you to specify several individual images, and then it glues them into a sprite sheet for you.

Loading a sprite sheet

The following code loads a sprite that has been stored as a sprite sheet:

```
robot_right_strip = new Sprite(1);
robot_right_strip->SetFrameSize(125.0f, 100.0f);
robot_right_strip->SetNumberOfFrames(4);
robot_right_strip->SetPosition(0, screen_height - 130.0f);
robot_right_strip->AddTexture("resources/robot_right_strip.png");
```

This code is very similar to the code that we used to create a sprite with individual textures previously. However, there are important differences:

- We only need to allocate space for one texture because we only load one texture. This is the main advantage of using a sprite sheet because it is much more efficient to load a single large texture than it is to load several smaller textures.

- Again, we set the width and height of each frame. Note that these are the same values as when loading individual textures because the important information is the width and height of each frame, not the width and height of the texture.

- Again, we store the number of frames for this sprite. This sprite still has four frames, although all of the four frames are stored in a single image.

- We then add a single image to the sprite.

> When we get ready to render each frame of the animation, the sprite class will take care of calculating exactly which part the sprite strip to render based on the current frame and the width of each frame.

Loading our sprites

The following code shows the full code that we will use to load the sprites into our game. Open the **RoboRacer2D** project and open `RoboRacer.cpp`. First we need to include the Sprite header:

```
#include "Sprite.h"
```

Next, we need some global variables to hold our sprites. Add this code in the variable declarations section of the code (before any functions):

```
Sprite* robot_left;
Sprite* robot_right;
Sprite* robot_right_strip;
```

```
Sprite* robot_left_strip;
Sprite* background;
Sprite* player;
```

We created pointers for each sprite that we will need in the game until this point:

- A sprite to move the robot left
- A sprite to move the robot right
- A sprite for the background

> In order to make it easy for you to work with both types of sprites, I defined two sprites for each robot direction. For example, `robot_left` will define a sprite made up of individual textures, while `robot_left_strip` will define a sprite made up of a single sprite sheet. Normally, you would not use both in a single game!

Now, add the `LoadTextures` function:

```
const bool LoadTextures()
{
  background = new Sprite(1);
  background->SetFrameSize(1877.0f, 600.0f);
  background->SetNumberOfFrames(1);
  background->AddTexture("resources/background.png", false);

  robot_right = new Sprite(4);
  robot_right->SetFrameSize(100.0f, 125.0f);
  robot_right->SetNumberOfFrames(4);
  robot_right->SetPosition(0, screen_height - 130.0f);
  robot_right->AddTexture("resources/robot_right_00.png");
  robot_right->AddTexture("resources/robot_right_01.png");
  robot_right->AddTexture("resources/robot_right_02.png");
  robot_right->AddTexture("resources/robot_right_03.png");

  robot_left = new Sprite(4);
  robot_left->SetFrameSize(100.0f, 125.0f);
  robot_left->SetNumberOfFrames(4);
  robot_left->SetPosition(0, screen_height - 130.0f);
  robot_left->AddTexture("resources/robot_left_00.png");
  robot_left->AddTexture("resources/robot_left_01.png");
  robot_left->AddTexture("resources/robot_left_02.png");
  robot_left->AddTexture("resources/robot_left_03.png");
```

```
robot_right_strip = new Sprite(1);
robot_right_strip->SetFrameSize(125.0f, 100.0f);
robot_right_strip->SetNumberOfFrames(4);
robot_right_strip->SetPosition(0, screen_height - 130.0f);
robot_right_strip->AddTexture("resources/robot_right_strip.png");

robot_left_strip = new Sprite(1);
robot_left_strip->SetFrameSize(125.0f, 100.0f);
robot_left_strip->SetNumberOfFrames(4);
robot_right_strip->SetPosition(0, screen_height - 130.0f);
robot_left_strip->AddTexture("resources/robot_left_strip.png");

background->IsVisible(true);
background->IsActive(true);
background->SetVelocity(-50.0f);

robot_right->IsActive(true);
robot_right->IsVisible(true);
robot_right->SetVelocity(50.0f);

player = robot_right;
player->IsActive(true);
player->IsVisible(true);
player->SetVelocity(50.0f);

return true;
}
```

This code is exactly the same as the code that I showed you earlier to load sprites. It is simply more comprehensive:

- `LoadTexures` loads all of the sprites needed in the game (including duplicate *strip* versions so that you can see the difference between using sprite sheets versus individual textures).

- `SetPosition` is used to set the initial position for the robot sprites. Notice that we don't do this for the background sprite because its position starts at (0, 0), which is the default.

- `SetVisible` and `SetActive` are used to set the `background` sprite and the `robot_left_strip` sprite as active and visible. All of the other sprites will remain inactive and invisible.

As the loading of textures only needs to occur once in the game, we will add the call to do this to the StartGame function. Modify the StartGame function in RoboRacer.cpp:

```
void StartGame()
{
   LoadTextures();
}
```

The final step in getting our textures loaded is to implement the AddTexture method in our sprite class. Open Sprite.cpp and add the following code:

```
const bool Sprite::AddTexture(const char* p_imageName, const bool p_
useTransparency)
{
   GLuint texture = SOIL_load_OGL_texture( p_imageName, SOIL_LOAD_AUTO,
SOIL_CREATE_NEW_ID, 0 );
   if (texture == 0)
   {
     return false;
   }

   m_textures[m_textureIndex] = texture;
   m_textureIndex++;
   if (m_textureIndex == 1 && m_numberOfFrames > 1)
   {
     m_isSpriteSheet= true;
   }
   else
   {
     m_isSpriteSheet = false;
   }
   m_useTransparency = p_useTransparency;
   return true;
}
```

AddTexture is used after a new sprite has been created. It adds the required textures to the m_textures array. Here's how it works:

- p_imageName holds the name and path of the image to load.

- p_useTransparency is used to tell the sprite class whether this image uses an alpha channel. As most of our sprites will use transparency, this is coded to default to true. However, if we set p_useTransparency to false, then any transparency information will be ignored.

- `SOIL_load_OGL_texture` does all of the work of loading the texture. The parameters for this call were described earlier in this chapter. Note that SOIL is smart enough to load image types based on the file extension.

- If the texture was successfully loaded, `SOIL_load_OGL_texture` will return an OpenGL texture handle. If not, it will return `0`. Generally, we would test this value and use some kind of error handling, or quit if any texture did not load correctly.

- As the `m_textures` array is allocated in the constructor, we can simply store texture in the `m_textureIndex` slot.

- We then increment `m_textureIndex`.

- We use a little trick to determine if this sprite uses a sprite sheet or individual sprites. Basically, if there is only one texture but many frames, then we assume that this sprite uses a sprite sheet and set `m_isSpriteSheet` to `true`.

- Finally, we set `m_useTransparency` to the value that was passed in. This will be used later in the `Render` method.

Rendering

We did a lot of work creating our sprites, but nothing is going to show up until we actually render the sprites using OpenGL. Rendering is done for every frame of the game. First, an `Update` function is called to update the state of the game, then everything is rendered to the screen.

Adding a render to the game loop

Let's start by adding a call to `Render` in the `GameLoop` RoboRacer.cpp:

```
void GameLoop()
{
  Render();
}
```

At this point, we are simply calling the main `Render` function (implemented in the next section). Every object that can be drawn to the screen will also have a `Render` method. In this way, the call to render the game will cascade down through every renderable object in the game.

Implementing the main Render function

Now, it is time to implement the main `Render` function. Add the following code to `RoboRacer.cpp`:

```cpp
void Render()
{
  glClear(GL_COLOR_BUFFER_BIT);
  glLoadIdentity();

  background->Render();
  robot_left->Render();
  robot_right->Render();
  robot_left_strip->Render();
  robot_right_strip->Render();

  SwapBuffers(hDC);
}
```

> Notice that we render the background first. In a 2D game, the objects will be rendered in a first come, first rendered basis. This way the robot will always render on top of the background.

Here's how it works:

- We always start our render cycle by resetting the OpenGL render pipeline. `glClear` sets the entire color buffer to the background color that we chose when initializing OpenGL. `glLoadIdentity` resets the rendering matrix.

- Next, we call `Render` for each sprite. We don't care if the sprite is actually visible or not. We let the sprite class `Render` method make that decision.

- Once all objects are rendered, we make the call to `SwapBuffers`. This is a technique known as double-buffering. When we render our scene, it is actually created in a buffer off screen. This way the player doesn't actually see the separate images as they are composited to the screen. Then, a single call to `SwapBuffers` makes a fast copy of the offscreen buffer to the actual screen buffer. This makes the screen render appear much more smoothly.

Implementing Render in the Sprite class

The last step in our render chain is to add a render method to the Sprite class. This will allow each sprite to render itself to the screen. Open Sprite.h and add the following code:

```cpp
void Sprite::Render()
{
  if (m_isVisible)
  {
    if (m_useTransparency)
    {
      glEnable(GL_BLEND);
      glBlendFunc(GL_SRC_ALPHA, GL_ONE_MINUS_SRC_ALPHA);
    }

    glBindTexture(GL_TEXTURE_2D, GetCurrentFrame());

    glBegin(GL_QUADS);

    GLfloat x = m_position.x;
    GLfloat y = m_position.y;

    GLfloat w = m_size.width;
    GLfloat h = m_size.height;

    GLfloat texWidth = (GLfloat)m_textureIndex / (GLfloat)m_
numberOfFrames;
    GLfloat texHeight = 1.0f;
    GLfloat u = 0.0f;
    GLfloat v = 0.0f;
    if (m_textureIndex < m_numberOfFrames)
    {
      u = (GLfloat)m_currentFrame * texWidth;
    }
    glTexCoord2f(u, v); glVertex2f(x, y);
    glTexCoord2f(u + texWidth, v); glVertex2f(x + w, y);
    glTexCoord2f(u + texWidth, v + texHeight); glVertex2f(x + w, y +
h);
    glTexCoord2f(u, v + texHeight); glVertex2f(x, y + h);

    glEnd();

    if (m_useTransparency)
    {
```

```
        glDisable(GL_BLEND);
    }
  }
}
```

This is probably one of the more complex sections of the code because rendering has to take many things into consideration. Is the sprite visible? Which frame of the sprite are we rendering? Where on screen should the sprite be rendered? Do we care about transparency? Let's walk through the code step by step:

- First, we check to see if `m_visible` is `true`. If not, we bypass the entire render.

- Next, we check to see if this sprite uses transparency. If it does, we have to enable transparency. The technical term to implement transparency is blending. OpenGL has to blend the current texture with what is already on the screen. `glEnable(GL_BLEND)` turns on transparency blending. The call to `glBlendFunc` tells OpenGL exactly what type of blending we want to implement. Suffice to say that the `GL_SRC_ALPHA` and `GL_ONE_MIUS_SRC_ALPHA` parameters tell OpenGL to allow background images to be seen through transparent sections of the sprite.

- `glBindTexture` tells OpenGL which texture we want to work with right now. The call to `GetCurrentFrame` returns the OpenGL handle of the appropriate texture.

- `glBegin` tells OpenGL that we are ready to render a particular item. In this case, we are rendering a quad.

- The next two lines of code set up the x and y coordinates for the sprite based on the x and y values stored in `m_position`. These values are used in the `glVertex2f` calls to position the sprite.

- We will also need the `width` and `height` of the current frame, and the next two lines store these as `w` and `h` for convenience.

- Finally, we need to know how much of the texture we are going to render. Typically, we render the entire texture. However, in the case of a sprite sheet we will only want to render a section of the texture. We will discuss how this works in more detail later.

- Once we have the position, width, and portion of the texture that we want to render, we use for pairs of calls to `glTexCoord2f` and `glVertex2f` to map each corner of the texture to the quad. This was discussed in great detail in *Chapter 2, Your Point of View*.

- The call to `glEnd` tells OpenGL that we are finished with the current render.

- As alpha checking is computationally expensive, we turn it off at the end of the render with a call to `glDisable(GL_BLEND)`.

UV mapping

UV mapping was covered in detail in *Chapter 2, Your Point of View*. However, we'll do a recap here and see how it is implemented in code.

By convention, we assign the left coordinate of the texture to the variable **u**, and the top coordinate of the texture to the variable **v**. This technique is therefore known as **uv** mapping.

OpenGL considers the origin of a texture to be at **uv** coordinates of $(0, 0)$, and the farthest extent of the texture to be at **uv** coordinates of $(1, 1)$. So, if we want to render the entire texture, we will map the entire range from $(0, 0)$ to $(1, 1)$ the four corners of the quad. However, let's say that we only want to render the first half of the image width (but the entire height). In this case, we will map the range of **uv** coordinates from $(0, 1)$ to $(0.5, 1)$ to the four corners of the quad. Hopefully, you can visualize that this will only render one-half of the texture.

So, in order to render our sprite sheets, we first determine how wide each frame of the sprite is by dividing `m_textureIndex` by `m_numberOfFrames`. In the case of a sprite that has four frames, this will give us a value of 0.25.

Next, we determine which frame we are in. The following table shows the **uv** ranges for each frame of a sprite with four frames:

Frame	**u**	**v**
0	0.0 to 0.25	0.0 to 1.0
1	0.25 to 0.5	0.0 to 1.0
2	0.5 to 0.75	0.0 to 1.0
3	0.75 to 1.0	0.0 to 1.0

As our sprite sheets are set up horizontally, we only need to worry about taking the correct range of **u** from the whole texture, while the range for **v** stays the same.

So, here is how our algorithm works:

- If the sprite is not a sprite sheet, then each frame uses 100 percent of the texture, and we use a range of uv values from $(0,0)$ to $(1, 1)$
- If the sprite is based on a sprite sheet, we determine the width of each frame (`texWidth`) by dividing `m_textureIndex` by `m_numberOfFrames`
- We determine the starting u value by multiplying `m_currentFrame` by `texWidth`
- We determine the extent of **u** by adding `u + texWidth`

- We map u to the upper-corner of the quad, and u + texWidth to the lower corner of the quad

- v is mapped normally because our sprite sheets use 100 percent of the height of the texture

 If you are having a hard time understanding uv mapping, don't fret. It took me years of application to fully understand this concept. You can play around with the uv coordinates to see how things work. For example, try settings of .05, 1, and 1.5 and see what happens!

One more detail

We need to take a closer look at the call to GetCurrentFrame to make sure you understand what this function does. Here is the implementation:

```
const GLuint GetCurrentFrame()
{

    if(m_isSpriteSheet)
    {
        return m_textures[0];
    }
    else
    {
        return m_textures[m_currentFrame];
    }
}
```

Here is what is happening:

- If the sprite is a sprite sheet, we always return m_textures[0] because, by definition, there is only one texture at index 0

- If the sprite is not a sprite sheet, then we return the texture at index m_currentFrame. m_currentFrame is updated in the sprite update method (defined next)

A moving example

The code that we created until this point creates a basic scene with our robot and a background. Now, it's time to bring our robot to life using the power of animation.

Animation actually has two components. First, the sprite itself will appear to animate because we will play each frame of the sprite in sequence. If you use the stock files that were made for this book, you will see the robot's eyes and arms move.

The second component is movement across the screen. It is the combination of the robot's horizontal movement and body movements that will make a convincing animation.

Adding update to the game loop

As with rendering, we start by adding an Update call to the GameLoop function. Modify the GameLoop function in RoboRacer.cpp:

```
void GameLoop(const float p_deltatTime)
{
  Update(p_deltatTime);
  Render();
}
```

We now have two new features:

- We added p_deltaTime as a parameter. This represents the amount of time that has passed in milliseconds since the last frame. We will see how this is calculated in the following section.
- We added a call to the main Update function (defined in the following section). Every object in the game will also have an Update method. In this way, the call to update the game will cascade down through every object in the game. We pass p_deltatTime so that every subsequent call to Update will know how much time has passed in the game.

Implementing the main Update call

Our first task is to implement the Update function in RoboRacer.cpp. Add the following function to RoboRacer.cpp:

```
void Update(const float p_deltaTime)
{
  background->Update(p_deltaTime);
  robot_left->Update(p_deltaTime);
  robot_right->Update(p_deltaTime);
  robot_left_strip->Update(p_deltaTime);
  robot_right_strip->Update(p_deltaTime);
}
```

Notice that we make an Update call to every sprite. At this point, we don't care if the sprite really needs to be updated. This decision will be made inside the Sprite class.

 In a real game, we would probably have an array of sprites, and we would update them all by iterating through the array and calling update on each element. As this game uses so few sprites, I have coded each sprite individually.

Implementing Update in the Sprite class

Now it's time to implement the Update method in our Sprite class. This method does all of the work required to both position the sprite and update the sprite's internal animation. Add this code to Sprite.h:

```
void Sprite::Update(const float p_deltaTime)
{
   float dt = p_deltaTime;

   if (m_isActive)
   {
     m_animationElapsed += dt;
     if (m_animationElapsed >= m_animationDelay)
     {
       m_currentFrame++;
       if (m_currentFrame >= m_numberOfFrames) m_currentFrame = 0;
       m_animationElapsed = 0.0f;
     }
     m_position.x = m_position.x + m_velocity * dt;
   }
}
```

Here is what this code does:

- We store p_deltaTime into a local variable dt for convenience. This is useful because you sometimes want to hardcode the value of dt during testing.

- Next, we test m_active. If this if false, then we bypass the entire update.

- We now handle the sprite's internal animation. We first add dt to m_animationElapsed to see how much time has elapsed since the last frame change. If m_animationElapsed exceeds m_animationDelay, then it is time to increment to the next frame. This means that the higher the value of m_animationDelay, the slower the sprite will animate.

- If necessary, we increment `m_currentFrame` making sure that once we have exceeded the total number of frame, we reset to `0`.

- If we just did a frame increment, we also want to reset `m_animationElapsed` to `0`.

- Now ,we move the sprite based on `m_velocity` and `dt`. Look at the details on using delta time to calculate movement in the upcoming sections.

Character movement

In this version of the game, we programmed our robot to move across the screen from left to right. The key to making our character move is the **velocity** property. The velocity property tells the program how many pixels to move our robot each game cycle.

As the frames come pretty fast, the velocity is typically pretty small. For example, in a game running at 60 fps, a velocity of 1 would move the robot 60 pixels each game frame. The sprite would probably be moving too fast to interact with.

Using delta time

There is a small problem with setting the velocity as a fixed value. Obviously, some computers are faster than other computers. With a fixed velocity, the robot will move faster on faster computers. This is a problem because it means that people on faster computers will have to be much better at playing the game!

We can use the computer's clock to solve this problem. The computer keeps track of the time that has passed since the start of the previous frame. In game terminology, this is called **delta time**, and we assign this to a variable that we can access in the `Update` loop:

```
void Update(float deltaTime);
```

In the preceding function definition, `deltaTime` is a floating value. Remember, our game is typically running at 60 fps, so `deltaTime` is going to be a very small number.

 When we set up a game to run at 60 fps, it rarely runs at exactly that speed. Each frame may take slightly more or less time to finish its calculations. Delta time tells us exactly how much time has passed, and we can use that information to adjust the timing or speed of events.

Let's take a closer look at how we use velocity to position our sprites:

```
m_position.x += m_velocity * dt;
```

We multiply m_velocity times dt, and then add this to the current position. This technique automatically adjusts the velocity based on the amount of time that has passed since the last frame. If the last frame took a little less time to process, then the robot will move a little less. If the last frame took a little longer to process, then our robot will move a little further. The end result is that the robot moves consistently now on both faster and slower computers.

> For slower computers, this could cause other side effects, especially regarding collision detection. If too much time goes by, then the sprite will move farther. This could, for example, cause the sprite to go right through a wall before the collision detection is checked.

As dt is a very small number, we will now have to use a larger number for our velocity. The current code uses a value of 50. Of course, in the full game this value will change based on what is happening to our robot.

Calculating delta time

We already have all of the code in place except the actual code to calculate delta time. In order to calculate the time that has elapsed during each frame of the game, we must:

1. Store the time before the frame.
2. Store the time after the frame.
3. Calculate the difference between the two.

Open RoboRacer.cpp and add the following code right after the call to StartGame:

```
int previousTime = glutGet(GLUT_ELAPSED_TIME);
```

Notice that we are using GLUT to get the current elapsed time. Each call to glutGet(GLUT_ELAPSED_TIME) will give us the number of milliseconds that have elapsed since the game started.

> In order to use GLUT, remember to copy glut.h, glut32.dll, and glut32.lib from the OpenGLFun project to the source code folder of RoboRacer2D. include glut.h at the top of SpaceRacer2D.cpp.

Next, add the following lines directly above the call to GameLoop:

```
int currentTime = glutGet(GLUT_ELAPSED_TIME);
float deltaTime = (float)(currentTime - previousTime) / 1000;
previousTime= currentTime;
GameLoop(deltaTime);
```

Here is what we have done:

- First, we captured the current elapsed time and stored that in
  m_currentTime.

- We then calculated the time that elapsed since the last frame by subtracting
  m_currentTime from m_previousTime. We converted this to seconds to
  make it easier to deal with.

- We then set previousTime to equal current time so that we have a
  benchmark for our next calculation.

- Finally, we modified the call to GameLoop to pass the value of deltaTime.
  This will subsequently be passed to every Update call in the game.

Flipping

Today's games can be created for and played on a wide variety of devices, ranging
from supercharged PCs to mobile phones. Each of these devices has its own set of
advantages and disadvantages. However, one rule of thumb is that as the device gets
smaller its capabilities become more limited.

One area where these limitations become critical is texture memory. Texture memory
is the location in the memory that stores the textures that are being used in the game.
Mobile devices, in particular, are very limited by the amount of available texture
memory, and game programmers have to be very careful not to exceed this limitation.

2D games tend to use a lot of texture memory. This is because each frame of every
animation has to be stored in the memory to bring the 2D images to life. It is typical for
a 2D game to have thousands of frames of textures that have to be loaded into memory.

One simple way to almost cut the required amount of texture memory in half is to utilize texture flipping. Simply put, our robot moving to the left is a mirror image of our robot moving to the right. Instead of using one set of textures to move to the left and another to move to the right, we can use code to flip the texture when it is rendered.

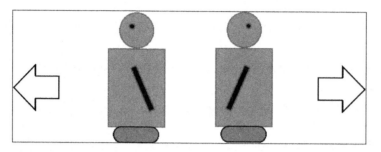

If you want to try it out sometime, flipping would be implemented by changing the way you mapped the sprite's **uv** coordinates to the texture.

Scrolling the background

You may be wondering why we set up our background as a sprite. After all, we defined sprites as objects that the player interacts with in the game, and the background is basically ignored by the robot.

The main reason to set up the background as a sprite is that this allows us to handle all of our textures in a uniform manner. The advantage of this is that we can then apply the same properties to all of our images. For example, what if we decided that we wanted our background to move?

Scrolling backgrounds are used in 2D games to give the impression of a continuously changing background. In fact, the 2D side-scrolling game is considered its own genre. There are basically two requirements to create a scrolling background:

1. Create a large texture that is wider than the screen.
2. Assign a velocity to the texture so that it moves sideways.

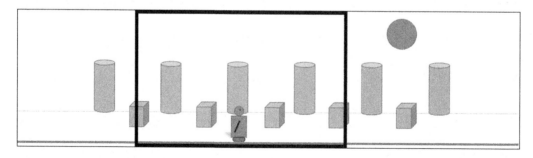

The parts of the texture background that exceeds the screen width will not be rendered. As the image moves, the background appears to slide either to the left or the right. If you set the velocity of the background image to be exactly the same as the velocity of the player, you get the illusion of a background that is flying by as the robot runs left or right.

As we already implemented our background image as a sprite, the only thing that we have to do to make it scroll is to set its velocity. This was already done in the code for `AddTextures`:

```
background->SetVelocity(-50.0f);
```

By setting the background velocity to `-50`, the background scrolls to the left as the robot moves to the right.

Using an atlas

As I have mentioned already, texture memory is one of your core resources. In fact, it is common to run out of memory because of all the textures required to animate a typical 2D game. It is also time-consuming to load individual textures rather than loading on a larger texture. So, we have to come up with methods to use texture memory more efficiently.

One common technique designed to pack more textures into less space is known as **atlasing**. A texture atlas works much like a sprite sheet described earlier in this chapter. Instead of storing each texture as its own image, we pack all of the textures for the entire game into one or more textures known as **atlases**.

As the word suggests, an atlas works much like a map. We simply need to know the location of any particular image, and we can find and extract it out of the atlas. Every atlas consists of two parts:

- The texture that contains all of the images
- A text file that contains the positions of each image in the atlas

As you can imagine, efficiently packing thousands of images into an atlas and then keeping track of each image's position within the atlas would be almost impossible to manage manually. This is why there are programs to do this for us.

I use a free texture atlas tool called **Texture Atlas Generator**. You can download this at http://www.gogo-robot.com/2010/03/20/texture-atlas-sprite-sheet-generator/.

A detailed example of atlasing is beyond the scope of this chapter. If you want to explore this on your own, here are the steps that you require:

1. Use a program, such as the one just mentioned, to create your atlas.

2. Save your data as an XML file.

3. Write a class to parse the XML saved in the previous step (I suggest **TinyXML** at http://www.grinninglizard.com/tinyxml/ as a starter).

4. Using the code to work with sprite sheets, modify the sprite class to be able to handle sub-textures from any arbitrary position in a larger texture.

Summary

This chapter has covered a lot of ground. You created a new class specifically to work with sprites. Consider this class a huge part of your utility box for any game that you will create. This class handles all of the requirements that you will need to load, move, and handle textures as objects in your game.

In the next chapter, you will learn how to how to handle input, and actually control your robot.

4
Control Freak

Most games are designed to be interactive. This means that the player must have some way to control what happens during the game. In the last chapter, you wrote code that displayed the robot and moved him across the screen. Now, you will control the robot!

This chapter will explain how to implement an input system to control the game's character, and interact with the game. Topics will include:

- **Types of input**: There are many ways to interact with your game. Typically, games written for the PC depended on the mouse and keyboard. Direct touch input has now become the standard for mobile and tablet devices, and soon every PC will also have a touch-enabled display. We will cover the most common methods to receive input in your game.

- **Using the mouse and keyboard**: In this section, you will write code to receive input from the mouse and keyboard to control both the game and our friendly robot.

- **Creating the user interface**: In addition to controlling our robot, we also need a way to interact with the game. You will learn how to create an onscreen interface that allows you to control the game and choose the game options.

- **Controlling the character**: We want our robot to be able to walk, run, jump, and play! You will learn how to use the mouse and keyboard to control how your robot moves about on the screen.

A penny for your input

It's likely that at some point in your life, you have been part of a conversation that seemed one-sided. The other party was talking and talking, and it didn't seem you could get a word in. After a while, such a conversation becomes quite boring!

The same would happen with a computer game that didn't allow any **input**. Input is a set of techniques that allows you to control the game. There are many ways to implement an input system, and we will cover them here.

The keyboard input

The most common form of input for most computers is the keyboard. Obviously, the keyboard can be used to enter text, but the keyboard can also be used to directly control the game.

Some examples of this include the following:

- Using the right arrow, left arrow, up arrow, and down arrow keys to control the character (we'll be using this)
- Using the *W*, *A*, *S*, and *D* keys as to move the character (these keys almost form a cross on the keyboard, making them a good substitute to move up, left, down, and right, respectively)
- Using certain keys to perform predefined actions, such as:
  - Using the *Esc* key or *Q* to quit
  - Using the Spacebar or *Enter key* to fire a projectile

These are just a few examples. In fact, there are some games that seem to use every key on the keyboard!

Using the mouse

The mouse has been around for a long time, so it makes sense that the mouse is used in many games. The mouse can be used in several ways:

- The left and right mouse buttons can perform specific actions.
- The wheel can be pushed and used as a third button.
- The mouse wheel can be used to scroll.
- The position of the mouse pointer can be tracked and used in conjunction with any of the previous actions. We will use a combination of the left mouse button and the mouse pointer position to click onscreen buttons when we design our user interface.

Touch

More and more devices now respond to touch. Many input systems treat touch very similarly to the mouse:

- A single touch is equivalent to using the left mouse button
- A single touch that is held is equivalent to using the right mouse button
- The position of the finger can be used in the same way as the mouse pointer

However, there are many features of touch that cannot be easily equated to the mouse. For example, most touch interfaces allow several touches to be handled simultaneously. This feature is known as multitouch. This has led to many standard gestures, including:

- The swipe or flick (moving one or more fingers quickly across the screen)
- The pinch (moving two fingers together)
- The zoom (moving two fingers apart)

Unfortunately, we won't be implementing touch in this game because the target device for this book is the PC.

Other inputs

The advent of mobile devices was followed by an explosion of input techniques. Some of the more common ones include:

- The accelerometer, which can be used to track the physical motion of the device
- Geolocation, which can be used to detect the physical location of the device
- The compass, which can be used to detect the orientation of the device
- The microphone, which can be used to accept voice input

There are many other input techniques, and there is a lot of overlap. For example, most PCs have a microphone. Again, while many games in the mobile market are taking advantage of these alternative input methods, our game will be limited to the keyboard and mouse.

Someone is listening

Now, it's time to actually write some code to implement input for our game. It turns out that some rudimentary input has already been implemented. This is because Windows is an **event driven** operating system and is already looking for input to occur. From a simplistic point of view, the main task of Windows (or any modern operating system) is to listen for **events**, and then do something based on those events.

So, whenever you hit a key on your keyboard, an event is triggered that wakes up Windows and says, "Hey, someone hit the keyboard!" Windows then passes that information to any programs that happen to be listening to keyboard events. The same occurs when you use the mouse.

The WndProc event listener

We have already told our program that we want it to listen to events. Open RoboRacer.cpp and locate the WndProc function. WndProc is part of the code that was created for us when use used the **Win32 Project template** to start our game. WndProc is known as a **callback function**.

Here is how a callback function works:

- First, the function name is registered with the operating system. In our case, this occurs in CreateGLWindow:

  ```
  wc.lpfnWndProc = (WNDPROC)WndProc;
  ```

  This line tells our window class to register a function called WndProc as the event handler for our program.

- Now, any events that are caught by Windows are passed to the WndProc function. The code in WndProc then decides which events to handle. Any events that aren't handled by WndProc are simply ignored by the program.

As WndProc was created for a typical Windows application, it contains some things that we don't need, while there are some things that we can use:

```
LRESULT CALLBACK WndProc(HWND hWnd, UINT message, WPARAM wParam,
LPARAM lParam)
{
  int wmId, wmEvent;
  PAINTSTRUCT ps;
  HDC hdc;

  switch (message)
  {
```

```
     case WM_COMMAND:
     wmId     = LOWORD(wParam);
     wmEvent = HIWORD(wParam);
     // Parse the menu selections:
     switch (wmId)
     {
       case IDM_ABOUT:
       DialogBox(hInstance, MAKEINTRESOURCE(IDD_ABOUTBOX), hWnd,
About);
       break;
       case IDM_EXIT:
       DestroyWindow(hWnd);
       break;
       default:
       return DefWindowProc(hWnd, message, wParam, lParam);
     }
     break;
     case WM_PAINT:
     hdc = BeginPaint(hWnd, &ps);
     // TODO: Add any drawing code here...
     EndPaint(hWnd, &ps);
     break;
     case WM_DESTROY:
     PostQuitMessage(0);
     break;
     default:
     return DefWindowProc(hWnd, message, wParam, lParam);
   }
   return 0;
}
```

The main work is done by switch, which handles various windows events (all prefixed by **WM**, which is an abbreviation for **Windows Message**):

- The WM_COMMAND events can all be ignored. In a typical Windows application, you would create a menu and then assign various command events to be triggered when the user clicks on a command on the menu (for example, IDM_ABOUT to click on the **About** command). Games almost never use the standard Windows menu structure (and so, neither do we).

- We also ignore the WM_PAINT event. This event is triggered whenever the window containing the program needs to be redrawn. However, we are constantly redrawing our window using OpenGL via the Render function, so we don't need to add code to do that here.

- We are already handling the WM_DESTROY event. This event is triggered when you click the close icon (**X**) in the upper-right corner of the Windows. Our handler responds to this by posting its own message using PostQuitMessage(0). This tells our program that it is time to quit.

Handling the message queue

We discussed the Windows messaging system in *Chapter 1, Building the Foundation* but this discussion warrants a recap. If you take a look at the _wWinMain function, you will see this block of code that sets up the main messaging loop:

```
bool done = false;
while (!done)
{
  if (PeekMessage(&msg, NULL, 0, 0, PM_REMOVE))
  {
    if (msg.message == WM_QUIT)
    {
      done = true;
    }
    else
    {
      TranslateMessage(&msg);
      DispatchMessage(&msg);
    }
  }
  else
  {
    int currentTime = glutGet(GLUT_ELAPSED_TIME);
    float deltaTime = (float)(currentTime - previousTime) / 1000;
    previousTime= currentTime;
    GameLoop(deltaTime);
  }
}
```

The relevant part of this discussion is the call to PeekMessage. PeekMessage queries the message queue. In our case, if the WM_QUIT message has been posted (by PostQuitMessage), then done is set to true and the while loop exits, ending the game. As long as WM_QUIT has not been posted, the while loop will continue and GameLoop will be called.

The event driven system is a great way to handle input and other actions for most programs, but it doesn't work well with games. Unlike games, most programs just sit around waiting for some kind of input to occur. For example, a word processing program waits for either a keystroke, a mouse button click, or a command to be issued. With this type of system, it makes sense to wake up the program every time an event happens so that the event can be processed.

Games, on the other hand, do not sleep! Whether or not you are pressing a button, the game is still running. Furthermore, we need to be able to control the process so that an input is only processed when we are ready for it to be handled. For example, we don't want input to interrupt our render loop.

The following diagram shows how Windows is currently rigged to handle input:

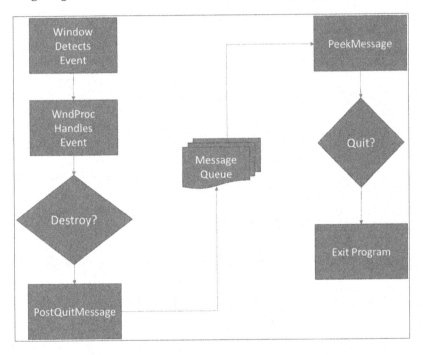

Handling mouse and keyboard inputs

We could expand `WndProc` to handle all of the input events. However, this is a terribly inefficient way to handle input, especially in a real-time program, such as a game. We will let Windows handle the case when the user closes the Window. For everything else, we are going to create our own input class that directly polls for input.

There are many different ways to design an input system, and I am not going to presume that this is the best system. However, our input system accomplishes two important tasks:

- We define a consistent input interface that handles both mouse and keyboard input
- We handle input by directly polling for mouse and keyboard events during each frame (instead of waiting for Windows to send them to us)

Creating the Input class

Create a new class called Input. Then add the following code into Input.h:

```cpp
#pragma once
#include <Windows.h>

class Input
{
  public:
  enum Key
  {
    K_ESC = VK_ESCAPE,
    K_SPACE = VK_SPACE,
    K_LEFT = VK_LEFT,
    K_RIGHT = VK_RIGHT,
    K_UP = VK_UP,
    K_DOWN = VK_DOWN,
    K_W = 87,
    K_A = 65,
    K_S = 83,
    K_D = 68,
    K_Q = 81,
    K_ENTER = VK_RETURN,
    K_LB = VK_LBUTTON,
    K_RB = VK_RBUTTON
  };

  enum Command
  {
    CM_LEFT,
    CM_RIGHT,
    CM_STOP,
    CM_UP,
```

```
    CM_DOWN,
    CM_QUIT
};

#define KEYDOWN(vk_code) ((GetAsyncKeyState(vk_code) & 0x8000) ? 1 :
0)

protected:
Command m_command;
HWND m_hWnd;

public:
Input(const HWND m_hWnd);
~Input();

void Update(const float p_detlaTime);

const Command GetCommand() const { return m_command; }
};
```

As with all of our code, let's take a close look to see how this is designed:

- We include Windows.h because we want access to the Windows API virtual key constants. These are constants that have been defined to represent special keys on the keyboard and mouse.

- We create the Key enum so that we can easily define values to poll the keys that we want to handle.

- We create the Command enum so that we can easily map input to command actions that we want to support.

- We define a C++ macro named KEYDOWN. This greatly simplifies our future code (see the next step for details).

- The class only has one member variable, m_command, which will be used to hold the last action that was requested.

- We define three member functions: the constructor, the destructor, Update, and GetCommand.

Virtual key codes

In order to understand how our input system works, you must first understand virtual key codes. There are a lot of keys on a keyboard. In addition to letters and numbers, there are special keys, including shift, control, escape, enter, arrow keys, and function keys. Coming up with a simple way to identify each key is quite a task!

Windows uses two techniques to identify keys; for the normal keys (letters and numbers), each key is identified by the ASCII code of the value that is being tested. The following table shows the ASCII value for the keys that we use in our game:

ASCII Value	Key
87	*W*
65	*A*
83	*S*
68	*D*
81	*Q*

For special keys, Windows defines integer constants to make them easier to work with. These are known as virtual key codes. The following table shows the virtual key codes that we will work with in our game:

Virtual key code	Key
VK_ESC	*Esc*
VK_SPACE	Spacebar
VK_LEFT	Left arrow
VK_RIGHT	Right arrow
VK_UP	Up arrow
VK_DOWN	Down arrow
VK_RETURN	*Enter*
VK_LBUTTON	Left mouse button
VK_RBUTTON	Right mouse button

Notice that there are even virtual key codes for the mouse buttons!

Querying for input

The GetAsyncKeyState function is used to query the system for both keyboard and mouse input. Here is an example of that command:

```
if ( (getAsyncKeyState(VK_ESC) & 0x8000) == true )
{
    PostQuitMessage(0);
}
```

First, we pass in a virtual key code (or ASCII value), then we do a logical and with the hex value 8000 to strip out information that we don't need. If the result of this call is true, then the queried key is being pressed.

It's a pretty awkward command to have to use over and over again! So, we create a C++ macro to make things simpler:

```
#define KEYDOWN(vk_code) ((GetAsyncKeyState(vk_code) & 0x8000) ? 1 :
0)
```

KEYDOWN executes the GetAsyncKeyState command. The macro accepts a key code as a parameter, and returns true if that key is being pressed or false if that key is not being pressed.

Implementing the Input class

All of the actual work is for our input system is done in the Update function, so let's implement the Input class. Open Input.cpp and enter the following code:

```
#include "stdafx.h"
#include "Input.h"

Input::Input(const HWND p_hWnd)
{
  m_command = Command::CM_STOP;
m_hWnd = p_hWnd;
}

Input::~Input()
{
}

void Input::Update(const float p_deltaTime)
{
  m_command = Command::CM_STOP;
  if (KEYDOWN(Key::K_LEFT) || KEYDOWN(Key::K_A))
  {
    m_command = Command::CM_LEFT;
  }
  if (KEYDOWN(Key::K_RIGHT) || KEYDOWN(Key::K_D))
  {
    m_command = Command::CM_RIGHT;
  }
  if (KEYDOWN(Key::K_UP) || KEYDOWN(Key::K_LB))
  {
```

```
    m_command = Command::CM_UP;
  }
  if (KEYDOWN(Key::K_DOWN) || KEYDOWN(Key::K_RB))
  {
    m_command = Command::CM_DOWN;
  }
  if (KEYDOWN(Key::K_ESC) || KEYDOWN(Key::K_Q))
  {
    m_command = Command::CM_QUIT;
  }
}
```

In a nutshell, the `Update` function queries all of the keys that we want to check simultaneously, and then maps those keys to one of the command enums that we have defined in the class header. The program then calls the class `GetCommand` method to determine the current action that has to be taken.

If you are really paying attention, then you may have realized that we only store a single command result into `m_command`, yet we are querying many keys. We can get away with this for two reasons:

- This is an infinitely simple input system with few demands
- The computer cycles through the input at 60 frames per second, so the process of the player pressing and releasing keys is infinitely slow in comparison

Basically, the last key detected will have its command stored in `m_command`, and that's good enough for us.

Also, notice that we set the initial command to `Input::Command::STOP`. As a result, if no key is currently being held down, then the `STOP` command will be the final value of `m_command`. The result of this is that if we are not pressing keys to make our robot move, then he will stop.

Adding input to the game loop

Now that we have an input class, we will implement it in our game. We will handle input by adding it to `Update`. This gives us total control over when and how we handle input. We will only rely on the Windows event listener to tell us if the Window has been closed (so that we can still shut the game down properly).

Open `RoboRacer.cpp` and modify the `Update` function so that it looks like the following code:

```
void Update(const float p_deltaTime)
{
  inputManager->Update(p_deltaTime);
```

```
    ProcessInput (p_deltaTime);

    background->Update(p_deltaTime);
    robot_left->Update(p_deltaTime);
    robot_right->Update(p_deltaTime);
    robot_left_strip->Update(p_deltaTime);
    robot_right_strip->Update(p_deltaTime);
}
```

Before now, our Update function only updated the game's sprites. If you recall, the sprite Update method modifies the position of the sprites. So, it makes sense to perform the input before we update the sprites. The Update method of the Input class queries the system for input, and then we run a ProcessInput to decide what to do.

Processing our input

Just before we update all of our sprites, we need to process the input. Remember, the Input class Update method only queries the input and stores a command. It doesn't actually change anything. This is because the Input class does not have access to our sprites.

First, open RoboRacer.cpp and include the Input header file:

```
include "Input.h"
```

We need to add a variable to point to our Input class. Add the following line in the variable declarations section:

```
Input* inputManager;
```

Then, modify StartGame to instantiate the Input class:

```
void StartGame()
{
  inputManager = new Input(hWnd);
  LoadTextures();
}
```

Now, we will create a function to process the input. Add the following function to RoboRacer.cpp:

```
void ProcessInput (const float p_deltaTime);
{
  switch (inputManager->GetCommand())
  {
    case Input::Command::CM_STOP:
```

```
player->SetVelocity(0.0f);
background->SetVelocity(0.0f);
break;

case Input::Command::CM_LEFT:
if (player == robot_right)
{
  robot_right->IsActive(false);
  robot_right->IsVisible(false);
  robot_left->SetPosition(robot_right->GetPosition());
}

player = robot_left;
player->IsActive(true);
player->IsVisible(true);
player->SetVelocity(-50.0f);
background->SetVelocity(50.0f);
break;

case Input::Command::CM_RIGHT:
if (player == robot_left)
{
  robot_left->IsActive(false);
  robot_left->IsVisible(false);
  robot_right->SetPosition(robot_left->GetPosition());
}

player = robot_right;
player->IsActive(true);
player->IsVisible(true);
player->SetVelocity(50.0f);
background->SetVelocity(-50.0f);
break;

case Input::Command::CM_UP:
player->Jump(Sprite::SpriteState::UP);
break;

case Input::Command::CM_DOWN:
player->Jump(Sprite::SpriteState::DOWN);
break;

case Input::Command::CM_QUIT:
PostQuitMessage(0);
```

```
        break;
    }
}
```

`ProcessInput` is where the changes to our game actually take place. Although it seems like a lot of code, there are really only two things that are happening:

- We query the input system for the latest command using `inputManager->GetCommand()`
- Based on that command we perform the required actions

The following table shows the commands that we have defined, followed by a description of how this affects the game:

Command	Actions
CM_STOP	• Set the velocity of `player` to 0 • Set the background velocity to 0
CM_LEFT	• If `player` is currently moving right, deactivate the right sprite and make it invisible, and set the left sprite to the right sprite's position • Set `player` to the left sprite • Activate the left sprite and make it visible • Set the velocity of the left sprite to -50 • Set the velocity of the background to 50
CM_RIGHT	• If `player` is currently moving left, deactivate the left sprite and make it invisible, and set the right sprite to the left sprite's position • Set `player` to the right sprite • Activate the right sprite and make it visible • Set the velocity of the right sprite to 50 • Set the velocity of the background to -50
CM_UP	• Call the sprite's `Jump` method with the parameter set to UP
CM_DOWN	• Call the sprite's `Jump` method with the parameter set to DOWN
CM_QUIT	• Quit the game

Changes to the Sprite class

Now that the robot can jump, we need to add a new method to the Sprite class to give the robot the ability to jump:

First, we will add an enum to Sprite.h to track the sprite state:

```
enum SpriteState
{
  UP,
  DOWN
};
```

Next, we need a new member variable to track if an element has been clicked. Add:

```
bool m_isClicked;
```

Now go to the constructor in Sprite.cpp and add a line to initialize the new variable:

```
m_isClicked = false;
```

Add the following code to Sprite.h:

```
void Jump(SpriteState p_state);
void IsClicked(const bool p_value) { m_isClicked = p_value; }
const bool IsClicked() const { return m_isClicked; }
```

Then add the following code to Sprite.cpp:

```
void Sprite::Jump(SpriteState p_state)
{
  if (p_state == SpriteState::DOWN )
  {
    if (m_position.y < 470.0f) m_position.y += 75.0f;
  }
  else if (p_state == SpriteState::UP)
  {
    if (m_position.y >= 470.0f) m_position.y -= 75.0f;
  }
}
```

Our robot is a little unique. When he jumps, he hovers at an elevated level until we tell him to come back down. The Jump method moves the robot 75 pixels higher when the player presses the up arrow, and moves him 75 pixels back down when the player presses the down arrow. However, we want to make sure that we don't allow a double-jump up or a double-jump down, so we check the current y position before we apply the change.

Now that we are going to use input to control our robot, we no longer need to set the initial velocity as we did in the previous chapter. Locate the following two lines of code in LoadTextures and delete them:

```
background->SetVelocity(-50.0f);
player->SetVelocity(50.0f);
```

Run the game. You should now be able to control the robot with the arrow keys, moving him left and right, up and down. Congratulations, you're a control freak!

Graphical User Interface

It is now time to turn our attention to the graphical user interface, or GUI. The GUI allows us to control other elements of the game, such as starting or stopping the game, or setting various options.

In this section, you will learn how to create buttons on the screen that can be clicked by the mouse. We'll keep it simple by adding a single button to pause the game. While we are at it, we will learn important lessons about game state.

Creating a button

A button is nothing more than a texture that is being displayed on the screen. However, we have to perform some special coding to detect whether or not the button is being clicked. We will add this functionality to the sprite class so that our buttons are being handled by the same class that handles other image in our game.

We will actually create two buttons: one to Pause and one to Resume. I have used a simple graphics program to create the following two buttons:

I have saved these buttons as, you guessed it, `pause.png` and `resume.png` in the `resources` folder.

Enhancing the Input class

In order to integrate UI into our existing `Input` class, we are going to have to add some additional features. We will add a dynamic array to the `Input` class to hold a list of UI elements that we need to check for input.

Start by adding the following line to the includes for `Input.h`:

```
#include "Sprite.h"
```

We need to include the `Sprite` class so that we can work with sprites in the `Input` class.

Next, we add a new command. Modify the `Command` enum so that it looks like the following list:

```
enum Command
{
CM_INVALID,
CM_LEFT,
   CM_RIGHT,
   CM_STOP,
   CM_UP,
   CM_DOWN,
   CM_QUIT,
   CM_UI
};
```

We have added `CM_UI`, which will be set as the current command if any UI element is clicked.

Now, we define a member variable to hold the list of UI elements. Add this line of code to the member variables in `Input.h`:

```
Sprite** m_uiElements;
unsigned int m_uiCount;
```

`m_uiElements` will be a dynamic list of pointers to our elements, while `m_uiCount` will keep track of the number of elements in the list.

The final change to `Input.h` is to add the following line in the public methods:

```
void AddUiElement(Sprite* m_pElement);
```

Adding UI elements to the list

We need to be able to add a list of elements to our `Input` class so that they can be checked during the input handling.

First, we have to allocate memory for our list of elements. Add the following lines to the `Input` constructor in `Input.cpp`:

```
m_uiElements = new Sprite*[10];
m_uiCount = 0;
```

I could probably get cleverer than this, but for now, we will allocate enough memory to hold 10 UI elements. We then initialize m_uiCount to 0. Now, we need to add the following method to Input.cpp:

```
void Input::AddUiElement(Sprite* p_element)
{
  m_uiElements[m_uiCount] = p_element;
  m_uiCount++;
}
```

This method allows us to add a UI element to our list (internally, each UI element is a pointer to a sprite). We add the element to the m_uiElements array at the current index and then increment m_uiCount.

Checking each UI element

Eventually, the Input class will contain a list of all UI elements that it is supposed to check. We will need to iterate through that list to see if any of the active elements have been clicked (if we want to ignore a particular element, we simply set its active flat to false).

Open Input.cpp and add the following code to Update above the existing code:

```
for (unsigned int i = 0; i < m_uiCount; i++)
{
  Sprite* element = m_uiElements[i];
  if (element->IsActive() == true)
  {
    if (CheckForClick(element))
    {
      element->IsClicked(true);
      m_command = Input::Command::CM_UI;
      return;
    }
  }
}
```

This code iterates through each item in the m_uiElements array. If the element is active, then CheckForClick is called to see if this element has been clicked. If the element has been clicked, the IsClicked property of the element is set to true and m_command is set to CM_UI.

We put this code above the existing code because we want checking the UI to take priority over checking for game input. Notice in the preceding code that we exit the function if we find a UI element that has been clicked.

Pushing your buttons

In order to see if an element has been clicked, we need to see if the left mouse button is down while the mouse pointer is inside the area bounded by the UI element.

First, open `Input.cpp` and add the following code:

```
const bool Input::CheckForClick(Sprite* p_element) const
{
  if (KEYDOWN(Key::K_LB))
  {
    POINT cursorPosition;
    GetCursorPos(&cursorPosition);
    ScreenToClient(m_hWnd, &cursorPosition);
    float left = p_element->GetPosition().x;
    float right = p_element->GetPosition().x + p_element->GetSize().
width;
    float top = p_element->GetPosition().y;
    float bottom = p_element->GetPosition().y + p_element->GetSize().
height;

    if (cursorPosition.x >= left  &&
      cursorPosition.x <= right &&
    cursorPosition.y >= top &&
    cursorPosition.y <= bottom)
    {
      return true;
    }
    else
    {
      return false;
    }
  }
  return false;
}
```

Here is what we are doing:

- We first make sure that the left mouse button is down.
- We need to store the current position of the mouse. To do this, we create a POINT called cursorPosition, then pass that by reference into GetCursorPos. This will set cursorPosition to the current mouse position in screen coordinates.

- We actually need the mouse position in client coordinates (the actual area that we have to work with, ignoring windows borders and fluff). To get this, we pass `cursorPosition` along with a handle to the current window into `ScreenToClient`.

- Now that we have the `cursorPosition`, want to test to see if it is inside the rectangle that bounds our UI element. We calculate the left, right, top, and bottom coordinates of the sprite.

- Finally, we check to see if `cursorPosition` is within the boundaries of the UI element. If so, we return `true`; otherwise, we return `false`.

Ensure to add the following declaration to `Sprite.h`:

```
const bool CheckForClick(Sprite* p_element) const;
```

Adding our pauseButton

We now need to add the code to our game to create and monitor our pause and resume buttons.

First, we will add two variables for our two new sprites. Add the following two lines to the variable declaration block of `RoboRacer.cpp`:

```
Sprite* pauseButton;
Sprite* resumeButton;
```

Then, add the following lines to `LoadTextures` (just before the `return` statement):

```
pauseButton = new Sprite(1);
pauseButton->SetFrameSize(75.0f, 38.0f);
pauseButton->SetNumberOfFrames(1);
pauseButton->SetPosition(5.0f, 5.0f);
pauseButton->AddTexture("resources/pauseButton.png");
pauseButton->IsVisible(true);
pauseButton->IsActive(true);
inputManager->AddUiElement(pauseButton);

resumeButton = new Sprite(1);
resumeButton->SetFrameSize(75.0f, 38.0f);
resumeButton->SetNumberOfFrames(1);
  resumeButton->SetPosition(80.0f, 5.0f);
resumeButton->AddTexture("resources/resumeButton.png");
inputManager->AddUiElement(resumeButton);
```

This code sets up the pause and resume sprites exactly like we set up the other sprites in our game. Only the pause sprite is set to be active and visible.

You will notice one important addition: we add each sprite to the `Input` class with a call to `AddUiElement`. This adds the sprite to the list of UI elements that need to be checked for input.

We must also add code to the `Update` function in `RoboRacer.cpp`:

```
pauseButton->Update(p_deltaTime);
resumeButton->Update(p_deltaTime);
```

Similarly, we must add code to the `Render` function in `RoboRacer.cpp` (just before the call to `SwapBuffers`):

```
pauseButton->Render();
resumeButton->Render();
```

That's it! If you run the game now, you should see the new pause button in the upper-left corner. Unfortunately, it doesn't do anything yet (other than change the button from Pause to Resume. Before we can actually pause the game, we need to learn about state management.

State management

Think about it. If we want our game to pause, then we have to set some kind of flag that tells the game that we want it to take a break. We could set up a Boolean:

```
bool m_isPaused;
```

We would set `m_isPaused` to `true` if the game is paused, and set it to `false` if the game is running.

The problem with this approach is that there are a lot of special cases that we may run into in a real game. At any time the game might be:

- Starting
- Ending
- Running
- Paused

These are just some example of **game states**. A game state is a particular mode that requires special handling. As there can be so many states, we usually create a state manager to keep track of the state we are currently in.

Creating a state manager

The simplest version of a state manager begins with an enum that defines all of the game states. Open `RoboRacer.cpp` and add the following code just under the include statements:

```
enum GameState
{
  GS_Running,
  GS_Paused
};
```

Then go to the variable declarations block and add the following line:

```
GameState m_gameState;
```

To keep things simple, we are going to define two states: running and paused. A larger game will have many more states.

Enums have a big advantage over Boolean variables. First, their purpose is generally clearer. Saying that the game state is `GS_Paused` or `GS_Running` is clearer than if we just had set a Boolean to `true` or `false`.

The other advantage is that enums can have more than two values. If we need to add another state to our game, it is as simple as adding another value to our `GameState` enum list.

Our game will start in the running state, so add the following line of code to the `StartGame` function:

```
m_gameState = GS_Running;
```

Pausing the game

Think about it for a minute. What do we want to do when the game is paused? We still want to see things on the screen, so that means that we still want to make all of our Render calls. However, we don't want things to change position or animate. We also don't want to process game input, though we do need to handle UI input.

All of this should have you thinking about the update calls. We want to block updates to everything except the UI. Modify the `Update` function in `RoboRacer.cpp` so that it contains the following code:

```
void Update(const float p_deltaTime)
{
  inputManager->Update(p_deltaTime);
```

```
ProcessInput(p_deltaTime);

if (m_gameState == GS_Running)
{
  background->Update(p_deltaTime);
  robot_left->Update(p_deltaTime);
  robot_right->Update(p_deltaTime);
  robot_left_strip->Update(p_deltaTime);
  robot_right_strip->Update(p_deltaTime);

  pauseButton->Update(p_deltaTime);
  resumeButton->Update(p_deltaTime);
}
}
```

Notice that we will only process the sprite updates if the game state is GS_Running.

We are going to get ready to accept mouse input. First, we are going to setup a timer. Add the following code in the variable declarations of RoboRacer2d.cpp:

```
float uiTimer;
const float UI_THRESHOLD = 0.2f;
```

Then add the line of code below to StartGame:

```
uiTimer = 0.0f;
```

The time will be used to add a small delay to mouse input. Without the delay, each click on the mouse would be registered several times instead of a single time.

We still need to handle input, but not all input. Go to the ProcessInput function in RoboRacer.cpp and make the following changes:

```
void ProcessInput(const float p_deltaTime)
{
  Input::Command command = inputManager->GetCommand();
  if (m_gameState == GS_Paused) command = Input::Command::CM_UI;

  uiTimer += p_deltaTime;
  if (uiTimer > UI_THRESHOLD)
  {
    uiTimer = 0.0f;
    switch (command)
    {
    case Input::Command::CM_STOP:
      player->SetVelocity(0.0f);
      background->SetVelocity(0.0f);
      break;
```

```
case Input::Command::CM_LEFT:
 if (player == robot_right)
 {
  robot_right->IsActive(false);
  robot_right->IsVisible(false);
  robot_left->SetPosition(robot_right->GetPosition());
 }

 player = robot_left;
 player->IsActive(true);
 player->IsVisible(true);
 player->SetVelocity(-50.0f);
 background->SetVelocity(50.0f);
 break;

case Input::Command::CM_RIGHT:
 if (player == robot_left)
 {
  robot_left->IsActive(false);
  robot_left->IsVisible(false);
  robot_right->SetPosition(robot_left->GetPosition());
 }

 player = robot_right;
 player->IsActive(true);
 player->IsVisible(true);
 player->SetVelocity(50.0f);
 background->SetVelocity(-50.0f);
 break;

case Input::Command::CM_UP:
 player->Jump(Sprite::SpriteState::UP);
 break;

case Input::Command::CM_DOWN:
 player->Jump(Sprite::SpriteState::DOWN);
 break;

case Input::Command::CM_QUIT:
 PostQuitMessage(0);
 break;

case Input::Command::CM_UI:
 if (pauseButton->IsClicked())
 {
  pauseButton->IsClicked(false);
  pauseButton->IsVisible(false);
```

```
      pauseButton->IsActive(false);

      resumeButton->IsVisible(true);
      resumeButton->IsActive(true);
      m_gameState = GS_Paused;
    }

    if (resumeButton->IsClicked())
    {
      resumeButton->IsClicked(false);
      resumeButton->IsVisible(false);
      resumeButton->IsActive(false);

      pauseButton->IsVisible(true);
      pauseButton->IsActive(true);
      m_gameState = GS_Running;
    }
  }
}
  command = Input::Command::CM_INVALID;
}
```

Take a look at the second line. It sets the command to CM_UI if the game is paused. This means that only UI commands will be processed while the game is paused. A hack? Perhaps, but it gets the job done!

We only have two more changes to make. When the pause button is clicked, we need to change the game state to GS_Paused, and when the resume button is clicked, we need to change the game state to GS_Running. Those changes have already been made in the CS_UI case in the preceding code!

When you run the program now, you will see that the game pauses when you click the pause button. When you click the resume button, everything picks up again.

Summary

Again, you have traveled far! We implemented a basic input class, then modified our sprite class to handle UI. This unified approach allows one class to handle sprites as game objects as well as sprites as part of the user interface. The same approach to see if a button has been pushed, can also be used for collision detection for a game object too. Then you learned how to create a state machine to handle the various states that the game may be in.

In the next chapter, we will learn to detect when game objects collide.

5
Hit and Run

You've already come a long way since beginning the book at the first chapter! You have managed to render moving images to the screen and control their movement. You are well on your way toward creating a great game. The next step is to code the interactions between various objects in the game.

This chapter will explain how to implement collision detection. Collision detection determines how objects interact with each other when they are in the same location. Topics will include:

- **Boundary detection**: When an object reaches the top, bottom, left, or right edge of the screen, what should happen? There are a surprising number of choices and you get to choose what to do.

- **Collision detection**: There are various scenarios that we often need to check to determine whether two objects have hit each other. We will cover circular and rectangular collision detection algorithms. We will also discuss when each type of collision detection is appropriate to use.

Out of bounds!

If you run our current game, you will notice that the robot will go off the screen if you allow him to continue moving to the left or right. When he reaches the edge of the screen, he will keep on moving until he is no longer visible. If you reverse his direction and make him move the same number of steps now, he will reappear on the screen.

Whenever an object reaches the edge of the screen, we often want it to do something special, such as stopping, or turning around. The code that determines when an object has reached a screen edge is known as **boundary checking**. There are many possibilities for what we can do when an object reaches a boundary:

- Stop the object
- Allow the object to continue past the border (and therefore, disappear)
- Allow the object to continue past the border and reappear at the opposite border (ever played the arcade version of Asteroids?)
- Scroll the camera and the screen along with the object (aka Mario)
- Allow the object to rebound off the border (ever played Breakout?)

As our Robo is controlled by the player, we will simply force him to stop moving when he has reached the edge of the screen.

Getting anchored

In order to implement boundary checking, you must first know the exact anchor point of the image. Technically, the anchor point could be anywhere, but the two most common locations are the top-left corner and the center of the image.

First, let's see what happens if we just ignore the anchor point. Open the **RoboRacer2D** project and then open RoboRacer2D.cpp.

Insert the following function:

```
void CheckBoundaries(Sprite* p_sprite)
{
  if (p_sprite->GetPosition().x < 0)
  {
    p_sprite->SetVelocity(0.0f);
  }
  else if (p_sprite->GetPosition().x > screen_width)
  {
    p_sprite->SetVelocity(0.0f);
  }
}
```

Here is what this code is doing for us:

- The function accepts a sprite as its parameter
- The function first checks to see whether the x position of the sprite is less than 0, where 0 is the x coordinate of the far-left edge of the screen
- The function then checks to see whether the x position of the sprite is greater than the screen width, where `screen_width` is the x coordinate of the far-right edge of the screen
- If either check is `true`, the sprite's velocity is set to 0, effectively stopping the sprite in its tracks

Now, add the highlighted line of code to the `Update` function right after `ProcessInput` in `RoboRacer2D.cpp`:

```
inputManager->Update(p_deltaTime);
ProcessInput();
CheckBoundaries(player);
```

This simply calls the `CheckBoundaries` function that we just created and passes in the `player` object.

Now, run the program. Move Robo until he reaches the far left of the screen. Then run him to the far right of the screen. Does anything seem wrong about the way we have implemented our boundary checking?

[Ignore the way the background scrolls off to the side. We'll fix this shortly.]

Problem 1: Robo doesn't seem to hit the boundary on the left.

The following screenshot shows you what happens if you allow Robo to go to the far left of the screen. He appears to stop just before reaching the edge. Although you can't see it in the following screenshot, there is a shadow that always extends to the left edge of the robot. It is the left edge of the shadow that is being detected as the edge of the image.

It turns out that the default anchor point for images loaded by our image loading routine is, in fact, the upper-left corner.

Problem 2: Robo moves completely off the screen to the right.

The following screenshot shows you what occurs if you allow Robo to continue traveling to the right. Now that you understand that the anchor point is at the upper-left, you may already understand what is happening.

As the boundary checking is based on the x coordinate of the sprite, by the time the upper-left hand corner exceeds the screen width, the entire sprite has already moved off the screen. The grayscale image of the robot shows us where his actual position would be if we could see him:

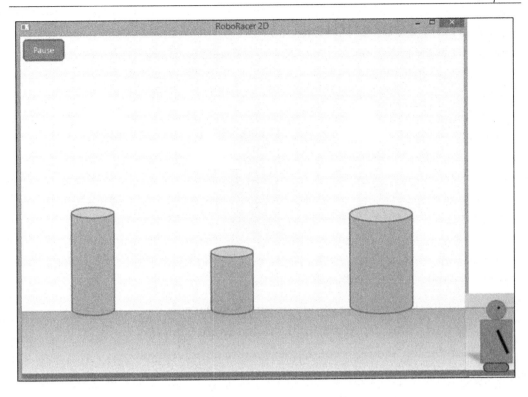

Problem 3: Once Robo reaches the far left or far right of the screen, he gets stuck. Changing his direction seems to have no effect!

This problem is known as **embedding**. Here is what has happened:

- We continued check Robo's position until his *x* coordinate exceeded a threshold.
- Once he exceeded that threshold, we set his velocity to 0.
- Now that Robo's *x* coordinate exceeds that threshold, it will always exceed that threshold. Any attempt to move him in the opposite direction will trigger the boundary check, which will discover that Robo's *x* coordinate still exceeds the threshold and his velocity will be set to 0.

The solution is to set Robo's position to the other side of threshold as soon as we discover he has crossed it. We will add this correction, but first we have to understand collision rectangles.

Collision rectangles

Take a look at the following image of Robo. The solid rectangle represents the boundaries of the texture. The dotted rectangle represents the area that we actually want to consider for boundary and collision detection. This is known as the **collision rectangle**.

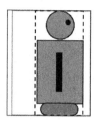

Comparing the two rectangles, here is what we would have to do to convert the texture rectangle to be the collision rectangle:

- Add about 34 pixels to the left texture boundary
- Subtract about 10 pixels from the right texture boundary
- Both the top and right boundaries require no adjustment

Let's enhance the sprite class by adding functionality to define a collision rectangle.

Open `Sprite.h` and add the following member variable:

```
Rect m_collision;
```

Then add the two accessor methods:

```
const Rect GetCollisionRect() const;
void SetCollisionRectOffset(const Rect p_rect) { m_collision = p_rect;
}
```

The implementation for `GetCollisionRect` is a little more complex, so we will put that code into `Sprite.cpp`:

```
const Sprite::Rect Sprite::GetCollisionRect() const
{
  Rect rect;
  rect.left = m_position.x + m_collision.left;
  rect.right = m_position.x + m_size.width + m_collision.right;
  rect.top = m_position.y + m_collision.top;
  rect.bottom = m_position.y + m_size.height + m_collision.bottom;

  return rect;
}
```

Here's what we are doing:

- `m_collision`: This will hold four offset values. These values will represent a number that must be added to the texture's bounding rectangle to get to the collision rectangle that we desire.

- `SetCollisionRectOffset`: This accepts a `Rect` parameter that contains the four offsets—top, bottom, left, and right—that must be added to the top, bottom, left, and right of the texture boundaries to create the collision rectangle.

- `GetCollisionRect`: This returns the collision rectangle that we can actually use when checking boundaries and checking for collisions. This is calculated by adding the width and height to the sprite's current anchor point (the top-left corner), and then adjusting it by the values in `m_collision`.

Note that `GetCollisionRect` is dynamic; it always returns the current collision rectangle based on the sprite's current position. Thus, we are returning the actual top, bottom, left, and right boundaries that need to be checked at any moment in the game.

If you look closely at the design, you should be able to see that if no collision rectangle is defined, `GetCollisionRect` will return a collision rectangle determined by the texture's rectangle. Therefore, this new design allows us to use the texture rectangle as the collision rectangle by default. On the other hand, if we want to specify our own collision rectangle, we can do so using `SetCollisionRectOffset`.

Just to be safe, we will want to initialize m_collision by adding the following lines to the constructor:

```
m_collision.left = 0.0f;
m_collision.right = 0.0f;
m_collision.top = 0.0f;
m_collision.bottom = 0.0f;
```

Now that we have the code to support a collision rectangle, we need to define the collision rectangle for the robot's sprites. Go to the `LoadTextures` function in `RoboRacer2D.cpp` and add the following highlighted lines just before the `return true` line of code:

```
Sprite::Rect collision;
collision.left = 34.0f;
collision.right = -10.0f;
collision.top = 0.0f;
collision.bottom = 0.0f;
robot_left->SetCollisionRectOffset(collision);
robot_right->SetCollisionRectOffset(collision);

return true;
```

Remember, only add the preceding code that is highlighted. The last line of the code is shown to provide context.

We are now going to rewrite our boundary detection function to take advantage of the collision rectangle. Along the way we will solve all three of the problems that we encountered in our first attempt. The current code uses the anchor point of the image, which doesn't accurately reflect the actual boundaries that we want to check. The new code will use the collision rect. Replace the CheckBoundaries function in RoboRacer2D with the following code:

```
void CheckBoundaries(Sprite* p_sprite)
{
  Sprite::Rect check = p_sprite->GetCollisionRect();

  if (check.left < 0.0f)
  {
    p_sprite->SetVelocity(0.0f);
  }
  else if (check.right > screen_width)
  {
    p_sprite->SetVelocity(0.0f);
  }
}
```

This code uses the collision rectangle defined for the sprite that is being checked. As we already discussed earlier, GetCollisionRect returns the top, bottom, left, and right boundaries for us based on the current position of the sprite. This greatly simplifies our code! Now, we just check to see whether the left edge of the sprite is less than zero or whether the right edge of the sprite is greater than zero, and we're done!

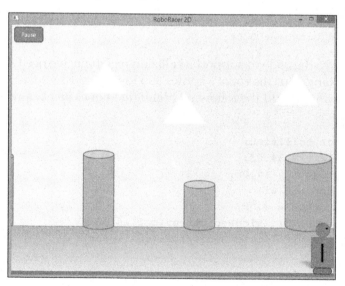

Embedding

Hurrah! Robo now successfully stops at the edge of the screen (only the right-hand side is shown in the preceding image). But boo! He still gets stuck! As we mentioned earlier, this problem is called embedding. If we zoom in, we can see what's going on:

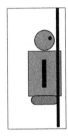

The vertical line represents the edge of the screen. By the time Robo has stopped, his right edge has already exceeded the right edge of the screen, so we stop him. Unfortunately, even if we try to turn him around to go in the other direction, the CheckBoundaries function will check on the very next frame, before Robo has a chance to start moving back:

According to the boundary check, the right edge of Robo is still beyond the right edge of the screen, so once again Robo's velocity is set to zero. Robo is stopped before he can even take a step!

Here is the solution; as soon as we detect that Robo has exceeded the boundary, we set his velocity to zero and we reposition Robo to just the other side of the boundary:

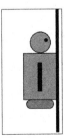

Now, Robo will be able to move as long as he goes in the other direction.

To implement this change, we are once again going to change the CheckBoundaries function:

```
void CheckBoundaries(Sprite* p_sprite)
{
  Sprite::Rect check = p_sprite->GetCollisionRect();
  float offset;
  float x;
  float y;

  if (check.left < 0.0f)
  {
    p_sprite->SetVelocity(0.0f);
    offset = check.left;
    x = p_sprite->GetPosition().x - offset;
    y = p_sprite->GetPosition().y;
    p_sprite->SetPosition(x, y);
  }
  else if (check.right > screen_width)
  {
    p_sprite->SetVelocity(0.0f);
    offset = screen_width - check.right;
    x = p_sprite->GetPosition().x + offset;
    y = p_sprite->GetPosition().y;
    p_sprite->SetPosition(x, y);
  }
  if (check.top < 0.0f)
  {
    p_sprite->SetVelocity(0.0f);
    offset = check.top;
    y = p_sprite->GetPosition().y - offset;
    x = p_sprite->GetPosition().x;
    p_sprite->SetPosition(x, y);
  }
  else if (check.bottom > screen_height)
  {
    p_sprite->SetVelocity(0.0f);
    offset = screen_height - check.bottom;
    y = p_sprite->GetPosition().y + offset;
    x = p_sprite->GetPosition().x;
    p_sprite->SetPosition(x, y);
  }
}
```

The highlighted lines show the added code. Basically, we perform the following actions:

- Calculate how far past the boundary Robo has gone
- Adjust his position by that much so that he is now positioned right at the boundary

You'll notice that we also filled out the function to handle the top and bottom boundaries so that the boundary checking can be used for any sprite travelling in any direction.

Fixing the background

Now that we have Robo moving the way we want him to, two new problems have cropped up for the background image:

1. When Robo stops, the background keeps scrolling.
2. When the background image ends at either the right or the left, it slides off the screen and we are left with a black background.

Before we continue on with collision detection, let's fix the background. First, we will add the following function to `RoboRacer2D.cpp`:

```cpp
void CheckBackground()
{
  float leftThreshold = 0.0f;
  float rightThreshold = -(background->GetSize().width - screen_
width);
  if (background->GetPosition().x > 0)
  {
    background->SetPosition(0.0f, background->GetPosition().y);
  }
  else if (background->GetPosition().x < rightThreshold)
  {
    background->SetPosition(rightThreshold, background-
>GetPosition().y);
  }
}
```

This code is very similar to the boundary checking code. If the background anchor point moves far enough to the left to expose the right edge of the texture, it will be reset. If the background anchor point moves far enough to the right to expose the left edge of the texture, it will be reset.

Now, add the highlighted line of code to the Update function right after the call to CheckBoundaries in RoboRacer2D.cpp:

```
inputManager->Update(p_deltaTime);
ProcessInput();
CheckBoundaries(player);
CheckBackground();
```

The background should now run from edge to edge. Play the game and take a coffee break. You deserve it!

Collideables

There are many times that we may want to check and see whether objects in the game have collided with each other. We may want to see whether the player has struck an obstacle or an enemy. We may have objects that the player can pick up, often called **pickups** or **powerups**.

Collectively, objects in the game that can collide with other objects are known as collideables. When we created our Sprite class, we actually it designed for this. Looking at the class constructor, you will notice that member variable m_isCollideable is set to false. When we write our collision detection code, we will ignore objects that have m_isCollideable set to false. If we want to allow an object to collide with other objects, we have to make sure to set m_collideable to true.

Ready to score

To keep our design simple, we are going to create one enemy and one pickup. Running into an enemy will subtract points from the player's score, while running into the pickup will increase the player's score. We will add some additional code to the sprite class to support this feature.

First, let's add some new member variables. Declare a new variable in Sprite.h:

```
int m_value;
```

Then add the following methods:

```
void SetValue(const int p_value) { m_value = p_value; }
const int GetValue() const { return m_value; }
```

With these changes, every sprite will have an intrinsic value. If the value is positive, then it is a reward. If the value is negative, then it is a penalty.

Don't forget to initialize m_value to zero in the Sprite class constructor!

A friend indeed

Let's add the sprite for our pickup. In this case, the pickup is a can of oil to keep Robo's joints working smoothly.

Add the following sprite definitions to RoboRacer2D:

```
Sprite* pickup;
```

Now, we will set up the sprite. Add the following code to `LoadTextures`:

```
pickup = new Sprite(1);
pickup->SetFrameSize(26.0f, 50.0f);
pickup->SetNumberOfFrames(1);
pickup->AddTexture("resources/oil.png");
pickup->IsVisible(false);
pickup->IsActive(false);
pickup->SetValue(50);
```

This code is essentially the same code that we used to create all of our sprites. One notable difference is that we use the new `SetValue` method to add a value to the sprite. This represents how many points the player will earn for the collection of this pickup.

Time to spawn

Note that we have set the sprite as inactive and invisible. Now, we will write a function to randomly spawn the pickup. First, we need to add two more C++ headers. In `RoboRacer2D.cpp` add the following headers:

```
#include <stdlib.h>
#include <time.h>
```

We need `stdlib` for the `rand` function and `time` to give us a value to seed the random generator.

> Random numbers are generated from internal tables. In order to guarantee that a different random number is chosen each time the program is started, you first seed the random number generator with a value that is guaranteed to be different each time you start the program. As the time that the program is started will always be different, we often use time as the seed.

Next, we need a timer. Declare the following variables in `RoboRacer2D.cpp`:

```
float pickupSpawnThreshold;
float pickupSpawnTimer;
```

The threshold will be the number of seconds that we want to pass before a pickup is spawned. The timer will start and zero and count up to that number of seconds.

Let's initialize these values in the `StartGame` function. The `StartGame` function is also a great place to seed our random number generator. Add the following three lines of code to the end of `StartGame`:

```
srand(time(NULL));
pickupSpawnThreshold = 15.0f;
pickupSpawnTimer = 0.0f;
```

The first line seeds the random number generator by passing in an integer representing the current time. The next line sets a spawn threshold of 15 seconds. The third line sets the spawn timer to 0.

Now, let's create a function to spawn our pickups. Add the following code to `RoboRacer2D.cpp`:

```
void SpawnPickup(float p_DeltaTime)
{
  if (pickup->IsVisible() == false)
  {
    pickupSpawnTimer += p_DeltaTime;
    if (pickupSpawnTimer > pickupSpawnThreshold)
    {
      float marginX = pickup->GetSize().width;
      float marginY = pickup->GetSize().height;
      float spawnX = (rand() % (int)(screen_width - (marginX * 2))) +
marginX;
      float spawnY = screen_height - ((rand() % (int)(player-
>GetSize().height - (marginY * 1.5))) + marginY);
      pickup->SetPosition(spawnX, spawnY);
      pickup->IsVisible(true);
      pickup->IsActive(true);
      pickupSpawnTimer = 0.0f;
    }
  }
}
```

This code does the following:

- It checks to make sure that the pickup is not already on the screen
- If there is no pickup, then the spawn timer is incremented
- If the spawn timer exceeds the spawn threshold, the pickup is spawned at a random position somewhere within the width of the screen and within the vertical reach of Robo

Don't get too worried about the particular math being used. Your algorithm to position the pickup could be completely different. The key here is that a single pickup will be generated within Robo's reach.

Make sure to add a call to SpawnPickup in the Update function as well as a line to update the pickup:

```
if (m_gameState == GS_Running)
{
  background->Update(p_deltaTime);
  robot_left->Update(p_deltaTime);
  robot_right->Update(p_deltaTime);
  robot_left_strip->Update(p_deltaTime);
  robot_right_strip->Update(p_deltaTime);

  pause->Update(p_deltaTime);
  resume->Update(p_deltaTime);

  pickup->Update(p_deltaTime);
  SpawnPickup(p_deltaTime);
}
```

We also need to add a line to Render to render the pickup:

```
void Render()
{
  glClear(GL_COLOR_BUFFER_BIT);
  glLoadIdentity();

  background->Render();
  robot_left->Render();
  robot_right->Render();
  robot_left_strip->Render();
  robot_right_strip->Render();

  pause->Render();
```

```
    resume->Render();

    pickup->Render();
    SwapBuffers(hDC);
}
```

If you run the game right now, then an oil can should be spawned about five seconds after the game starts.

> The current code has one flaw. It could potentially spawn the pickup right on top of Robo. Once we implement collision detection, the result will be that Robo immediately picks up the oil can. This will happen so quickly that you won't even see it happen. In the name of keeping it simple, we will live with this particular flaw.

Circular collision detection

One way to detect collision is to see how far each of the objects are from each other's center. This is known as circular collision detection because it treats each object as if it is bound by a circle, and uses the radius of that circle to determine whether the objects are close enough to collide.

Take a look at the following diagram:

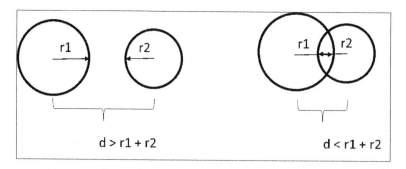

The circles on the left are not colliding, while the circles on the right are colliding. For the non-colliding circles, the distance (d) between the center points of the two circles is greater than the sum of the two radii ($r1 + r2$). For the colliding circles, the distance (d) between the two centers is less than the sum of the two radii ($r1 + r2$). We can use this knowledge to test any two objects for collision based on the radii of the circles and the distance between the objects center point.

So, how do we use this information?

1. We will know **r1** and **r2** because we set them when we create the sprite.
2. We will calculate two legs of a right-triangle using the x and y coordinates for the center of each circle.
3. We will calculate d, the distance between two center points, using a variant of the **Pythagorean Theorem**.

It will probably hurt your brain a little, but I'd like to refresh your memory one tenet of basic geometry.

The Pythagorean Theorem

The Pythagorean Theorem allows us to find the distance between any two points in a two-dimensional space if we know the lengths of the line segments that form a right-angle between the points.

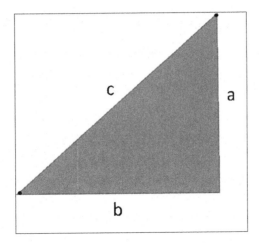

$a^2 + b^2 = c^2$

In our case, we are trying to calculate the distance (c) between the two points.

A little algebra will transform this equation to:

$$\Box = \sqrt{\Box^2 + \Box^2}$$

It is computationally expensive to perform the square root. A nice mathematical trick will actually allow us to perform our collision detection without calculating the square root.

If we were to use square roots to do this calculation, here is what that might look like:

```
c = sqrt(a * a + b * b);
if (c <= r1 + r2) return true;
```

Although this would work, there is a nice little mathematical trick that allows us to accomplish this test without taking the square root. Take a look at this:

```
c = a * a + b * b;
if (c<= r1 * r1 + r2 * r2) return true;
```

It turns out that we can just keep everything in the equation at the power of 2 and the comparison still works. This is because we are only interested in the relative comparison between the distance and the sum of the radii, not the absolute mathematical values.

> If the math we presented here boggles your brain, then don't worry too much. Circular collision detection is so common that the math to detect it is generally already built into the game engine that you will use. However, I wanted you to take a little look under the hood. After all, game programming is inherently mathematical, and the more you understand the math, the better you will be at coding.

Adding the circular collision code

Now, it's time to modify `Sprite.h` to add support for the circular collision detection. First, we need to add some member variables to hold the center point and radius. Add these two properties to `Sprite.h`:

```
float m_radius;
Point m_center;
```

Then add the following methods declarations:

```
void SetRadius(const GLfloat p_radius) { m_radius = p_radius; }
const float GetRadius() const { return m_radius; }
void SetCenter(const Point p_center) { m_center = p_center; }
const Point GetCenter() const;
const bool IntersectsCircle(const Sprite* p_sprite) const;
```

These methods allow us to set and retrieve the center point and radius of the sprite. The `GetCenter` method is more than one line, so we will implement it in `Sprite.cpp`:

```cpp
const Sprite::Point Sprite::GetCenter() const
{
    Point center;
    center.x = this->GetPosition().x + m_center.x;
    center.y = this->GetPosition().y + m_center.y;

    return center;
}
```

An important point to note here is that `m_center` represents an x and y offset from the sprite's anchor point. So, to return the center point we will add `m_center` to the current position of the sprite and this will give us the current center point of the sprite exactly where it is in the game.

We now need to add the code to perform the collision detection. Add the following code to `Sprite.cpp`:

```cpp
const bool Sprite::IntersectsCircle(const Sprite* p_sprite) const
{
 if (this->IsCollideable() && p_sprite->IsCollideable() && this-
>IsActive() && p_sprite->IsActive())
 {
  const Point p1 = this->GetCenter();
  const Point p2 = p_sprite->GetCenter();
  float y = p2.y - p1.y;
  float x = p2.x - p1.x;
  float d = x*x + y*y;
  float r1 = this->GetRadius() * this->GetRadius();
  float r2 = p_sprite->GetRadius() * p_sprite->GetRadius();
  if (d <= r1 + r2)
  {
   return true;
  }
 }
 return false;
}
```

As we have already explained the use of the Pythagorean Theorem, this code should actually seem a little familiar to you. Here is what we are doing:

The function accepts one sprite to compare with itself.

- First, we check to make sure both sprites are collideable.
- p1 and p2 represent the two centers.
- x and y represent the lengths of the *a* and *b* sides of a right-angled triangle. Notice that the calculation is simply the difference between the x and y position of each sprite, respectively.
- r1 and r2 are the radii of the two circles (left as a power of 2).
- d is the distance between the two centers (left as a power of 2).
- If d is less than or equal to the sum of the two radii, then the circles are intersecting.

Why use circular collision detection?

As we discussed many times, textures are represented as rectangles. In fact, we will take advantage of this when we cover rectangular collision detection later in the chapter. The following figure illustrates how rectangular and circular collision detection differ (the relative sizes are exaggerated to make a point):

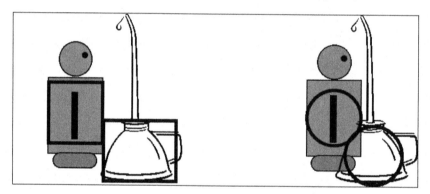

The sprites on the left are colliding using a rectangular bounding box. The sprites on the right are colliding using a bounding circle. In general, using a bounding circle is visually more convincing when we are dealing with rounder shapes.

I'll admit the difference in this example is not that big. You could get away with rectangular or circular collision detection in this example. The round nature of the oil can made it a good candidate for circular collision detection. Circular collision detection is really essential if the two objects that are colliding are actually circles (that is, two balls colliding).

With the code that we developed, we need to define the center and radius for any sprites that will use circular collision detection. Add the following code to the LoadTextures function in RoboRacer.cpp:

```
Sprite::Point center;
float radius;

center.x = robot_right->GetSize().width / 2.0f;
center.y = robot_right->GetSize().height / 2.0f;
radius = (center.x + center.y) / 2.0f;

robot_right->SetCenter(center);
robot_right->SetRadius(radius);
robot_left->SetCenter(center);
robot_left->SetRadius(radius);

center.x = pickup->GetSize().width / 2.0f;
float yOffset = (pickup->GetSize().height / 4.0f) * 3.0f;
center.y = yOffset;
pickup->SetCenter(center);
radius = pickup->GetSize().width / 2.0f;
pickup->SetRadius(radius);
```

Don't get too worried about the exact values that we are using here. We are basically setting up a bounding circle for Robo and the oil can that match the preceding figure. Robo's bounding circle is set to the middle of the robot, while the oil can's circle is set to the bottom half of the texture.

Wiring in the collision detection

We are now going to add a new function that will perform all of our collision detection. Add the following function to RoboRacer2D.cpp:

```
void CheckCollisions()
{
 if (player->IntersectsCircle(pickup))
 {
  pickup->IsVisible(false);
  pickup->IsActive(false);
  player->SetValue(player->GetValue() + pickup->GetValue());
  pickupSpawnTimer = 0.0f;
 }
}
```

The purpose of this code is to check to see whether the player has collided with the pickup:

- If the call to `player->IntersectsCircle(pickup)` returns `true`, then the player has collided with the pickup
- The pickup is deactivated and made invisible
- The pickup's value is added to the player's value (this will be the base for scoring in a future chapter)
- The spawn timer is reset

We have two small details left. First, you must add a call to `CheckCollisions` to the `Update` function:

```
if (m_gameState == GS_Running)
{
   background->Update(p_deltaTime);
   robot_left->Update(p_deltaTime);
   robot_right->Update(p_deltaTime);
   robot_left_strip->Update(p_deltaTime);
   robot_right_strip->Update(p_deltaTime);

   pause->Update(p_deltaTime);
   resume->Update(p_deltaTime);

   pickup->Update(p_deltaTime);
   SpawnPickup(p_deltaTime);

   CheckCollisions();
}
```

Secondly, you need to make the player and pickup `collideable`. Add these three lines to the bottom of `LoadTextures` just before the return statement:

```
robot_left->IsCollideable(true);
robot_right->IsCollideable(true);
pickup->IsCollideable(true);
```

Now, the real fun starts! Play the game and when the oil can spawns, and use Robo to pick it up. Five seconds later another oil can spawns. The fun never ends!

Rectangular collision detection

Now, we are going to learn how to implement rectangular collision detection. It turns out that both Robo and our enemy (a water bottle) are very rectangular, making rectangular collision detection the best choice.

The enemy within

Let's introduce our Robo's enemy—a bottle of water to rust his gears. The code for this is included next.

Add the following sprite definition to `RoboRacer2D`:

```
Sprite* enemy;
```

Now, we will setup the sprite. Add the following code to `LoadTextures`:

```
enemy = new Sprite(1);
enemy->SetFrameSize(32.0f, 50.0f);
enemy->SetNumberOfFrames(1);
enemy->AddTexture("resources/water.png");
enemy->IsVisible(false);
enemy->IsActive(false);
enemy->SetValue(-50);
enemy->IsCollideable(true);
```

This code is essentially the same code that we used to create all of our sprites. One notable difference is that we use the new `SetValue` method to add a negative value to the sprite. This is how many points the player will lose if they hit this enemy. We also make sure that we set the enemy to be collideable.

Spawning the enemy

Just like the pickups, we need to spawn our enemies. We could use the same code as the pickups, but I thought it would be nicer if our enemies worked on a different timer.

Declare the following variables in `RoboRacer2D.cpp`:

```
float enemySpawnThreshold;
float enemySpawnTimer;
```

The threshold will be the amount of seconds that we want to pass before an enemy is spawned. The timer will start and zero and count up to that number of seconds.

Let's initialize these values in the StartGame function. Add the following two lines of code to the end of StartGame:

```
enemySpawnThreshold = 7.0f;
enemySpawnTimer = 0.0f;
```

We set a spawn threshold of 7 seconds, and set the spawn timer to 0.

Now, let's create a function to spawn our enemies. Add the following code to RoboRacer2D.cpp:

```
void SpawnEnemy(float p_DeltaTime)
{
   if (enemy->IsVisible() == false)
   {
      enemySpawnTimer += p_DeltaTime;
      if (enemySpawnTimer >enemySpawnThreshold)
      {
         float marginX = enemy->GetSize().width;
         float marginY = enemy->GetSize().height;
         float spawnX = (rand() % (int)(screen_width - (marginX * 2))) +
marginX;
         float spawnY = screen_height - ((rand() % (int)(player-
>GetSize().height - (marginY * 2))) + marginY);
         enemy->SetPosition(spawnX, spawnY);
         enemy->IsVisible(true);
         enemy->IsActive(true);
      }
   }
}
```

This code does the following:

- It checks to make sure that the enemy is not already on the screen
- If there is no enemy, then the spawn timer is incremented
- If the spawn timer exceeds the spawn threshold, the enemy is spawned at a random position somewhere within the width of the screen and within the vertical reach of Robo

Don't get too worried about the particular math being used. Your algorithm to position the enemy can be completely different. The key here is that a single enemy will be generated within Robo's path.

Make sure to add a call to SpawnEnemy in the Update function as well as a line to update the enemy:

```
if (m_gameState == GS_Running)
{
  background->Update(p_deltaTime);
  robot_left->Update(p_deltaTime);
  robot_right->Update(p_deltaTime);
  robot_left_strip->Update(p_deltaTime);
  robot_right_strip->Update(p_deltaTime);

  pause->Update(p_deltaTime);
  resume->Update(p_deltaTime);

  pickup->Update(p_deltaTime);
  SpawnPickup(p_deltaTime);

  enemy->Update(p_deltaTime);
  SpawnEnemy(p_deltaTime);

  CheckCollisions();

}
```

We also need to add a line to Render to render the enemy:

```
void Render()
{
  glClear(GL_COLOR_BUFFER_BIT);
  glLoadIdentity();

  background->Render();
  robot_left->Render();
  robot_right->Render();
  robot_left_strip->Render();
  robot_right_strip->Render();

  pause->Render();
  resume->Render();

  pickup->Render();
  enemy->Render();
  SwapBuffers(hDC);
}
```

If you run the game right now, then a water bottle should be spawned about seven seconds after the game starts.

Adding the rectangular collision code

As we have mentioned several times, all sprites are essentially rectangles. Visually, if any border of these rectangles overlap, we can assume that the two sprites have collided.

We are going to add a function to our `Sprite` class that determines whether two rectangles are intersecting. Open `Sprite.h` and add the following method declaration:

```
const bool IntersectsRect(const Sprite*p_sprite) const;
```

Now, let's add the implementation to `Sprite.cpp`:

```cpp
const bool Sprite::IntersectsRect(const Sprite* p_sprite) const
{
  if (this->IsCollideable() && p_sprite->IsCollideable() && this-
>IsActive() && p_sprite->IsActive())
  {
    const Rect recta = this->GetCollisionRect();
    const Rect rectb = p_sprite->GetCollisionRect();
    if (recta.left >= rectb.left && recta.left <= rectb.right && recta.
top >= rectb.top && recta.top <= rectb.bottom)
    {
      return true;
    }
    else if (recta.right >= rectb.left && recta.right <= rectb.right &&
recta.top >= rectb.top && recta.top <= rectb.bottom)
    {
      return true;
    }
    else if (recta.left >= rectb.left && recta.right <= rectb.right &&
recta.top < rectb.top && recta.bottom > rectb.bottom)
    {
      return true;
    }
    else if (recta.top >= rectb.top && recta.bottom <= rectb.bottom &&
recta.left < rectb.left && recta.right > rectb.right)
    {
      return true;
    }
    else if (rectb.left >= recta.left && rectb.left <= recta.right &&
     rectb.top >= recta.top && rectb.top <= recta.bottom)
    {
      return true;
    }
```

```
    else if (rectb.right >= recta.left && rectb.right <= recta.right &&
rectb.top >= recta.top && rectb.top <= recta.bottom)
    {
     return true;
    }
    else if (rectb.left >= recta.left && rectb.right <= recta.right &&
rectb.top < recta.top && rectb.bottom > recta.bottom)
    {
     return true;
    }
    else if (recta.top >= rectb.top && recta.bottom <= rectb.bottom &&
recta.left < rectb.left && recta.right > rectb.right)
    {
     return true;
    }
    else if (rectb.top >= recta.top && rectb.bottom <= recta.bottom &&
rectb.left < recta.left && rectb.right > recta.right)
    {
     return true;
    }
   }
  return false;
}
```

Here's how this code works:

- This function looks really complicated, but it is really only doing a few things.
- The function accepts a sprite parameter.
- We set `recta` to be the collision rectangle of the sprite that called the `IntersectsRect` method and set `rectb` to be the collision rectangle of the sprite that was passed in.
- We then test every possible combination of the position of the vertices in of `recta` to those of `rectb`. If any test is `true`, then we return `true`. Otherwise we return `false`.

The following figure illustrates some of the ways that two rectangles could interact:

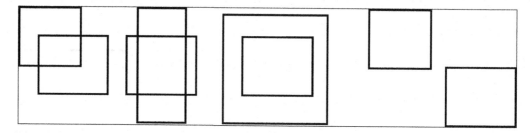

Wiring continued

We have already wired in the collision check using `CheckCollisions`. We just need to add the following code to `CheckCollisions` to the check whether the player is colliding with an enemy:

```
if (player->IntersectsRect(enemy))
{
  enemy->IsVisible(false);
  enemy->IsActive(false);
  enemy->SetValue(player->GetValue() + enemy->GetValue());
  enemySpawnTimer = 0.0f;
}
```

Now, the real fun starts! Play the game and when the water can enemy spawns make sure Robo avoids it! If you collide with an enemy, you will lose points (as the value of enemy is set to a negative number). Until we implement a visible score, you may want to write the score out to the console.

Summary

I'm sure you can now understand that most games would not be possible without collision detection. Collision detection allows objects in the game to interact with each other. We used collision detection to get pickups and detect whether we ran into an enemy.

We also discussed the essential task of boundary checking. Boundary checking is a special form of collision detection that checks to see whether an object has reached the screen boundaries. Another type of boundary checking is used to manage the scene background.

In the next chapter, we will wrap up the game by adding some finishing touches, including a heads-up display!

6
Polishing the Silver

I'm sure that you are as excited as I am about the progress that you have made on your game. It's almost ready to publish, right? Well, not quite! There is a lot of work that goes into polishing your game before it is ready, and that's what this chapter is all about.

Many people have a great idea for a game, and lots of enthusiastic coders, such as you, actually code their game to the point where we have reached so far. Unfortunately, this is where a lot of projects die. For some reason, many first-time game coders don't take the time to really finish their game. There are lots of things that still need to be done to make your game presentable:

- **Game state**: We already touched on game state a little bit when you learned how to pause your game. This chapter will continue the discussion of how you use game state to manage your game at various stages of gameplay.

- **Splash screen**: Most games display one or more screens before the game starts. These screens, known as splash screens, often display the logo and name of the studios that were involved in creating the game. A splash screen shows that you went the extra mile in polishing your game.

- **Menu screen**: Most games start with a menu of choices for the player. We will create a simple menu that loads after our splash screen and gives the player a few options.

- **Scoring and statistics**: You probably noticed that our game currently doesn't keep score. Although it is possible to design a game that doesn't involve scoring, most players want to know how they are doing in the game.

- **Winning and losing**: Again, while there are certainly games out there where no one wins or loses, most games have win-or-lose conditions that signal that the game is over.

- **Game progression**: Most games allow the player to continue playing as long as the player has achieved certain goals. Many games are broken down into a series of levels, with each level becoming a little more difficult than the previous one. You will learn how to add this type of progression to your game.

- **Credits**: Everyone likes to get credit for their work! Just like the movies, it is traditional to include a screen that shows each person that was involved in creating the game and what their role was. I'll show you how to create a simple credits screen.

The state of the game

Remember when we coded the pause button back in *Chapter 4, Control Freak*? We had to add some code that told the game whether it was active or paused. In fact, we defined the following enums:

```
enum GameState
{
  GS_Running,
  GS_Paused
};
```

These enums defined two game states: GS_Running, and GS_Paused. We then set the default game state to GS_Running in the StartGame function:

```
void StartGame()
{
  inputManager = new Input(hWnd);
  LoadTextures();
  m_gameState = GS_Running;

  srand(time(NULL));
  pickupSpawnThreshold = 5.0f;
  pickupSpawnTimer = 0.0f;
}
```

As long as the game state is set to GS_Running, then the game continues to cycle through the game loop, processing updates, and rendering the scene. However, when you click the pause button, the game state is set to GS_Paused. When the game is paused, we no longer update the game objects (that is, the robot, pickups, and enemies), but we do continue to render the scene and process the UI (user interface) so that buttons can be clicked.

State machines

The mechanism used to set up and control game states is known as a **state machine**. A state machine sets up separate and distinct stages (or **states**) for the game. Each state defines a certain set of rules for what is supposed to happen or not happen during each state. For example, our simple state machine has two states with the following rules, illustrated by the following matrix:

	GS_Running	**GS_Paused**
Input	All input	Only UI input
Objects Updating	All objects	Only UI objects
Collision Detection	All collideables	No need to check for collisions
Spawning	All spawnables	No spawning
Rendering	All objects	All objects

The state machine also defines the progression from one state to another. Here is a simple diagram showing the progression in our current state machine:

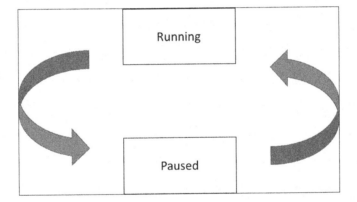

This state diagram is pretty simple. If you are in the running state, then it is legal to go to the paused state. If you are in the paused state, then it is legal to go to the running state. As we will see, most games are much more complex than this!

Why do we need a state machine?

At first glance, you may wonder why we even need a state machine. You could, for example, set up several Boolean flags (maybe one called `running` and one called `paused`), and then insert them into the code in the same way that we are using our enums.

This solution may work considering that our current game only has two states, but even then, it starts to get complicated if you choose to use Booleans. For example, to change the state from running to paused, I would always have to make sure to properly set both Booleans:

```
running = false;
paused = true;
```

When I went from the running state to the paused state, I would have to set both Booleans again:

```
running = true;
paused = false;
```

Imagine the problem if I forgot to change both Booleans and left the game in a state where it was both running and paused! Then imagine how complicated this becomes if my game has three, four, or ten states!

Using enums is not the only way to set up a state engine, but it does have immediate advantages over using Booleans:

- Enums have a descriptive name associated with their value (for example, GS_Paused), whereas Booleans only have true and false.
- Enums are already mutually exclusive. In order to make a set of Booleans mutually exclusive, I have to set one to true and all the others to false.

The next consideration as to why we need a state machine is that it simplifies the coding of the control of the game. Most games have several game states, and it is important that we are able to easily manage which code runs in which state. An example of game states that are common to most games includes:

- Loading
- Starting
- Running
- Paused
- Ending
- GameWon
- GameLost
- GameOver
- NextLevel
- Exiting

Of course, this is just a representative list, and each coder picks his or her own names for their game states. But I think that you get the idea: there are a lot of states that a game can be in, and that means it is important to be able to manage what happens during each state. Players tend to get angry if their character dies while the game was paused!

Planning for state

We are going to expand our simple state machine to include several more game states. This is going to help us to better organize the processing of the game, and better define which processes should be running at any particular time.

The following table shows the game states that we are going to define for our game:

State	Description
Loading	The game is loading and the Splash screen should be displayed
Menu	The main menu is showing
Running	The game is actively running
Paused	The game is paused
NextLevel	The game is loading the next level
GameOver	The game is over and the stats are being displayed
Credits	Showing the Credits screen

Here is our state diagram machine:

	Splash	Loading	Menu	Running	Paused	Next	GameOver	Credits
Input	None	None	UI	All	UI	UI	UI	UI
Updating	Splash	Splash	UI	All	UI	UI	UI	UI
Collision Detection	None	None	None	All	None	None	None	None
Spawning	None	None	None	All	None	None	None	None
Rendering	Splash	Splash	Menu	Game	Game	Game	GameOver	Credits

Finally, here is our state diagram:

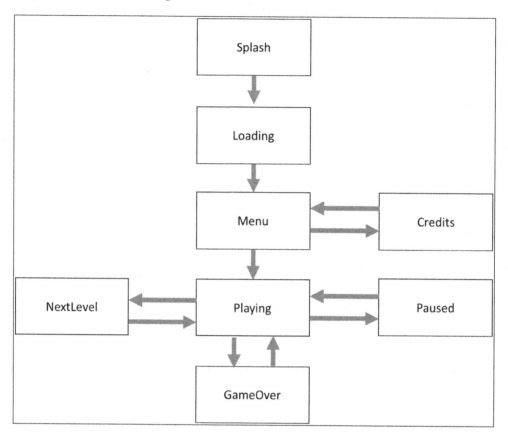

It turns out that our state diagram will also double as a UI diagram. A UI diagram is a diagram of all of the screens in a program and how they interact with each other. It turns out that each time that we want to change to a different screen in our game, we are also changing to a different screen. This isn't exactly the case – when the game is paused, it doesn't launch a completely new screen. However, there is often a very close correlation between the UI diagram and the state diagram.

Looking at the state diagram, you can easily see the legal state changes versus the illegal state changes. For example, it is legal to change the state from playing to paused, but you can't change the state from playing to credits.

Having this structure in place will guide us as we implement all of the final polish features that we want to add to our game.

Defining the new state

The first step in expanding our game state machine is adding the required enums. Replace the GameState enum code with the following code:

```
enum GameState
{
  GS_Splash,
  GS_Loading,
  GS_Menu,
  GS_Credits,
  GS_Running,
  GS_NextLevel,
  GS_Paused,
  GS_GameOver,
};
```

As we implement the polish features covered in this chapter, we will implement code that uses these game states.

Implementing the state machine

In order for our state machine to have any effect, we need to modify the code so that key decisions are made based on the game state. There are three functions that game state affects in a big way:

- **Update**: Some game states update game objects, while other game states update only the UI or a particular sprite
- **Render**: Different game states render different items
- **Input**: Some game states accept all input, while other game states only process UI input

It should come as no surprise then that we will be changing the Update, Render, and ProcessInput functions.

First, let's modify the Update function. Change the Update function in RoboRacer2D. cpp to match the following code:

```
void Update(const float p_deltaTime)
{
 switch (m_gameState)
 {
 case GameState::GS_Splash:
 case GameState::GS_Loading:
 {
```

```
          }
          break;
          case GameState::GS_Menu:
          {
           inputManager->Update(p_deltaTime);
           ProcessInput(p_deltaTime);
          }
          break;

          case GameState::GS_Credits:
          {
           inputManager->Update(p_deltaTime);
           ProcessInput(p_deltaTime);
          }
          break;
          case GameState::GS_Running:
          {
           inputManager->Update(p_deltaTime);
           ProcessInput(p_deltaTime);
           CheckBoundaries(player);
           CheckBackground();
           background->Update(p_deltaTime);
           robot_left->Update(p_deltaTime);
           robot_right->Update(p_deltaTime);
           robot_left_strip->Update(p_deltaTime);
           robot_right_strip->Update(p_deltaTime);
           pauseButton->Update(p_deltaTime);
           resumeButton->Update(p_deltaTime);
           pickup->Update(p_deltaTime);
           SpawnPickup(p_deltaTime);
           SpawnEnemy(p_deltaTime);
           enemy->Update(p_deltaTime);
           CheckCollisions();
          }
          break;
          case GameState::GS_Paused:
          {
           inputManager->Update(p_deltaTime);
           ProcessInput(p_deltaTime);
          }
          break;
          case GameState::GS_NextLevel:
          {
           inputManager->Update(p_deltaTime);
           ProcessInput(p_deltaTime);
          }
          break;
```

```
case GameState::GS_GameOver:
{
 inputManager->Update(p_deltaTime);
 ProcessInput(p_deltaTime);
}
break;
}
}
```

As you can see, we are now using a switch statement to handle each game state. This is a whole lot more readable than using if statements, and it keeps the code much more structured. If we need to add another game state, we just add another case to the switch statement.

Notice that each case has its code to run specific to that game state. Some lines of code are duplicated (almost every state has some input), but this is a small price to pay for clarity. GS_Running has the most work to do, while GS_Loading has the least work to do. We will be adding code to each switch as we add polish features.

Now, let's give the Render function an upgrade. Replace the Render function with the following code:

```
switch (m_gameState)
{
case GameState::GS_Splash:
case GameState::GS_Loading:
{
}
break;
case GameState::GS_Menu:
{
}
break;
case GameState::GS_Credits:
{
}
break;
case GameState::GS_Running:
case GameState::GS_Paused:
{
 background->Render();
 robot_left->Render();
 robot_right->Render();
 robot_left_strip->Render();
 robot_right_strip->Render();
 pauseButton->Render();
 resumeButton->Render();
```

```
    pickup->Render();
    enemy->Render();
    DrawScore();
    }
    break;
    case GameState::GS_NextLevel:
    {
    }
    break;
    case GameState::GS_GameOver:
    {
    }
    break;
    }

    SwapBuffers(hDC);
}
```

In this case, we have some work that needs to be done regardless of the game state. We need to clear the OpenGL buffer, and set the matrix to identity. Then we decide which items to render based on the game state, and finally, we swap the buffers.

If you look closely, GS_Running and GS_Paused render the same items. This is because the pause and render buttons are rendered over the top of the gameplay screen, so we still need to render the entire game even when we are paused. We will be adding code to each switch as we add polish features.

Finally, we need to apply our state machine to the ProcessInput function. As the function is so long, I am only showing the top lines of the function. Change all of the lines above the uiTimer += p_deltaTime; statement to the following code:

```
Replace highlighted code with:

switch (m_gameState)
{
case GameState::GS_Splash:
case GameState::GS_Loading:
{
  return;
}
break;
case GameState::GS_Menu:
case GameState::GS_Credits:
case GameState::GS_Paused:
case GameState::GS_NextLevel:
case GameState::GS_GameOver:
{
```

```
        command = Input::Command::CM_UI;
    }
    break;
    case GameState::GS_Running:
    {
    }
     break;
    }


    uiTimer += p_deltaTime;
```

First, we get the latest command. Then, depending on the game state, we perform the following actions:

- Ignore and return if we are still in the loading state
- Reset the command to only handle UI commands if the game state is menu, paused, next level, or game over
- Leave the command unchanged if we are in the running game state

This is exactly what we did in the prior versions, except we only had two game states to deal with in the prior versions. Once the command is handled, we move on to the uiTimer += p_deltaTime; (everything after this line is unchanged from the prior versions).

Making a splash

A splash menu adds a touch of class to your game and also does a little bragging. Typically, the splash screen shows off your company logo. In fact, many game projects have multiple studios that work on them, so there are often multiple splash screens. We will use just one!

It is important to get the splash screen up and running as soon as possible, so we will do that before we perform any other loading. Part of the function of a splash screen is to give the player something pretty to look at while the rest of the game is loading.

Creating the splash screen

It's up to you to create a splash screen that defines your game. For convenience, we have included one in the code resource package for this chapter called splash.png. Make sure you copy splash.png into your project. The only requirement for the splash image is that it is 800 x 600 pixels, the same resolution as our game screen.

Defining the splash screen

As with all images in this game, we will implement the splash screen as a sprite. Declare the splash sprite at the top of `RoboRacer2D.cpp`:

```
Sprite* splashScreen;
```

We also want to define some timers for the splash screen:

```
float splashDisplayTimer;
float splashDisplayThreshold;
```

As we want to define the splash screen separately, we will create a separate function just to load it. Create the `LoadSplash` function using the following code:

```
void LoadSplash()
{
  m_gameState = GameState::GS_Splash;

  splashScreen = new Sprite(1);
  splashScreen->SetFrameSize(800.0f, 600.0f);
  splashScreen->SetNumberOfFrames(1);
  splashScreen->AddTexture("resources/splash.png", false);
  splashScreen->IsActive(true);
  splashScreen->IsVisible(true);
}
```

We are not going to make a significant change to the `StartGame` function. We are going to only load the splash screen, and defer loading the other game resources. This will get our splash screen up as soon as possible. Change the `StartGame` function so that it looks like the following code:

```
void StartGame()
{
 LoadSplash();
 inputManager = new Input(hWnd);

 uiTimer = 0.0f;
 srand(time(NULL));

 pickupSpawnThreshold = 3.0f;
 pickupSpawnTimer = 0.0f;

 enemySpawnThreshold = 7.0f;
 enemySpawnTimer = 0.0f;
```

```
splashDisplayTimer = 0.0f;
splashDisplayThreshold = 5.0f;

}
```

Notice that we only load the splash resources and set a few variables here. We also set the splash timer so that it will show up for at least five seconds.

Next, modify the GS_Splash case in the Update function to look like the following code:

```
switch (m_gameState)
{
case GameState::GS_Splash:
case GameState::GS_Loading:
{
  splashScreen->Update(p_deltaTime);
  splashDisplayTimer += p_deltaTime;
  if (splashDisplayTimer > splashDisplayThreshold)
  {
    m_gameState = GameState::GS_Menu;
  }
}
break;
```

This code updates the splash timer. When the timer exceeds our threshold, then the game state changes to GS_Menu. We will define the code to load the next menu.

Modify the GS_Splash case in the Render function to look like the following code:

```
case GameState::GS_Loading:
splashScreen->Render();
break;
```

 As the splash sprite is only a static image, you may wonder why we update the splash sprite. While an update has no effect on our current code, consider a case where I wanted to implement a dynamic, animated splash screen.

Loading our resources

If you have been paying attention, then you should realize that we removed the LoadTextures call from the StartGame function. Instead, we are going to load the textures in the GameLoop function. Change GameLoop so that it looks like the following code:

```
void GameLoop(const float p_deltatTime)
{
```

```
    if (m_gameState == GameState::GS_Splash)
    {
      LoadTextures();
      m_gameState = GameState::GS_Loading;
    }
    Update(p_deltatTime);
    Render();
  }
```

If you recall, GameLoop is called every frame. We need GameLoop to be running to display our splash screen, which we have already loaded. But on the first call to GameLoop, we haven't loaded our other resources.

We check to see whether our game state is GS_Splash. If it is, we call load textures, and immediately change the game state to GS_Loading. If we didn't change the game state, then the game would attempt to load the textures every frame, which would be a very bad thing! This is another practical example of why we define different game states in our state machine.

> In a way, we haven't created a true splash screen. That is because our splash still depends on Windows and OpenGL initializing before the splash screen can even be loaded and rendered. True splash screens use a snippet of code that does not depend on all of this initialization so that they can load before everything else. Unfortunately, that level of detail is beyond the scope of our book. Sometimes, the splash screen will run on a separate thread so that it is independent of the startup code.

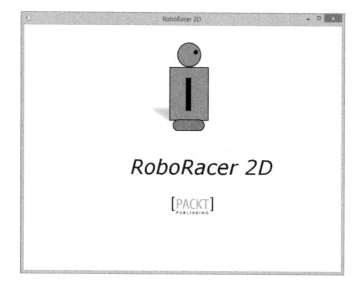

When you run the game now, you should see the splash screen display, but then nothing else happens. This is because we changed the game state to GS_Menu in the Update function, and we have not coded for that game state yet! If you want to test your splash screen, change m_gameState = GameState::GS_Menu to m_gameState = GameState::GS_Running in the Update function. Just don't forget to change it back before you move on.

> The ability to change your game state allows you to reroute the flow of your game. This is very useful, for example, when you are trying to code a new game state but you aren't ready to run it in the game yet. Once the new game state is coded, then you can wire it in.

What's on the menu?

Main menus may have disappeared in many applications, but they are still alive and well in games. The main menu gives the player a chance to decide what to do once the game has loaded. We are going to create a simple menu that allows the player to start the game, display the credits, or exit the game.

Creating the menu

Our menu will be built out of two components. First, we will load an image to use as the background. Next, we will load additional images to use as UI buttons. Together, these images will create a screen that will allow the player to navigate our game.

We will start by defining a sprite to represent the menu. Add the following line of code to the variable declarations in RoboRacer2D.cpp:

```
Sprite* menuScreen;
```

Next, we will instantiate the menu in the LoadTextures function. Add the following code to LoadTextures:

```
menuScreen = new Sprite(1);
menuScreen->SetFrameSize(800.0f, 600.0f);
menuScreen->SetNumberOfFrames(1);
menuScreen->AddTexture("resources/mainmenu.png", false);
menuScreen->IsActive(true);
menuScreen->IsVisible(true);
```

Make sure that you have downloaded the menu.png texture from the book website, or that you have created your own background at 800 by 600 pixels.

Now, we must modify the Update and Render functions. Modify the GS_Menu case in Update to the following code:

```
case GameState::GS_Menu:
  {
   menuScreen->Update(p_deltaTime);
   inputManager->Update(p_deltaTime);
   ProcessInput(p_deltaTime);
  }
  break;
```

Next, modify the GS_Menu case in the Render function:

```
case GameState::GS_Menu:
{
   menuScreen->Render();
}
break;
```

If you run the game now, the splash screen should display for five seconds, followed by the menu screen.

Defining the menu buttons

Our next task is to add buttons to the menu screen that the player can click. These buttons will work similar to the pause and resume buttons that we have already created.

We will start by declaring variables for the buttons. Add the following declarations to the variables section in RoboRacer2D.cpp:

```
Sprite* playButton;
Sprite* creditsButton;
Sprite* exitButton;
```

These three pointers will manage the three buttons on our main menu. Next, add the following code to LoadTextures to instantiate the buttons:

```
playButton = new Sprite(1);
playButton->SetFrameSize(75.0f, 38.0f);
playButton->SetNumberOfFrames(1);
playButton->SetPosition(390.0f, 300.0f);
playButton->AddTexture("resources/playButton.png");
playButton->IsVisible(true);
playButton->IsActive(false);
inputManager->AddUiElement(playButton);

creditsButton = new Sprite(1);
creditsButton->SetFrameSize(75.0f, 38.0f);
```

```
creditsButton->SetNumberOfFrames(1);
creditsButton->SetPosition(390.0f, 350.0f);
creditsButton->AddTexture("resources/creditsButton.png");
creditsButton->IsVisible(true);
creditsButton->IsActive(false);
inputManager->AddUiElement(creditsButton);

exitButton = new Sprite(1);
exitButton->SetFrameSize(75.0f, 38.0f);
exitButton->SetNumberOfFrames(1);
exitButton->SetPosition(390.0f, 500.0f);
exitButton->AddTexture("resources/exitButton.png");
exitButton->IsVisible(true);
exitButton->IsActive(false);
inputManager->AddUiElement(exitButton);
```

This code is mostly the same as the code that we used to instantiate the pause and resume buttons. One small difference is that we set all three buttons to be visible. Our code already enforces that these buttons will not render unless we are in the game state GS_Menu.

We do, however, want to set the buttons as inactive. This way the input class will ignore them until we want them to be activated.

As with all of our objects, we now need to wire them into the Update and Render functions. Change the GS_Menu case in the Update function to the following code:

```
case GameState::GS_Menu:
{
 menuScreen->Update(p_deltaTime);
 playButton->IsActive(true);
 creditsButton->IsActive(true);
 exitButton->IsActive(true);
 playButton->Update(p_deltaTime);
 creditsButton->Update(p_deltaTime);
 exitButton->Update(p_deltaTime);
 inputManager->Update(p_deltaTime);
 ProcessInput(p_deltaTime);
}
break;
```

This is where we set the buttons on our menu to be active. We want to guarantee that the buttons on the menu are active when we are in the game state GS_Menu.

Next, change the GS_Menu case in the Render function to the following code:

```
case GameState::GS_Menu:
{
 menuScreen->Render();
```

```
    playButton->Render();
    creditsButton->Render();
    exitButton->Render();
    }
  break;
```

In order for the buttons to actually do something, we need to add the following code to the CM_UI case in `ProcessInput`:

```
if (playButton->IsClicked())
{
  playButton->IsClicked(false);
  exitButton->IsActive(false);
  playButton->IsActive(false);
  creditsButton->IsActive(false);
  m_gameState = GameState::GS_Running;
}

if (creditsButton->IsClicked())
{
  creditsButton->IsClicked(false);
  exitButton->IsActive(false);
  playButton->IsActive(false);
  creditsButton->IsActive(false);
  m_gameState = GameState::GS_Credits;
}

if (exitButton->IsClicked())
{
  playButton->IsClicked(false);
  exitButton->IsActive(false);
  playButton->IsActive(false);
  creditsButton->IsActive(false);
  PostQuitMessage(0);
}
```

Notice that we change the game state if the play button or credits button are clicked (if the exit button is clicked, we simply post the quit message). Notice that we have to do a little button management, setting the buttons on the menu to be inactive once we are no longer in the GS_Menu game state. This is because our input class checks the input for all buttons that are active. Leaving the buttons active would mean that they could still be clicked even though they are not being displayed on the screen.

We don't have to set the buttons to be invisible. This is because changing the state will automatically stop these buttons from updating or rendering. The same is true of the menu screen. Once the game state is changed, it will not render or update. This is one of the big advantages of utilizing a state machine.

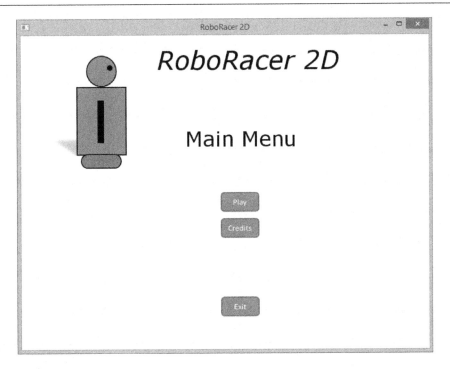

If you run the program right now, the main menu will display. If you click the play button, the game will start. If you click the exit button, the game will exit. We will implement the credit screen next.

Getting some credit

Everyone likes to get credit for their hard work! Most games will implement a credits screen that shows the name and function of each person involved in creating the game. For AAA titles, this list may be as long as a list for a movie. For smaller, independent games, this list might be three people.

Creating the credits screen

Similarly to the main menu, the credits screen will be based on a background image and a button that can be clicked. We will also need to add text to the screen.

Let's start by declaring a pointer for our screen. Add the following declaration to the variables section of `RoboRacer2D.cpp`:

```
Sprite* creditsScreen;
```

Then, we will instantiate the credits screen in `LoadTextures`:

```
creditsScreen = new Sprite(1);
creditsScreen->SetFrameSize(800.0f, 600.0f);
creditsScreen->SetNumberOfFrames(1);
creditsScreen->AddTexture("resources/credits.png", false);
creditsScreen->IsActive(false);
creditsScreen->IsVisible(true);
```

Next, we wire the credits screen into `Update`:

```
case GameState::GS_Credits:
{
 creditsScreen->Update(p_deltaTime);
 inputManager->Update(p_deltaTime);
 ProcessInput(p_deltaTime);
}
break;
```

We also update `Render`:

```
case GameState::GS_Credits:
{
 creditsScreen->Render();
}
break;
```

Getting back to the main menu

We now need to add a button that allows us to get from the credits screen back to the main menu. We first declare the pointer in the variables declaration section:

```
Sprite* menuButton;
```

We then instantiate the button in `LoadTextures`:

```
menuButton = new Sprite(1);
menuButton->SetFrameSize(75.0f, 38.0f);
menuButton->SetNumberOfFrames(1);
menuButton->SetPosition(390.0f, 400.0f);
menuButton->AddTexture("resources/menuButton.png");
menuButton->IsVisible(true);
menuButton->IsActive(false);
inputManager->AddUiElement(menuButton);
```

Let's add the button to `Update`:

```
case GameState::GS_Credits:
{
```

```
creditsScreen->Update(p_deltaTime);
menuButton->IsActive(true);
menuButton->Update(p_deltaTime);
inputManager->Update(p_deltaTime);
ProcessInput(p_deltaTime);
}
break;
```

We also update `Render`:

```
case GameState::GS_Credits:
{
creditsScreen->Render();
menuButton->Render();
}
break;
```

Similarly to the menu buttons, we now need to add code to the case
`Input::Command::CM_UI:` case in `ProcessInput` to handle clicking on
the menu button:

```
if (menuButton->IsClicked())
{
  menuButton->IsClicked(false);
  menuButton->IsActive(false);
  m_gameState = GameState::GS_Menu;
}
```

When the menu button is clicked, we change the game state back to menu, and set
the menu button to be inactive. Due to the code that we have already written, the
menu screen will automatically display.

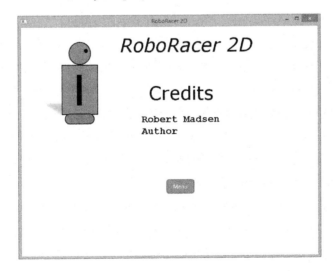

Working with fonts

Until now, we embedded any text that we needed inside of an existing texture. However, there are times when we may want to have the code decide what text to display. For example, on our credits screen, we don't want to make a graphic for each person's name who took part in creating the game.

Creating the font

We need a way to render text directly to the screen, and this means that we also need a way to define the font that we want to use when rendering the text. First, we need to add a global variable that services as a handle to our fonts. Add the following line to the variable declarations in the code:

```
GLuint fontBase;
```

Now, we need to add the following code to create the font:

```
GLvoid BuildFont(GLvoid)
{
  HFONT newFont;
  HFONT tempFont;

  fontBase = glGenLists(96);

  tempFont = CreateFont(-26, // Height
  0,                         // Width
  0,                         // Escapement
  0,                         // Orientation
  FW_BOLD,                   // Weight
  FALSE,                     // Italic
  FALSE,                     // Underline
  FALSE,                     // Strikeout
  ANSI_CHARSET,         // Character Set
  OUT_TT_PRECIS,             // Output Precision
  CLIP_DEFAULT_PRECIS, // Clipping Precision
  ANTIALIASED_QUALITY,// Output Quality
  FF_DONTCARE | DEFAULT_PITCH, // Family/Pitch
  "Courier New");            // Font Name

  newFont = (HFONT)SelectObject(hDC, tempFont);
  wglUseFontBitmaps(hDC, 32, 96, fontBase);
  SelectObject(hDC, newFont);
  DeleteObject(tempFont);
}
```

This code creates a font using three main elements.

First, we use `glGenLists` to create 96 display lists to hold each letter of our font. A display list is basically a buffer that can hold rendering data. Next, we call `CreateFont` to create a Windows font. The parameters of the `CreateFont` function specify the type of font that we want to create. Finally, we use `wglUseFontBitmaps` to assign our new font to the font handle that we created earlier.

One little twist is that we have to create a temporary `HFONT` object called `tempFont` with all the properties, then we assign `tempFont` to `newFont` and delete `tempFont`.

We will want to delete the display lists when the program closes down, so add the following utility function:

```
GLvoid KillFont (GLvoid)
{
  glDeleteLists(fontBase, 96);
}
```

This code simply uses `glDeleteLists` to delete the display lists that we created to hold our font.

Drawing text

Now that we have a font, we need to have a function that will render text to the screen. Add the following function to the code:

```
void DrawText(const char* p_text, const float p_x, const float p_y,
const float r, const float g, const float b)
{
 glBindTexture(GL_TEXTURE_2D, 0);
 glColor3f(r, g, b);

 glRasterPos2f(p_x, p_y);
 if (p_text != NULL)
 {
  glPushAttrib(GL_LIST_BIT);
  glListBase(fontBase - 32);
  glCallLists(strlen(p_text), GL_UNSIGNED_BYTE, p_text);
  glPopAttrib();
 }
 glColor3f(1.0f, 1.0f, 1.0f);

}
```

This code takes a string and an *x* and *y* position, and draws the text at that position. It also takes `r`, `g`, and `b` parameters to define the text color:

- `glBindTexture(GL_TEXTURE_2D, 0)`: This tells OpenGL that we are going to be working with 2D textures (i.e. the fonts) `glColor3f(r, g, b)`: This sets the color of the font.

- `glRasterPos2f`: This is used to set the current draw position on the screen.
- `glPushAttrib(GL_LIST_BIT)`: This tells OpenGL that we are going to render using display lists.
- `glListBase`: This sets the current start of the list. We subtract 32 because the ASCII value for a space is 32, and we don't use any characters with lower ASCII values.
- `glCallLists`: This is used to retrieve the lists for each character in the text.
- `glPopAttrib`: This returns the OpenGL attribute to its previous value.

Now, we are ready to draw our credits text:

```
void DrawCredits()
{
 float startX = 325.0f;
 float startY = 250.0f;
 float spaceY = 30.0f;
 DrawText("Robert Madsen", startX, startY, 0.0f, 0.0f, 1.0f);
 DrawText("Author", startX, startY + spaceY, 0.0f, 0.0f, 1.0f);
}
```

First, we set the position on the screen where we want to draw, then we use the `DrawText` function to actually perform the drawing. The first line adds me (a subtle indulgence), and the second line is for you!

Wiring in the font support

We have a few more book keeping tasks to perform to get the font support to work. First, modify the `GameLoop` code, adding the highlighted line:

```
if (m_gameState == GameState::GS_Splash)
{
  BuildFont();
  LoadTextures();
  m_gameState = GameState::GS_Loading;
}
```

This will create our fonts when the game starts up.

Next, fill out the `GS_Credits` case of the `m_gameState` switch in the `Render` function:

```
case GameState::GS_Credits:
{
 creditsScreen->Update(p_deltaTime);
 menuButton->IsActive(true);
 menuButton->Update(p_deltaTime);
 inputManager->Update(p_deltaTime);
```

```
    ProcessInput(p_deltaTime);
    }
    break;
```

This draws the credits text when the game state changes to `GS_Credits`. Congratulations! You can finally get the credit that you deserve!

Level up!

A lot of the fun in games is trying to increase your score. Part of good game design is to make the game challenging to play, but not so challenging that the player cannot score or improve.

Most players also get better at a game as they play, so if the game difficulty does not increase, the player will eventually get bored because the player will no longer be challenged.

We will start by simply displaying the score on the screen so that the player can see how well they are doing. Then we will discuss techniques that are used to continually increase the difficulty of the game, thus steadily increasing the challenge.

Displaying the score

We already learned how to display text on the screen when we were creating the credits screen. Now, we will use the same techniques to display the score.

If you recall, we already have a mechanism to keep track of the score. Every sprite has a value property. For pickups, we assign a positive value so that the player gains points for each pickup. For enemies, we assign a negative value so that the player loses points whenever they collide with an enemy. We store the current score in the value property of the player.

Add the following code to `RoboRacer2D.cpp` to create the `DrawScore` function:

```
void DrawScore()
{
  char score[50];
  sprintf_s(score, 50, "Score: %i", player->GetValue());
  DrawText(score, 350.0f, 25.0f, 0.0f, 0.0f, 1.0f);
}
```

This code works just like the `DrawCredits` function that we created earlier. First, we create a character string that holds the current score and a caption, then we use `DrawText` to render the text.

We also need to wire this into the main game. Modify the GS_Running case of the m_gameState switch in the Render function with the highlighted line:

```
case GameState::GS_Running:
case GameState::GS_Paused:
{
 background->Render();
 robot_left->Render();
 robot_right->Render();
 robot_left_strip->Render();
 robot_right_strip->Render();
 pauseButton->Render();
 resumeButton->Render();
 pickup->Render();
 enemy->Render();
 DrawScore();
}
break;
```

The score will display both when the game is running and when the game is paused.

Game progression

In order to add progression to the game, we need to have certain thresholds established. For our game, we will set three thresholds:

- Each level will last two minutes
- If the player receives less than five pickups during a level, the game will end, and the game over screen will be displayed
- If the player receives five or more pickups, then the level ends and the next level screen is displayed

For each level that the player successfully completes, we will make things a little more difficult. There are many ways that we could increase the difficulty of each level:

- Increase the spawn time for pickups
- Decrease the speed of the robot

To keep things simple, we will only do one of these. We will increase the spawn time threshold for pickups by .25 seconds for each level. With pickups spawning less often, the player will eventually receive too few pickups, and the game will end.

Defining game levels

Let's set up the code for level progression. We will start by defining a timer to keep track of how much time has passed. Add the following declarations to `RoboRacer2D.cpp`:

```
float levelTimer;
float levelMaxTime;
float pickupSpawnAdjustment;

int pickupsReceived;
int pickupsThreshold;
int enemiesHit;
```

We will initialize the variables in the `StartGame` function:

```
levelTimer = 0.0f;
levelMaxTime = 30.0f;
pickupSpawnAdjustment = 0.25f;

pickupsReceived = 0;
pickupsThreshold = 5;
enemiesHit =0;
```

We are setting up a timer that will run for 120 seconds, or two minutes. At the end of two minutes the level will end and the spawn time for pickups will be incremented by .25 seconds. We will also check to see whether the player has received five pickups. If not, the game will be over.

To handle the logic for the level progression, let's add a new function called `NextLevel` by adding the following code:

```
void NextLevel()
{
 if (pickupsReceived < pickupsThreshold)
 {
  m_gameState = GameState::GS_GameOver;
 }
 else
 {
  pickupSpawnThreshold += pickupSpawnAdjustment;
  levelTimer = 0.0f;
  m_gameState = GameState::GS_NextLevel;
 }
}
```

As stated previously, we check to see whether the number of pickups that the robot has is less than the pickup threshold. If so, we change the game state to `GS_GameOver`. Otherwise, we reset the level timer, reset the pickups received counter, increment the pickup spawn timer, and set the game state back to `GS_Running`.

We still need to add some code to update the level timer and check to see whether the level is over. Add the following code to the GS_Running case in the Update function:

```
levelTimer += p_deltaTime;
if (levelTimer > levelMaxTime)
{
  NextLevel();
}
```

This code updates the level timer. If the timer exceeds our threshold, then call NextLevel to see what happens next.

Finally, we need to add two lines of code to CheckCollisions to count the number of pickups received by the player. Add the following highlighted line of code to CheckCollisions:

```
if (player->IntersectsCircle(pickup))
{
  pickup->IsVisible(false);
  pickup->IsActive(false);
  player->SetValue(player->GetValue() + pickup->GetValue());
  pickupSpawnTimer = 0.0f;
  pickupsReceived++;
}

if (player->IntersectsRect(enemy))
{
  enemy->IsVisible(false);
  enemy->IsActive(false);
  player->SetValue(player->GetValue() + enemy->GetValue());
  enemySpawnTimer = 0.0f;
  enemiesHit++;
}
```

Game stats

It would be nice for the player to be able to see how they did between each level. Let's add a function to display the player stats:

```
void DrawStats()
{
 char pickupsStat[50];
 char enemiesStat[50];
 char score[50];
 sprintf_s(pickupsStat, 50, "Enemies Hit: %i", enemiesHit);
 sprintf_s(enemiesStat, 50, "Pickups: %i", pickupsReceived);
 sprintf_s(score, 50, "Score: %i", player->GetValue());
 DrawText(enemiesStat, 350.0f, 270.0f, 0.0f, 0.0f, 1.0f);
 DrawText(pickupsStat, 350.0f, 320.0f, 0.0f, 0.0f, 1.0f);
 DrawText(score, 350.0f, 370.0f, 0.0f, 0.0f, 1.0f);
}
```

We will now wire this into the next level screen.

The next level screen

Now that we have the logic in place to detect the end of the level, it is time to implement our next level screen. By now, the process should be second nature, so let's try an abbreviated approach:

1. Declare a pointer to the screen:

   ```
   Sprite* nextLevelScreen;
   ```

2. Instantiate the sprite in `LoadTextures`:

   ```
   nextLevelScreen = new Sprite(1);
   nextLevelScreen->SetFrameSize(800.0f, 600.0f);
   nextLevelScreen->SetNumberOfFrames(1);
   nextLevelScreen->AddTexture("resources/level.png", false);
   nextLevelScreen->IsActive(true);
   nextLevelScreen->IsVisible(true);
   ```

3. Modify the `GS_NextLevel` case in the `Update` function:

   ```
   case GameState::GS_NextLevel:
   {
     nextLevelScreen->Update(p_deltaTime);
     continueButton->IsActive(true);
     continueButton->Update(p_deltaTime);
     inputManager->Update(p_deltaTime);
     ProcessInput(p_deltaTime);
     break;
   }
   ```

4. Modify the `GS_NextLevel` case in the `Render` function to look like the following code::

   ```
   case GameState::GS_NextLevel:
   {
     nextLevelScreen->Render();
     DrawStats();
     continueButton->Render();
   }
   break;
   ```

Continuing the game

Now, we need to add a button that allows the player to continue the game. Again, you have done this so many times, so we will use a shorthand approach:

1. Declare a pointer for the button:

   ```
   Sprite* continueButton;
   ```

2. Instantiate the button in `LoadTextures`:

```
continueButton = new Sprite(1);
continueButton->SetFrameSize(75.0f, 38.0f);
continueButton->SetNumberOfFrames(1);
continueButton->SetPosition(390.0f, 400.0f);
continueButton->AddTexture("resources/continueButton.png");
continueButton->IsVisible(true);
continueButton->IsActive(false);
inputManager->AddUiElement(continueButton);
```

3. Add this code to `Update`:

```
case GameState::GS_NextLevel:
{
  nextLevelScreen->Update(p_deltaTime);
  continueButton->IsActive(true);
  continueButton->Update(p_deltaTime);
  inputManager->Update(p_deltaTime);
  ProcessInput(p_deltaTime);
}
break;
```

4. Add this code to `Render`:

```
case GameState::GS_NextLevel:
{
  nextLevelScreen->Render();
  DrawStats();
  continueButton->Render();
}
break;
```

5. Add this code to `ProcessInput`:

```
if (continueButton->IsClicked())
{
  continueButton->IsClicked(false);
  continueButton->IsActive(false);
  m_gameState = GameState::GS_Running;
pickupsReceived = 0;
enemiesHit = 0;
}
```

Clicking the continue button simply changes the game state back to `GS_Running`.
The level calculations have already occurred when `NextLevel` was called.

Game over

As the saying goes, all good things must come to an end. If the player doesn't meet
the pickup threshold, the game will end, and the game over screen will be displayed.
The player can choose to replay the game or exit.

The game over screen

Our last screen is the game over screen. By now, the process should be second nature, so let's try an abbreviated approach:

1. Declare a pointer to the screen:

```
Sprite* gameOverScreen;
```

2. Instantiate the sprite in `LoadTextures`:

```
gameOverScreen = new Sprite(1);
gameOverScreen->SetFrameSize(800.0f, 600.0f);
gameOverScreen->SetNumberOfFrames(1);
gameOverScreen->AddTexture("resources/gameover.png", false);
gameOverScreen->IsActive(true);
gameOverScreen->IsVisible(true);
```

3. Change the `GS_GameOver` case in the `Update` function to look like the following code:

```
case GameState::GS_GameOver:
{
  gameOverScreen->Update(p_deltaTime);
  replayButton->IsActive(true);
  replayButton->Update(p_deltaTime);
  exitButton->IsActive(true);
  exitButton->Update(p_deltaTime);
  inputManager->Update(p_deltaTime);
  ProcessInput(p_deltaTime);
}
break;
```

4. Add the following code to `Render`:

```
case GameState::GS_GameOver:
{
  gameOverScreen->Render();
  replayButton->Render();
  DrawStats();
}
break;
```

As a bonus, we will also draw the game stats on the game over screen.

Replaying the game

We need a way to reset the game to its initial state. So, let's create a function to do this:

```
void RestartGame()
{
    player->SetValue(0);
  robot_right->SetValue(0);
  robot_left->SetValue(0);

pickupSpawnThreshold = 5.0f;
    pickupSpawnTimer = 0.0f;
    enemySpawnThreshold = 7.0f;
    enemySpawnTimer = 0.0f;
    splashDisplayTimer = 0.0f;
    splashDisplayThreshold = 5.0f;

    levelTimer = 0.0f;

    pickupsReceived = 0;
    pickupsThreshold = 5;
pickupsReceived = 0;

    pickup->IsVisible(false);
    enemy->IsVisible(false);

    background->SetVelocity(0.0f);
    robot_left->SetPosition(screen_width / 2.0f - 50.0f, screen_height -
130.0f);
    robot_left->IsVisible(false);

    robot_right->SetPosition(screen_width / 2.0f - 50.0f, screen_height
- 130.0f);

    player = robot_right;
    player->IsActive(true);
    player->IsVisible(true);
    player->SetVelocity(0.0f);
}
```

Next, we need to add a button that allows the player to replay the game. Again, as you have done this so many times, we will use a shorthand approach:

1. Declare a pointer for the button:

```
Sprite* replayButton;
```

2. Instantiate the button in `LoadTextures`:

```
replayButton = new Sprite(1);
replayButton->SetFrameSize(75.0f, 38.0f);
replayButton->SetNumberOfFrames(1);
replayButton->SetPosition(390.0f, 400.0f);
replayButton->AddTexture("resources/replayButton.png");
replayButton->IsVisible(true);
replayButton->IsActive(false);
inputManager->AddUiElement(replayButton);
```

3. Add the following code to `Update`:

```
case GameState::GS_GameOver:
  {
    gameOverScreen->Update(p_deltaTime);
    replayButton->IsActive(true);
    replayButton->Update(p_deltaTime);
    exitButton->IsActive(true);
    exitButton->Update(p_deltaTime);
    inputManager->Update(p_deltaTime);
    ProcessInput(p_deltaTime);
  }
  break;
```

4. Add the following code to `Render`:

```
case GameState::GS_GameOver:
  {
    gameOverScreen->Render();
    replayButton->Render();
    DrawStats();
  }
  break;
```

5. Add the following code to `ProcessInput`:

```
if (replayButton->IsClicked())
{
    replayButton->IsClicked(false);
    replayButton->IsActive(false);
    exitButton->IsActive(false);
    RestartGame();
    m_gameState = GameState::GS_Running;
}
```

Notice how we are reusing the exit button in the Update function. Also, if the player wants to replay the game, we call the RestartGame function when the player clicks the replay button. This resets all of the game variables and allows the player to start all over.

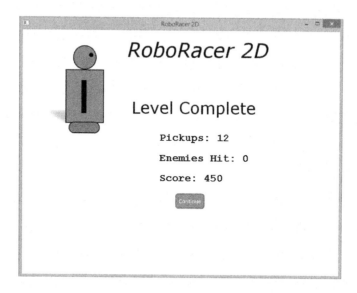

Summary

We covered a lot of ground in this chapter. The focus of the chapter is to add all of the final elements to the game that make it a truly polished game. This involves adding a lot of screens and buttons, and to manage all of this, we introduced a more advanced state machine. The state machine acts like a traffic director, routing the game to the correct routines depending on the game state.

In the next chapter, we will add sound effects and music to our game!

7
Audio Adrenaline

This is the final chapter on the 2D game that we have been working on. Although our Robo Racer 2D game is almost complete, there is one element that we have yet to include to make it a complete game. Unless you like silent movies, you have probably noticed that we don't have any audio in this game. Most games depend on audio, and ours is no exception. In this chapter, we will cover audio and a few other housekeeping items.

- **Audio formats**: It is important to understand how audio is represented in computers and how it is used in games. We will discuss sample rates and bits and help you understand how audio works.

- **Audio engine**: We need some kind of audio engine to integrate audio into our game. We will discuss FMOD, a very popular engine that allows you to easily integrate audio using C++.

- **SFX**: Sound effects play a huge role in most games and, we will add sound effects to our game to bring it to life.

- **Music**: Most games utilize some kind of music. Music is handled in a different way than sound effects, and you will learn the differences between the two.

- **Final housekeeping**: On a final note, for our game, we have left the game shutdown for this chapter. We have not been good programmers in that we have not properly released the objects in our game. We will learn why it is important to do so, and how to do it.

Bits and bytes

Audio is inherently an analog experience. Sound is created as compressed waves travel through the air and interact with our ear drums. Until recently, the techniques used to reproduce audio were also strictly audio as well. For example, a microphone records sound similarly to how our ears do by capturing changes in air pressure and converting them to electrical impulses. Speakers do the reverse by converting the electrical signals back into waves of air pressure.

Computers, on the other hand, are digital. Computers convert audio samples into bits and bytes by taking samples of the audio. To keep it simple, let's consider a system where the current frequency of the sound wave (that is, how fast the wave is moving) is captured as a 16 bit (2 byte) number. It turns out that a 16 bit number can capture numbers in a range from 0 to 65,536. Each sample of the sound wave must be encoded as a number in this range. Also, as we actually capture two samples each time (for stereo sound), we need 4 bytes to capture each sample.

The next important factor is how often you sample the sound. The range of audio frequencies run roughly from 20 to 20,000 Hz (*Hz = cycles per second*). A very smart person named Nyquist figured out that we have to sample audio at twice the frequency to accurately capture the wave. This means that we have to capture at least 40,000 samples each second to accurately capture a sound. Conversely, we have to play the sound back at the same frequency. This is why audio on compact discs are sampled at 44,100 Hz.

You should be able to see by now that it is going to take a lot of disk space and a lot of memory to work with sound. A one minute piece of audio will take about 10 MB of storage! This means that the same audio would require 10 MB of memory if we were to load the entire audio file at once.

You may wonder how modern games function at all. The music scores of some games are measured in hours, not minutes. Similarly, there may be hundreds or even thousands of sound effects, not to mention voice, which is also recorded as audio.

A sound by any other name

There are many formats that audio files can be stored in. We will deal with two common formats that are used in games: WAV files and MP3 files. A WAV file stores the audio data in an uncompressed format.

Although WAV files can be used for all of your audio, they are typically used for sound effects. Sound effects are typically very short, often less than 1 second. This means that the size of the file is going to be relatively small because the audio file is very short.

While sound effects are often saved as WAV files, music, typically, is not. This is because the length of music tends to be much longer than the length of sound effects. Loading a music file into memory that is three-to-five minutes long would take an exorbitant amount of memory.

There are two main techniques that are used to deal with larger audio files. First, data compression can be used to make the audio files smaller. One of the most common audio formats that provides data compression is the MP3 format. Using mathematical trickery, MP3 files store the sound data in less space without sacrificing any sound quality.

The second technique that is used to handle large files is streaming. Instead of loading the entire sound file into memory, the file is sent a piece at a time as a continuous stream of data, which is then played in the game.

There are some limitations to streaming. First, the transfer of data from a hard drive or another storage device is much slower that the transfer of data from memory. Streamed audio can suffer from lag, which is the amount of time that it takes for a sound to play from the time that the sound was triggered to play in code.

Lag is more critical for sound effects than it is for music. This is because a particular sound effect often coincides with something that just happened in the game. It would be disconcerting if the sound of a bullet occurred a half second after the bullet was fired! Music, on the other hand, often starts and runs for several minutes. A small lag in the start of the music can often be overlooked.

Making noise

Going into a full-blown course on creating sounds and music is, of course, beyond the scope of this book. However, I did want to give you a few resources to get you started.

The first question you may ask is where to find sounds. There are literally thousands of sites on the Web that provide sounds and music that can be used in games. Many charge a fee, while a few offer free audio.

One thing to keep in mind is that *royalty-free* doesn't necessarily mean free. Royalty-free audio means that once you obtain a license to use the audio, you won't have to pay any additional fees to use the music.

So, here's my big tip. Every site that I have found charges a small fee for both sound effects and music. But there is one way that I have found to obtain sounds for free using the **Unity Asset Store**. Go to `http://unity3d.com` and install the free version of Unity. Once you have started Unity, perform the following steps:

1. Create a new project by clicking **Create New Project** tab from the **Unity Project Wizard**. Click **Browse** and navigate to or create a folder to store your project in. Then click **Select Folder**.

2. Once Unity loads the project, click **Window** and then **Asset Store** from the menu.

3. When the **Asset Store** window appears, enter a relevant search term (for example, music or SFX) in the **Search Asset Store** text box and press *Enter*.

4. Browse the results for free assets. Click on any listing for more details. If you find something that you like, click the **Download** link.

5. Once Unity has downloaded the asset, the **Importing Package** screen will appear titled. Click the **Import** button.

6. You can now exit Unity and navigate to the folder where you created the new project. Then navigate inside the `Assets` folder. From here, it depends on the structure of the package that you imported, but if you browse around, you should be able to locate the audio files.

> In fact, we are using a musical piece titled Jolly Bot provided by Robson Cozendey (`www.cozendey.com`). We also found a great SFX package from.

7. You can now copy the audio files into your project!

> As you browse around for audio files, you will run across some files with the `ogg` extension. This is a common audio format similar to MP3. However, the engine that we will use does not support ogg files, so you will need to convert them to MP3 files. Audacity, which is described next, will allow you to convert audio files from one format to another.

You may find that you want to edit or mix your audio files. Or, you may need to convert your audio files from one format to another. The best free tool that I found to work with audio is **Audacity**, and you can download it at `http://audacity.sourceforge.net/`. Audacity is a full-featured audio mixer that will allow you to play, edit, and convert audio files.

To export files to the MP3 format, you will need a copy of **LAME** installed on your system. You can download LAME from `http://lame.buanzo.org/#lamewindl`.

Revving up your engine

Now that you have a better understanding of how audio works in your computer, it's time to write some code to bring audio into your game. We generally don't work with audio directly. Instead, there are audio engines that do all of the hard work for us, and one of the most popular ones is **FMOD**.

FMOD is a C and C++ API that allows us to load, manage, and play audio sources. FMOD is free to use for student and independent projects, so it is the perfect audio engine for our game. To use FMOD, you will have to go to the FMOD website, download the appropriate version of the API, and install it on your system:

1. To download FMOD, go to `http://www.FMOD.org/download/`.
2. There several downloads to choose from. Scroll down to the **FMOD Ex Programmer's API,** and click the **Download** button for Windows.
3. You will have to locate the exe file that you just downloaded and install it. Make a note of the folder that FMOD is installed in.
4. Once you have downloaded FMOD, you will have to incorporate it into the game project. Start by opening the `RoboRacer2D` project.

I'm sure that you would like to see the full documentation for the **FMOD API**. If you installed FMOD in the default location, you will find the documentation at `C:\Program Files (x86)\FMOD SoundSystem\FMOD Programmers API Windows\documentation`. The main documentation is found in the file fmodex.chm.

Now, it's time to set up our game to use FMOD. Similar to most third-party libraries, there are three steps to hooking things up:

1. Accessing the `.dll` file.
2. Linking to the library.
3. Point to the include files.

Let' walk through this process.

Accessing the FMOD .dll file

There are several .dll files that are included with FMOD, and it is important to use the correct file. The following table summarizes the dll files that come with FMOD and their associated library file:

Dll	Description	Library
fmodex.dll	32 bit FMOD API	fmodex_vc.lib
fmodexL.dll	32 bit FMOD API with debug logging	fmodexL_vc.lib
fmodex64.dll	64 bit FMOD API	fmodex64_vc.lib
fmodexL64.dll	64 bit FMOD API with debug logging	fmodexL64_vc.lib

It's up to you to decide whether or not to use the 32-bit or 64-bit versions of the library. The debug versions of the library write logging information out to a file. You can find more information in the documentation.

We are going to use the 32-bit file in our game. There are several places where we can place the file, but the simplest method is to simply copy the .dll file into our project:

1. Navigate to C:\Program Files (x86)\FMOD SoundSystem\FMOD Programmers API Windows\api.

 The preceding path assumes that you used the default install location. You may have to modify the path if you chose another location.

2. Copy fmodex.dll to the project folder that contains the RoboRacer2D source code.

Linking to the library

The next step is to tell Visual Studio that we want to access the FMOD library. This is done by adding the library to the project properties:

1. Right-click on the project and choose **Properties**.

2. Open the **Linker** branch under **Configuration Properties** and click on **Input**.

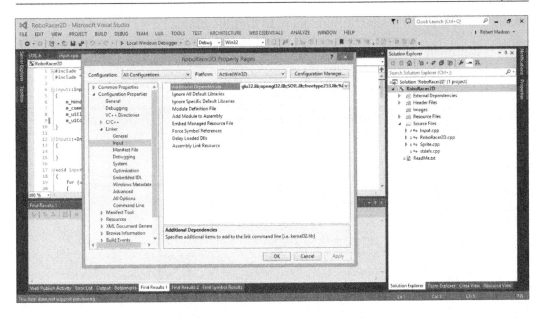

3. Click in the **Addition Dependencies** entry, then click the drop-down arrow and choose **<Edit...>**.

4. Add `fmodex_vc.lib` to the list of dependencies.

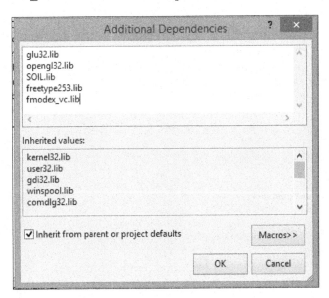

5. Click **OK** to close the `Additional Dependencies` window.

6. Click **OK** to close the `Property Pages` window.

Now, we have to tell Visual Studio where to find the library:

1. Right-click on the project and choose **Properties**.

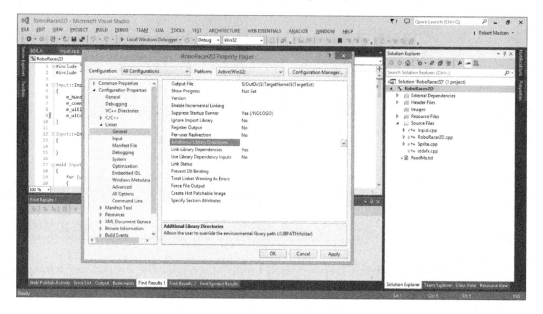

2. Open the **Linker** branch under **Configuration Properties** and click on **General**.

3. Click in the **Additional Library Directories** entry, then click the drop-down arrow and choose **<Edit...>**:

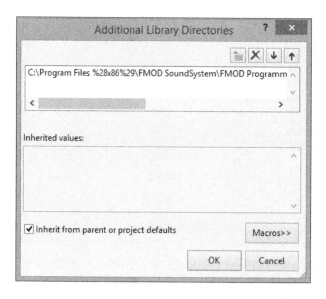

4. Click on the **New Line** icon, and then click the ellipses (**...**) that appear.

5. Navigate to `C:\Program Files (x86)\FMOD SoundSystem\FMOD Programmers API Windows\api\lib` and click **Select Folder**.

6. Click on **OK** to close the **Additional Library Directories** window.

7. Click on **OK** to close the **Property Pages** window.

Point to the include files

Whenever you use third-party code, you generally have to include C++ header files in your code. Sometimes, we just copy the relevant header files into the project folder (for example, this is what we did with `SOIL.h`).

With larger code bases, such as FMOD, we point Visual Studio to the location where the header files are installed:

1. Right-click on the project and choose **Properties**.

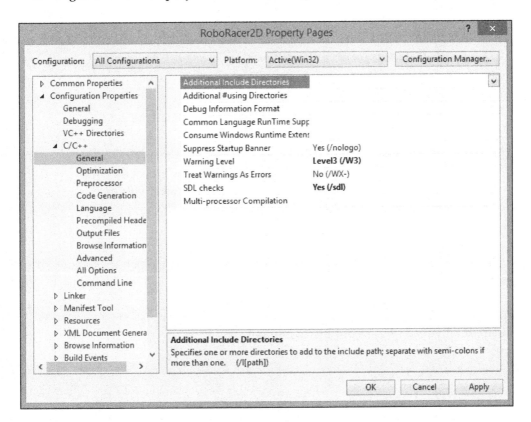

2. Open the **C/C++** branch under **Configuration Properties** and click on **General**.

3. Click on the **Additional Include Directories** entry, then click the drop-down arrow, and choose **<Edit...>**.

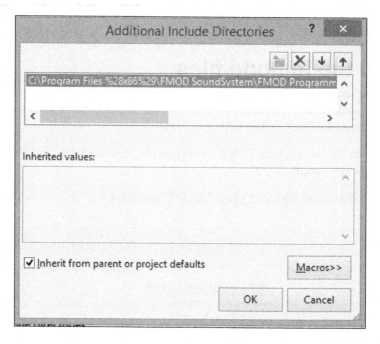

4. Click the **New Line** icon, and then click the ellipses (**...**) that appear.

5. Navigate to `C:\Program Files (x86)\FMOD SoundSystem\FMOD Programmers API Windows\api\inc` and click **Select Folder**.

6. Click **OK** to close the **Additional Include Directories** window.

7. Click **OK** to close the **Property Pages** window.

The final step is to include the header files into our program. Open `RoboRacer2D.cpp` and add the following line to include the header file:

```
#include "fmod.hpp"
```

You are finally ready to use our audio engine!

Initializing FMOD

The first code that we need to add is the code that will initialize the audio engine. Just like we must initialize OpenGL, the code will set up FMOD and check to see if there are any errors along the way.

Open `RoboRacer2D.cpp` and add the following code to the variable declarations area:

```
FMOD::System* audiomgr;
```

Then add the following function:

```
bool InitFmod()
{
  FMOD_RESULT result;
  result = FMOD::System_Create(&audiomgr);
  if (result != FMOD_OK)
  {
    return false;
  }
  result = audiomgr->init(50, FMOD_INIT_NORMAL, NULL);
  if (result != FMOD_OK)
  {
    return false;
  }
  return true;
}
```

This function creates the FMOD system and initializes it:

- First, we define a variable to catch FMOD error codes
- The `System_Create` call creates the engine and stores the results in `audiomgr`
- We then initialize FMOD with 50 virtual channels, normal mode, and

Finally, we need call the `InitAudio` function. Modify the `GameLoop` function, adding the highlighted line:

```
void GameLoop(const float p_deltatTime)
{
  if (m_gameState == GameState::GS_Splash)
  {
    InitFmod();
    BuildFont();
    LoadTextures();
```

```
      m_gameState = GameState::GS_Loading;
   }
   Update(p_deltatTime);
   Render();
}
```

Virtual channels

The most significant feature that FMOD provides for us is **virtual channels**. Each sound that you play has to have its own channel to play on. The number of physical channels to play audio varies from device to device. Early sound cards could only handle two to four channels of sound at a time. Modern sound cards may be able to handle eight, sixteen, or even more.

It used to be up to the developer to make sure that the number of sounds playing at any one time did not exceed the number of channels on the hardware. If the game triggered a new sound and no channel was available, then the sound wouldn't play. This led to choppy, unpredictable audio.

Fortunately, FMOD handles all of this for us. FMOD uses virtual channels, and allows you to decide how many virtual channels you want to use. Behind the scenes, FMOD decides which virtual channels need to be assigned to a hardware channel at any given time.

In our code example, we initialized FMOD with 50 virtual channels. This is actually way more that we will use in this game, but it wouldn't be outrageous for a full game. When considering how many virtual channels to assign, you should think about how many audio sources will be loaded at any particular time. These sounds won't all be playing at one time, just available to play.

Channel priority

FMOD can't make your hardware play more simultaneous sounds than it has physical sound channels, so you may wonder why you would ever assign more virtual channels than there are hardware channels.

The first answer to this question is that you really don't know how many hardware channels will be available on the system where a player is actually playing your game. The use of virtual channels takes this concern away from you.

The second answer is that virtual channels allow you to design your audio as if you really had 50 (or 100) channels available to you. FMOD then takes care of managing those channels behind the scenes.

So, what happens if your game needs to play a ninth sound and there are only eight physical channels? FMOD uses a priority system to decide which of the current eight channels is no longer needed. For example, channel seven may be assigned to a sound effect that is no longer playing. FMOD then assigns channel seven to the new sound that wants to play.

If all physical channels are actually playing a sound right now and FMOD needs to play a new sound, then it chooses the channel with the lowest priority, stops playing the sound on that channel, and plays the new sound. Factors that determine priority include:

- How long ago the sound was triggered
- Whether a sound is set to loop continuously
- The priority assigned by the programmer using the `Channel:setPriority` or `Sound::setDefaults` functions
- In 3D sound, how far away the sound is
- The current volume of the sound

So, you can still end up with sounds that drop out if your sound design exceeds the number of simultaneous, physical channels. But FMOD does its best to limit the impact this will have.

Bleeps and bloops

Imagine watching a move that has no sound. As the main character runs down the alley, there are no footsteps. There is no swishing sound as his arms rub his jacket. There is no screech as a car comes to a halt just before hitting him.

A movie without sound would be pretty boring, and so would most games. Sounds bring games to life. The best sound design is one where the player doesn't actually realize there is a sound design. This means crafting sound effects and music in a way that complement the game without being obnoxious.

Sound effects

Sound effects generally correspond to some event or action that is happening in the game. A particular sound often corresponds to something that the player can see, but sound effects may also occur for something that the player cannot see, perhaps just round the corner.

Let's add our first sound effects to the game. We'll keep it simple and add the following sounds:

- A rolling sound as Robo moves across the screen
- A sound when Robo jumps up or jumps down
- A happy sound when he collides with an oil can
- A not-so-happy sound when he collides with a water bottle

Setting up the sounds

We'll start by setting up some variables to act as pointers to our sounds. Open `RoboRacer2D.cpp` and add the following code in the variable declarations section:

```
FMOD::Sound* sfxWater;
FMOD::Sound* sfxOilcan;
FMOD::Sound* sfxJump;
FMOD::Sound* sfxMovement;
FMOD::Channel* chMovement;
```

We have three pointers to sound and one pointer to a channel. We only need one channel pointer because only one sound (`sfxMovement`) will be a looping sound. Looping sounds need a persistent channel pointer while one-shot sounds do not.

Next, we will load these sounds. Add the following function to `RoboRacer2D.cpp`:

```
const bool LoadAudio()
{
  FMOD_RESULT result;
  result = audiomgr-> createSound ("resources/oil.wav", FMOD_DEFAULT,
0, &sfxOilcan);
  result = audiomgr-> createSound ("resources/water.wav", FMOD_
DEFAULT, 0, &sfxWater);
  result = audiomgr-> createSound ("resources/jump.wav", FMOD_DEFAULT,
0, &sfxJump);
  result = audiomgr->createSound("resources/movement.wav", FMOD_LOOP_
NORMAL | FMOD_2D | FMOD_HARDWARE, 0, &sfxMovement);
  result = audiomgr->playSound(FMOD_CHANNEL_FREE, sfxMovement, true,
&chMovement);
return true; }
```

You can download these sounds from the book's website or you can replace them with your own. Just be sure that you are using very short sounds for oil, water, and jump because they are intended to play quickly.

This function loads our three sound effects files into the audio system.

- The createSound function allocates memory for the sound and sets the FMOD properties for the sound.
- FMOD_DEFAULT sets up the following FMOD properties:
    - FMOD_LOOP_OFF: The sound plays once and does not loop
    - FMOD_2D: This is a 2D sound
    - FMOD_HARDWARE: This uses the hardware features of the device to handle audio
- The result variable catches return value. In production games, you would test this each time to make sure that the sound had successfully loaded (we leave those error checks off here to save space).
- Notice that we call playSound on the movement SFX. We are going to start this sound, assign it to the next free hardware channel (FMOD_CHANNEL_FREE), but tell FMOD to immediately pause it (thus the true parameter). When we want to play the sound, we will play it, and when we want it to stop, we will pause it.
- We will call playSound on the other SFX as needed. As they are not looping sounds, we do not have to manage their paused state.

Notice that we set sfxJump, sfxOilcan, and sfxWater to use the FMOD_DEFAULT settings. However, we will need sfxMovement to loop, so we had to set its setting flags individually.

There are several flags that you can use to set the properties of a sound, and you can use the OR operator (|) to combine flags:

- FMOD_HARDWARE: This uses the device hardware to handle the audio.
- FMOD_SOFTWARE: This uses FMOD's software emulation to handle the audio (slower, but could give access to features not supported by the device).
- FMOD_2D: This is a 2D sound. This is the format we will use for this game!
- FMOD_3D: This is a 3D sound. 3D sounds can be placed in 3D space and appear to have both distance (for example, the sound gets softer as it is further away) and position (left, right, in front of, behind).
- FMOD_LOOP_OFF: The sound plays once and does not loop.
- FMOD_LOOP_NORMAL: The sound plays and then starts over again, looping indefinitely.

There are many other flags that can be set. Take a look at the FMOD documentation for additional details.

Now that we have a function to load our sounds, we have to wire it into the initialization for the game. Modify the `GameLoop` function, adding the following highlighted line:

```
void GameLoop(const float p_deltatTime)
{
  if (m_gameState == GameState::GS_Splash)
  {
    InitFmod();
    LoadAudio();
    BuildFont();
    LoadTextures();
    m_gameState = GameState::GS_Loading;
  }
  Update(p_deltatTime);
  Render();
}
```

Playing sounds

Now, we need to trigger the sound effects at the appropriate time. Let's start with Robo's movement SFX. Basically, we want to play this sound any time Robo is actually moving.

We are going to modify the CM_STOP, CM_LEFT, and CM_RIGHT cases in the ProcessInput function. Update the code inserting the highlighted lines indicated as follows:

```
case Input::Command::CM_STOP:
player->SetVelocity(0.0f);
background->SetVelocity(0.0f);
chMovement->setPaused(true);
break;

case Input::Command::CM_LEFT:
if (player == robot_right)
{
  robot_right->IsActive(false);
  robot_right->IsVisible(false);
  robot_left->SetPosition(robot_right->GetPosition());
  robot_left->SetValue(robot_right->GetValue());
}
player = robot_left;
player->IsActive(true);
player->IsVisible(true);
```

```
player->SetVelocity(-50.0f);
background->SetVelocity(50.0f);
chMovement->setPaused(false);
break;

case Input::Command::CM_RIGHT:
if (player == robot_left)
{
  robot_left->IsActive(false);
  robot_left->IsVisible(false);
  robot_right->SetPosition(robot_left->GetPosition());
  robot_right->SetValue(robot_left->GetValue());
}
player = robot_right;
player->IsActive(true);
player->IsVisible(true);
player->SetVelocity(50.0f);
background->SetVelocity(-50.0f);
chMovement->setPaused(false);
break;
```

Remember, we already loaded sfxMovement and assigned it to a virtual channel (chMovement), then told it to start playing as a paused sound. Actually, in FMOD, you pause and play the channel, not the sound. So, all we have to do now is call chMovement->setPaused(true) when Robo is moving and chMovement->setPaused(false) when he is not moving.

Now, we need to handle the oil and water pickups. These can both be handled in the CheckCollisions function. Modify CheckCollisions by adding the following highlighted lines of code:

```
void CheckCollisions()
{
  if (player->IntersectsCircle(pickup))
  {
    FMOD::Channel* channel;
    audiomgr->playSound(FMOD_CHANNEL_FREE, sfxOilcan, false,
&channel);
    pickup->IsVisible(false);
    pickup->IsActive(false);
    player->SetValue(player->GetValue() + pickup->GetValue());
    pickupSpawnTimer = 0.0f;
    pickupsReceived++;
  }
```

```
if (player->IntersectsRect(enemy))
{
  FMOD::Channel* channel;
  audiomgr->playSound(FMOD_CHANNEL_FREE, sfxWater, false, &channel);
  enemy->IsVisible(false);
  enemy->IsActive(false);
  player->SetValue(player->GetValue() + enemy->GetValue());
  enemySpawnTimer = 0.0f;
}
}
```

Finally, we will add a sound effect for Robo when he jumps up or jumps down. These changes will be applied to the CM_UP and CM_DOWN cases in the ProcessInput function. Modify the existing code with the following highlighted lines:

```
case Input::Command::CM_UP:
{
  FMOD::Channel* channel;
  audiomgr->playSound(FMOD_CHANNEL_FREE, sfxJump, false, &channel);
  player->Jump(Sprite::SpriteState::UP);
}
break;

case Input::Command::CM_DOWN:
{
  FMOD::Channel* channel;
  audiomgr->playSound(FMOD_CHANNEL_FREE, sfxJump, false, &channel);
  player->Jump(Sprite::SpriteState::DOWN);
}
break;
```

These sound effects are one-shot sounds. When they are done playing, we don't need to worry about them any more until it is time to play them again. For this type of sound, we create a channel (FMOD::channel* channel), then call playSound using:

- FMOD_CHANNEL_FREE: This lets FMOD pick the next available hardware sound channel.

- Sound pointer: sfxWater for the water bottle, sfxOilcan for the oil, and sfxJump for the jump SFX.

- false: Don't pause the sound!

- &channel: This is the virtual channel handle. Notice that this is just a local variable. We don't need to store this anywhere for one-shot SFX.

That's it! If you play the game now, the four SFX should trigger according to our design.

UI feedback

So far, we created sound effects to respond to events and actions in the game. Sound effects are also used to provide feedback from the user interface. For example, when the player clicks a button, there should be some kind of audio that plays so that the player immediately knows that the click was registered.

Fortunately, we already trap each time the user has clicked a UI button, so it's easy to trigger a sound each time it happens. Let's start by adding a new sound pointer. In RoboRacer2D.cpp, add the following line to the variable declarations:

```
FMOD::Sound* sfxButton;
```

Then add the following code to LoadAudio:

```
result = audiomgr->createSound("resources/button.wav", FMOD_DEFAULT,
0, &sfxButton);
```

Finally, add the following highlighted lines of code to the CM_UI case in ProcessInput:

```
case Input::Command::CM_UI:
FMOD::Channel* channel;
if (pauseButton->IsClicked())
{
   audiomgr->playSound(FMOD_CHANNEL_FREE, sfxButton, false, &channel);
   pauseButton->IsClicked(false);
   pauseButton->IsVisible(false);
   pauseButton->IsActive(false);

   resumeButton->IsClicked(false);
   resumeButton->IsVisible(true);
   resumeButton->IsActive(true);
   m_gameState = GS_Paused;
}

if (resumeButton->IsClicked())
{
   audiomgr->playSound(FMOD_CHANNEL_FREE, sfxButton, false, &channel);
   resumeButton->IsClicked(false);
   resumeButton->IsVisible(false);
   resumeButton->IsActive(false);

   pauseButton->IsClicked(false);
   pauseButton->IsVisible(true);
   pauseButton->IsActive(true);
```

```
      m_gameState = GS_Running;
   }

   if (playButton->IsClicked())
   {
     audiomgr->playSound(FMOD_CHANNEL_FREE, sfxButton, false, &channel);
     playButton->IsClicked(false);
     exitButton->IsActive(false);
     playButton->IsActive(false);
     creditsButton->IsActive(false);
     m_gameState = GameState::GS_Running;
   }

   if (creditsButton->IsClicked())
   {
     audiomgr->playSound(FMOD_CHANNEL_FREE, sfxButton, false, &channel);
     creditsButton->IsClicked(false);
     exitButton->IsActive(false);
     playButton->IsActive(false);
     creditsButton->IsActive(false);
     m_gameState = GameState::GS_Credits;
   }

   if (exitButton->IsClicked())
   {
     audiomgr->playSound(FMOD_CHANNEL_FREE, sfxButton, false, &channel);
     playButton->IsClicked(false);
     exitButton->IsActive(false);
     playButton->IsActive(false);
     creditsButton->IsActive(false);
     PostQuitMessage(0);
   }

   if (menuButton->IsClicked())
   {
     audiomgr->playSound(FMOD_CHANNEL_FREE, sfxButton, false, &channel);
     menuButton->IsClicked(false);
     menuButton->IsActive(false);
     m_gameState = GameState::GS_Menu;
   }

   if (continueButton->IsClicked())
   {
```

```
audiomgr->playSound(FMOD_CHANNEL_FREE, sfxButton, false, &channel);
continueButton->IsClicked(false);
continueButton->IsActive(false);
m_gameState = GameState::GS_Running;
}

if (replayButton->IsClicked())
{
    audiomgr->playSound(FMOD_CHANNEL_FREE, sfxButton, false, &channel);
    replayButton->IsClicked(false);
    replayButton->IsActive(false);
    exitButton->IsActive(false);
    RestartGame();
    m_gameState = GameState::GS_Running;
}
break;
```

At this point, when you run the game you will now hear an SFX each time a button is clicked.

The sound of music

We now turn to the audio soundtrack for our game. Just like a movie soundtrack, the music that is played during a game sets the tone for the game. Many games have huge, orchestrated productions, while others have synthesized or 8-bit music.

As we have already discussed, music files are handled in a different manner from sound effects. This is because sound effects are usually very short sounds that can be best stored as wav files. Music files tend to be much longer, and are stored as MP3 files because the data can be compressed, taking less storage and less memory.

We are going to add a single music track to our game. To keep things simple, we will tell the track to loop so that it runs continuously throughout the game.

We will start by adding a sound pointer. Open RoboRacer2D.cpp and add the following line of code to the variable declarations:

```
FMOD::Sound* musBackground;
```

Next, go to the LoadAudio function and add the following line:

```
result = audiomgr->createSound("resources/jollybot.mp3", FMOD_LOOP_
NORMAL | FMOD_2D | FMOD_HARDWARE, 0, &musBackground);
FMOD::Channel* channel;
result = audiomgr->playSound(FMOD_CHANNEL_FREE, musBackground, false,
&channel);
```

Notice that we use `createStream` instead of `createSound` to load our music file. As music is so much longer than sound effects, music is streamed from storage rather than loaded directly into memory.

We want the sound track to start when the game starts, so we start playing the music in right after it is loaded using `playSound`.

That's all there is to it! Our game is now enhanced by a vibrant soundscape.

Cleaning up the house

We have a pretty complete game. Sure, it's not going to set any records or make anyone rich, but if this is your first game, then congratulations!

We have been remiss in one area: good programming dictates that any time we create an object, we delete it when we are done using it. Up to now, you may be wondering if we were ever going to do this! Well, now is the time.

We made a placeholder for all of these operations in the `EndGame` function. Now, we will add the necessary code to properly release our resources.

Release sprites

Let's start by clearing out our sprites. It is important to remember that when we remove any resource, we need to make sure that it is also releasing its own resources. This is the purpose of the class destructor. Let's use the `Sprite` class as an example. Open `Sprite.cpp` and you should see a destructor defined using the following code:

```cpp
Sprite::~Sprite()
{
  for (int i = 0; i < m_textureIndex; i++)
  {
    glDeleteTextures(1, &m_textures[i]);
  }
  delete[] m_textures;
  m_textures = NULL;
}
```

We first want to release all of the textures in the `m_textures` array. Then we use `delete[]` to release the `m_textures` array. It is also good programming practice to set the variable to `NULL` once an object has been deleted.

The `Sprite` destructor will be called when we call `delete` on a sprite object. So, the first thing we need to add to `EndGame` is a `delete` operation for each sprite that was created for our game. Add the following lines of code to the `EndGame` function:

```
delete robot_left;
delete robot_right;
delete robot_right_strip;
delete robot_left_strip;
delete background;
delete pickup;
delete enemy;
delete pauseButton;
delete resumeButton;
delete splashScreen;
delete menuScreen;
delete creditsScreen;
delete playButton;
delete creditsButton;
delete exitButton;
delete menuButton;
delete nextLevelScreen;
delete continueButton;
delete gameOverScreen;
delete replayButton;
```

> If you look closely, you will notice that we did not delete the player object. This is because player was only used as a pointer to sprites that had already been created. Put another way, we never used player to create a new Sprite. A good rule of thumb is that there should be exactly one delete for every new.

Release input

Our next system to shut down is the input system. First, let's complete the `Input` destructor. Add the highlighted code to the destructor in the `Input` class:

```
Input::~Input()
{
  delete[] m_uiElements;
  m_uiElements = NULL;
}
```

We have to delete the `uiElements` array, which was an array of pointers to the sprites that were part of the input system. Note that we did not delete the actual sprites here because they were not created by the input system.

Now, add the following line of code to `EndGame`:

```
delete inputManager;
```

Releasing fonts

Add this line to release the display lists we used to store our fonts:

```
KillFont();
```

Releasing audio

Our final cleanup is the audio system. Add the following lines of code to `EndGame`:

```
sfxWater->release();
sfxOilcan->release();
sfxJump->release();
sfxMovement->release();
sfxButton->release();
musBackground->release();
audiomgr->release();
```

Congratulations! Your house is all cleaned up.

Summary

We covered a lot of material in this chapter, and in the process, we completed our 2D game. You learned a little about how audio is represented in the computer. Then we installed the FMOD API and learned how to integrate it into our project. Finally, we used FMOD to set up and play sound effects and music in our game.

This chapter completes our discussion of game programming in 2D. As you should now be aware, there is a lot more to completing a game than using the OpenGL library. Remember, OpenGL is a rendering library. We had to write our own class to handle input and we used a third-party class to handle audio.

In the next chapter, we begin our foray into the world of 3D programming!

8
Expanding Your Horizons

Until this point, we have limited our coding to two dimensions. Now, it is time to expand to the third dimension. In many ways, this will not be as intimidating as it sounds. After all, instead of specifying a position using two coordinates (x and y), we will now simply add a third coordinate (z). However, there are some areas where the third dimension will add considerable complexity, and it is my job to help you master that complexity. In this chapter, we will start with the basic understanding of placing an object in a 3D world, including:

- **3D coordinate systems**: You already mastered the Cartesian coordinate system (x and y coordinates). We will discuss how to expand this into a third axis.

- **3D cameras**: The camera in a 2D game is pretty much fixed while the objects move past it. In 3D game programming, we often move the camera forward, backward, side-to-side, or even in circles around the objects in the game.

- **3D views**: How exactly does a 2D computer screen represent 3D games? You will learn the basics of how 3D gets transformed by the graphics pipeline.

- **3D transformations**: Moving around in 3D space is quite a bit more complicated than moving in 2D space. In fact, we use a whole new form of mathematics to do so. You will learn the basics of matrices, and how they can be used to move, rotate, and change the size of 3D objects.

Into the third dimension!

You already live in a world with three dimensions. You can walk forward and backward, side to side, and jump up or duck. The reality of three dimensions becomes even more apparent if you are flying or even swimming.

Most 2D games operate by allowing the player to move left and right, or jump up or down. This is what we did when we created RoboRacer2D. In this type of 2D game, the missing dimension is depth. Our Robot could not move further away from us or closer to us. Considering that we were drawing him on a flat screen, it shouldn't be too surprising that he was limited to two dimensions.

Simulating 3D

Of course, artists found a way around this limitation hundreds of years ago by observing that as an object gets farther away from us, it gets smaller, and as it gets closer to us it gets larger. So, a simple way to represent 3D in a 2D world is to simply draw the more distant objects as smaller objects. 2D games learned this trick early on and used it to simulate 3D:

In the preceding image, the larger tank appears to be closer than the smaller tank.

Another important aspect of depth is **perspective**. Artists learned that parallel lines appear to converge toward the center as they move farther away. The point where they seem to converge is known as the **vanishing point**:

In the preceding image, the walls and floor panels are all parallel, but they appear to converge inward toward the center of the image.

A third aspect of 3D motion is that objects that are farther away appear to travel more slowly than objects that are closer. Thus, when you are driving, the telephone poles pass you by much faster than the distant mountains. Some 2D games take advantage of this phenomenon, called **parallax**, by creating a background layer in the game that moves much slower than the foreground. In fact, this is exactly what we did in RoboRacer2D because the Robot in the foreground moves more quickly than the objects in the background.

2D games have used all of these features — size, perspective, and parallax — to simulate 3D long before we ever had hardware and graphics cards to do them for us. One of the first games to do this in a convincing way was Pole Position. The game that really blew everyone away was Doom, which was probably the first game that allowed the player to freely move in a 3D world.

Real 3D

Modern 3D games take the idea of simulating 3D to the next level. In the simulating 3D section that we just discussed, it is the programmers' task to scale the image so that it appears smaller as it gets further away, take care of perspective, and handle parallax. This is now handled by the 3D graphics card.

The preceding image shows a 3D **model** of a tank. These models are created using special software, such as Maya or 3ds Max. This model is fundamentally different than the 2D tank image we showed you previously because it represents the tank in three dimensions.

We will discuss 3D modeling in more detail in a future chapter. For now, the important concept is that the data for a 3D tank is sent to the graphics card, and the graphics card takes care of size, perspective, and parallax as the tank is positioned in a 3D space. This takes a lot of the load off the programmer!

3D Coordinate Systems

Now that you have a fundamental idea of how the illusion of 3D is created on a 2D screen, let's learn how adding another dimension affects our coordinate system.

In *Chapter 2, Your Point of View* I introduced you to the 2D coordinate system that is used by many game systems.

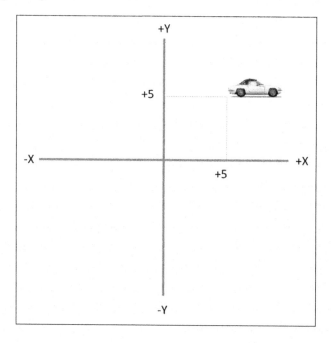

The preceding diagram shows a car placed at coordinate position (**5, 5**). Let's add the third dimension and see how it compares:

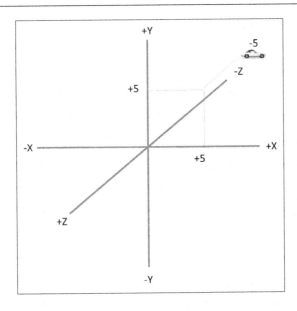

Notice that we added a third axis and labeled it as the Z-axis. Positive values on the Z-axis are closer to us, while negative values on the Z-axis are farther away. The car is now placed at coordinate (**5, 5, -5**) in 3D space. As the car is farther away, it also appears smaller than it did in the previous 2D image (you can think of 2D space as a space where all of the *z* coordinates are 0).

The preceding diagram shows the Z-axis at an angle, but it is important to understand that the Z-axis is actually perpendicular to the plane of the computer screen.

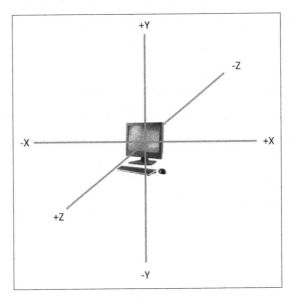

Think of the Z-axis as a line the pierces through the center of the monitor from the front and travels out the back!

There are actually many ways to represent the axes in a 3D world. One distinction between OpenGL and DirectX is the Z-axis. In OpenGL, positive *z* values are closer to the player. In DirectX, Microsoft's 3D rendering engine, negative *z* values are closer to the player. It's just a good thing to know because you will very likely work with both systems. OpenGL is known as a **right-hand** coordinate system, while DirectX is a **left-hand** coordinate system. It's a little hard to explain how they got these names, so perform an Internet search if you would like to learn more!

The camera

In *Chapter 2, Your Point of View* we compared creating games to making a video recording. Your video camera captures a part of the view in front of you. If objects move into or out of that field of view, they are no longer in the video recording.

3D games use a camera as well. OpenGL allows you to move the game camera on six axes: up, down, left, right, in, and out. As you move the game camera, the objects that are in its view change.

Let's say that you center the camera on the car in the scene and pan to the left or right. The car will move in and out of the field of view. Of course the same occurs if you pan the camera up or down. Move back (or zoom out) and the car appears smaller. Move forward (or zoom in) and the car appears larger. Tilt the camera and the car will appear to be going uphill, downhill, or even appear upside down!

Remember those home movies?

Remember those home movies where the whole scene would jump around as the camera moved? Obviously, the position and movement of the camera has a lot to do with the appearance of the car. The same is true in the game world.

OpenGL uses the concept of a camera to determine exactly what shows up on the screen, and how it shows up. You have the ability to move the camera up or down, and left or right. You can rotate or tilt the camera. You have complete control!

Steady as she goes!

Although you have complete control over moving the camera, some games simply place the camera at a particular spot and then leave it fixed. This is similar to taking your home video camera and attaching it to a tripod.

Many 2D games use a fixed camera, and this is exactly what we did in RoboRacer2D. All of the motion in the game came from changing the position of the objects in the game, not from changing the position of the camera.

In 3D games, it is very common to move both the camera and objects in the game. Imagine that we have a 3D scene with a moving car. If the camera remained fixed, the car would eventually move out of the scene. In order to keep the car in the scene, we need to move the camera so that it follows the car. Both the car and the camera need to move.

The viewport

In game terminology, the area that can be seen by the camera at any time is called the **viewport**. The viewport defines the area of the game world that the camera can see:

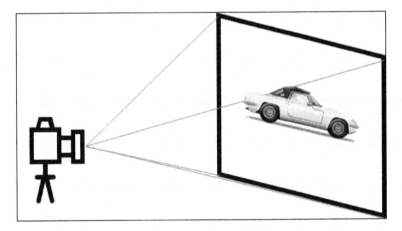

The preceding illustration shows a viewport with a certain width and height. If the car moves outside of these boundaries, it will no longer be visible. In a 3D world, we must also define the depth of the image that we want to capture.

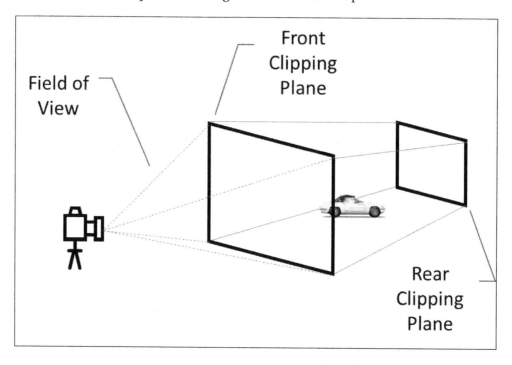

The preceding image shows how the 3D viewport is defined:

- The front clipping plane defines how close things can get to the camera. Anything closer than the front clipping plane will not be rendered on the screen.

- The rear clipping plane defines how far things can get from the camera. Anything beyond the rear clipping plane will not be rendered on the screen.

- The area between the front and back clipping planes is called the frustum. Objects inside the frustum will be rendered to the screen.

- The field of view determines how tall and wide the angle of view is from the camera. A wide field of view will render more area, while a narrow field of view will render less area. A wider angle will also introduce more distortion to the image.

Entering the matrix

Now for the topic that strikes fear into the heart of all new game programmers: **matrices**. Matrices are a mathematical device (part of linear algebra) that makes it easier to work with large sets of related numbers.

In its simplest form, a **matrix** is a table of numbers. Let's say that I wanted to represent a coordinate in space. I could write its value down as follows:

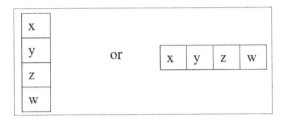

Vectors

A single row or single column of a matrix is called a **vector**. Vectors are important because they can be used to both position things and move things.

The typical matrix used in games contains four values: x, y, z, and w. These x, y, and z components typically refer to a position in the 3D coordinate system, while the w is a switch:

- The value 1 means that this vector is a position
- The value 0 means that this vector is a velocity

Here's an example:

- The vector, (1, 5, 10, 1), represents a point at x = 1, y = 5, and z = 10 in a 3D coordinate system.

- The vector, (1, 5, 10, 0), is a point that moves 1 unit in the *x* direction, 5 units in the *y* direction, and 10 units in the *z* direction

 Notice that vectors can be represented as a series of numbers inside of a parenthesis. This is much easier than having to draw a table every time you need to write down a vector!

Combining vectors

The real power of vectors comes when they are combined. The most common way to combine vectors is to multiply them. Look at the following example:

1	0	0	1
0	1	0	5
0	0	1	6
0	0	0	1

*

2
1
0
1

=

3
6
6
1

The matrix on the left is known as a **translation matrix** because when you multiply it by a positional vector, the result will be a new position (moving things in a 3D space is known as **translation**). In this case, the point at (**2, 1, 0**) has been translated to a new position at (**3, 6, 6**).

 Remember: the last **1** in (**1, 5, 6, 1**) and (**2, 1, 0, 1**) is the *w* value that simply tells us we are working with a position. Notice that the *w* value remained **1** in the final result as well!

If you are paying attention, you must be wondering how we got the third matrix! It turns out that multiplying two matrices is actually more complex that it seems. In order to multiply the two matrices shown earlier, the following operations had to occur:

- $(1 * 2) + (0 * 1) + (0 * 0) + (1 * 1) = 3$
- $(0 * 2) + (1 * 1) + (0 * 0) + (5 * 1) = 6$
- $(0 * 2) + (0 * 1) + (1 * 0) + (6 * 1) = 6$
- $(0 * 2) + (0 * 1) + (0 * 0) + (1 * 1) = 1$

Each cell in each row of the first matrix is multiplied by each cell in each column of the second matrix.

This might seem like a lot of trouble just to move a point, but when it comes to quickly moving 3D objects around in a game, matrix math is much faster than other techniques.

Don't worry! This is about all we are going to say about matrices and vectors. You should know that OpenGL uses matrices to calculate **transformations**, including:

- Moving
- Scaling
- Rotating

If you ever work with both OpenGL and DirectX, you will need to be aware that there is a difference in the way they handle matrices. OpenGL uses a **row major** order, while DirectX users a **column major order**. In a row major matrix, all of the cells in the first column are adjacent, followed by all of the cells in the next row, and so forth. In a column major matrix, all of the cells in the first column are adjacent, followed by all of the cells in the next column, and so forth. This makes a huge difference in how you manipulate and calculate the matrices!

Identity matrix

I will mention one more special matrix:

1	0	0	0
0	1	0	0
0	0	1	0
0	0	0	1

The preceding matrix is known as an identity matrix. If you multiply any matrix by an identity matrix, the result is the original matrix (just like multiplying any number by 1 results in the original number). Whenever we want to initialize a matrix, we set it to an identity matrix.

There are special matrices in OpenGL, and you will be introduced to some of them in the next code.

Coding in 3D

It's time for us to put our theory into practice and create our first 3D scene. To keep things simple, we will go through the steps of placing a cube in 3D space. This is also going to be the start of our 3D game, so let's start by creating a brand new project in Visual Studio.

Creating the project

When we created a project for our 2D game, we started with a standard Windows project and then removed (or ignored) the items that we didn't need to use. In fact, the standard Windows project has a lot of overhead that we don't need. This is because the Windows project template assumes that Windows is going to be in charge of rendering and processing. This came in useful for our 2D project, but just adds a lot of extra code that we don't need.

For this project, we will start with a blank Windows project and then add the necessary code to initialize and create an OpenGL window. Then, we will work our way up from there:

1. Begin by opening Visual Studio.

2. Once Visual Studio is open, create a new project by clicking on **File**, **New**, **Project**. From the **Visual C++** branch choose **Empty Project**.

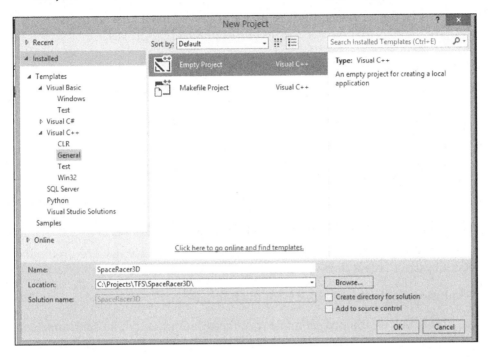

3. **Name** the project `SpaceRacer3D`, place it in the location of your choice, and click **OK**. The result is a project that has no code. Let's solve that problem by creating our main game file.

4. Right-click on the **Source Files** folder in the **Solution Explorer** panel.

5. Choose **Add**, **New Item…**.

6. Click on **C++ File (.cpp)**.

7. Type `SpaceRacer3D.cpp` for **Name** and click **Add**.

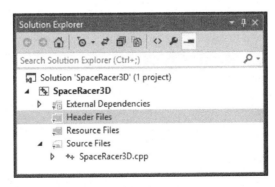

Retrieving OpenGL files

The standard OpenGL library is already installed when you install Visual Studio. However, the OpenGL utilities library may not be. To make things simple, we will simply copy the files that we need from our RoboRacer2D project.

Open the **RoboRacer2D** project folder and select the following files:

- `glut.h`
- `glut32.dll`
- `glut32.lib`

Now copy these files into the **SpaceRacer3D** source folder. This will be the same folder that your `SpaceRacer3D.cpp` file is located.

Linking projects to OpenGL libraries

Now that we have a project and the relevant OpenGL files, we need to link to the OpenGL libraries. This is done by accessing the project properties.

In the **Solution Explorer** panel perform the following actions:

1. Right-click on the project name (not the solution), and choose **Properties**.
2. Open the **Linker** branch under **Configuration Properties**, and select **Input**.
3. Click on **Additional Dependencies** and then click the drop-down arrow that appears.
4. Click on **<Edit...>**.

5. Add `OpenGL32.lib` and `GLu32.lib` in the **Additional Dependencies** dialog window.

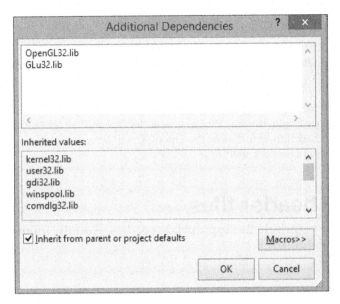

Setting up the OpenGL window

We are now going to add the code required to create an OpenGL window. We did this once for RoboRacer2D, but now, we are creating a 3D game and there will be some differences. Here's a look at what we need to do:

1. Include header files.
2. Define global variables.
3. Create the OpenGL window.
4. Initialize the OpenGL window.
5. Size the OpenGL window.
6. Remove the OpenGL window.
7. Create the Windows event handler.
8. Create the `WinMain` function.

Notice that we still have to create some code to satisfy Windows. We need an event handler to process Windows events, and we still need a main function to serve as the program entry point and run the main program loop. Everything else in this list is used to set up the OpenGL environment.

> I listed the functions tasks that we need in an order that makes logical sense. When we actually implement the code, we will create things in a slightly different order. This is because some functions require another function to already be defined. For example, the function to create the OpenGL window calls the function to initialize the OpenGL window, so the initialize function is coded first.

Including header files

The first step is to in include the appropriate headers. Add the following headers at the top of SpaceRacer3D.cpp:

```
#include <windows.h>
#include <gl\GL.h>
#include <gl\GLU.h>
#include "glut.h"
```

These are the same files that we used in the 2D project, but here is a quick description of each one so that you don't have to flip back:

- We are still running in Windows, so we must include windows.h

- The core header for OpenGL is GL.h

- There are some great utilities to make our lives easier in GLU.h

- There are also useful utilities in glut.h

Defining global variables

We need some global variables to hold onto references to Windows and OpenGL objects. Add the following lines of code just under the header lines:

```
HINSTANCE hInstance = NULL;
HDC hDC = NULL;
HGLRC hRC = NULL;
HWND hWnd = NULL;
bool fullscreen = false;
```

Here is a quick list of what these variables are for:

- hInstance: This holds a reference to this instance of the application
- hDC: This holds a reference to the GDI device context which is used for drawing in native Windows
- hRC: This holds a reference to the OpenGL rendering context, used for rendering 3D
- hWnd: This holds a reference to the actual window the application is running in

We have also included a global fullscreen variable. If you set this to true, the game will run in fullscreen mode. If you set this to false, the game will run in windowed mode.

Creating a function to create the OpenGL window

We will also include a forward reference to the Windows event handler. Add the following line of code:

```
LRESULT CALLBACK WndProc(HWND, UINT, WPARAM, LPARAM);
```

A forward reference allows us to define a function whose actual implementation will appear later in the code. The code for WndProc will be added later.

Sizing the OpenGL window

Next, we will create the function to size the OpenGL window. This function is called when the program starts as well as any time the window that the application is running in is resized. Add the following code:

```
void ReSizeGLScene(const GLsizei p_width, const GLsizei p_height)
{
  GLsizei h = p_height;
  GLsizei w = p_width;
  if (h == 0)
  {
    h = 1;
  }
  glViewport(0, 0, w, h);

  glMatrixMode(GL_PROJECTION);
  glLoadIdentity();
```

```
gluPerspective(45.0f, (GLfloat)w / (GLfloat)h, 0.1f, 100.0f);

glMatrixMode(GL_MODELVIEW);
glLoadIdentity();
}
```

This code sets the size of the OpenGL window and prepares the window for rendering in 3D:

- First, we take the width and height (ensuring that the height is never equal to 0), and use them to define the size viewport using the `glViewport` function. The first two parameters are the *x* and *y* value of the lower left-hand corner of the viewport, followed by the width and the height. These four parameters define the size and location of the viewport.

- Next, we have to define the frustum. After telling OpenGL to use the projection matrix, we use the `gluPerspective` function, which takes four parameters: the field of view (in degrees, not radians), the aspect ratio, the distance of the front clipping plane, and the distance of the rear clipping plane. The field of view is the angle from the center of the camera. The aspect ratio is the width divided by the height. These four parameters define the size of the frustum.

 After you complete this chapter, you may try playing with the values of this function to see how it changes the rendering.

- Finally, we tell OpenGL to use the model view from this point forward.

If you compare this function to the `GLSize` function that we used in RoboRacer2D, you will note one significant difference: we do not make a call to `glOrtho`. Remember, RoboRacer2D was a 2D game. 2D games use an **orthographic projection** that removes perspective when the scene is rendered. You don't need perspective in a 2D game. Most 3D games use a **perspective projection**, which is defined by the `gluPerspective` call.

OpenGL Matrices

Just before the `gluPerspective` call, you will notice two functions: `glMatrixMode`, and `glLoadIdentity`. Remember from our discussion of matrices that a matrix is used to hold a set of values. OpenGL has many standard matrices, and one of them is the projection matrix, which is used to define the view frustum.

If we want to set the values of a matrix, we must first tell OpenGL that we want to work with this matrix. Next, we typically initialize the matrix, and finally, we make a call that sets the values of the matrix.

Looking at the code to set the view frustum, this is exactly what we do:

- `glMatrixMode(GL_PROJECTION)`: This tells OpenGL that we want to work with the projection matrix. Any matrix operations after this call will be applied to the projection matrix.
- `glLoadIdentity()`: This sets the projection matrix to an identity matrix, thus, clearing any previous values.
- `gluPerspective(45.0f, (GLfloat)w / (GLfloat)h, 0.1f, 100.0f)`: This sets the values of the projection matrix.

You should get used to this pattern because it is used often in OpenGL: set a matrix to work with, initialize the matrix, then set the values of the matrix. For example, at the end of this function we tell OpenGL to use the model view matrix and initialize it. Any operations after this will affect the model view.

Initializing the OpenGL window

Add the following code to initialize OpenGL:

```
const bool InitGL()
{
  glShadeModel(GL_SMOOTH);
  glClearColor(0.0f, 0.0f, 0.0f, 0.0f);
  glClearDepth(1.0f);
  glEnable(GL_DEPTH_TEST);
  glDepthFunc(GL_LEQUAL);
  glHint(GL_PERSPECTIVE_CORRECTION_HINT, GL_NICEST);
  return true;
}
```

This function initializes OpenGL by defining important settings that determine how a scene will be rendered:

- `glShadeModel`: This tells OpenGL that we want it to smooth the edges of the vertices. This greatly improves the look of our images.

- `glClearColor`: This sets the color that is used each time `glClear` is called to clear out the rendering buffer. It is also the default color that will show in the scene.

- `glClearDepth(1.0f)`: This tells OpenGL that we want the entire depth buffer cleared each time `glClear` is called. Remember, we are working in 3D now, and the depth buffer is roughly synonymous with the Z-axis.

- `glEnable(GL_DEPTH_TEST)`: This turns on depth checking. Depth checking is used to determine if a particular piece of data will be rendered.

- `glDepthFunc(GL_LEQUAL)`: This tells OpenGL how you want to perform the depth test. LEQUAL tells OpenGL to write the data only if the z value of the incoming data is less than or equal to the z value of the existing data.

- `glHint((GL_PERSPECTIVE_CORRECTION_HINT, GL_NICEST))`: This is an interesting function. `glHint` means that this function is going to suggest that OpenGL use the settings passed as parameters. However, as there are many different types of devices, there is no guarantee that these settings will actually be enforced. The `GL_PERSPECTIVE` hint tells OpenGL to use the highest quality when rendering perspective, while `GL_NICEST` means focus on rendering quality rather than speed.

Creating a function to remove the OpenGL window

Eventually, we will want to shut things down. Good programming dictates that we release the resources that were being used by the OpenGL window. Add the following function to our code:

```
GLvoid KillGLWindow(GLvoid)
{
  if (fullscreen)
  {
    ChangeDisplaySettings(NULL, 0);
    ShowCursor(TRUE);
  }
  if (hRC)
  {
    wglMakeCurrent(NULL, NULL);
```

```
        wglDeleteContext(hRC);
        hRC = NULL;
    }
    if (hDC)
    {
        ReleaseDC(hWnd, hDC)
        hDC = NULL;
    }

    if (hWnd)
    {
        DestroyWindow(hWnd);
        hWnd = NULL;
    }
    UnregisterClass("OpenGL", hInstance)
    hInstance = NULL;
}
```

First, we tell Windows to exit fullscreen mode (if we were running fullscreen) and turn the cursor back on. Then, we check each object that had a resource attached, release that object, then set it to null. The objects that need to be released are:

- hRC: This is the OpenGL rendering context
- hDC: This is the Windows device context
- hWnd: This is the handle to the Window
- hInstance: This is the handle to the application

> You may notice the two functions that start with wgl (wglMakeCurrent and wglDeleteContext). This stands for Windows GL and these are special OpenGL functions that only work in Windows.

Creating the OpenGL window

Now that we have the other OpenGL support functions defined, we can add the function to actually create the OpenGL window. Add the following code:

```
const bool CreateGLWindow(const char* p_title, const int p_width,
const int p_height, const int p_bits, const bool p_fullscreenflag)
{
    GLuint  PixelFormat;
    WNDCLASS wc;
    DWORD  dwExStyle;
```

```
    DWORD   dwStyle;
    RECT   WindowRect;
    WindowRect.left = (long)0;
    WindowRect.right = (long)p_width;
    WindowRect.top = (long)0;
    WindowRect.bottom = (long)p_height;

    fullscreen = p_fullscreenflag;
    GLfloat screen_height = (GLfloat)p_height;
    GLfloat screen_width = (GLfloat)p_width;

    hInstance = GetModuleHandle(NULL);
    wc.style = CS_HREDRAW | CS_VREDRAW | CS_OWNDC;
    wc.lpfnWndProc = (WNDPROC)WndProc;
    wc.cbClsExtra = 0;
    wc.cbWndExtra = 0;
    wc.hInstance = hInstance;
    wc.hIcon = LoadIcon(NULL, IDI_WINLOGO);
    wc.hCursor = LoadCursor(NULL, IDC_ARROW);
    wc.hbrBackground = NULL;
    wc.lpszMenuName = NULL;
    wc.lpszClassName = "OpenGL";

    RegisterClass(&wc);

    if (fullscreen)
    {
      DEVMODE dmScreenSettings;
      memset(&dmScreenSettings, 0, sizeof(dmScreenSettings));
      dmScreenSettings.dmSize = sizeof(dmScreenSettings);
      dmScreenSettings.dmPelsWidth = p_width;
      dmScreenSettings.dmPelsHeight = p_height;
      dmScreenSettings.dmBitsPerPel = p_bits;
      dmScreenSettings.dmFields = DM_BITSPERPEL | DM_PELSWIDTH | DM_
PELSHEIGHT;

      ChangeDisplaySettings(&dmScreenSettings, CDS_FULLSCREEN);
    }

    if (fullscreen)
    {
      dwExStyle = WS_EX_APPWINDOW;
      dwStyle = WS_POPUP;
      ShowCursor(false);
```

```
  }
  else
  {
    dwExStyle = WS_EX_APPWINDOW | WS_EX_WINDOWEDGE;
    dwStyle = WS_OVERLAPPEDWINDOW;
  }

  AdjustWindowRectEx(&WindowRect, dwStyle, FALSE, dwExStyle);

  hWnd = CreateWindowEx(dwExStyle,"OpenGL", p_title,
  dwStyle | WS_CLIPSIBLINGS | WS_CLIPCHILDREN,
  0, 0, WindowRect.right - WindowRect.left, WindowRect.bottom -
WindowRect.top,
  NULL, NULL, hInstance, NULL);

  static PIXELFORMATDESCRIPTOR pfd =
  {
    sizeof(PIXELFORMATDESCRIPTOR),
    1,
    PFD_DRAW_TO_WINDOW | PFD_SUPPORT_OPENGL | PFD_DOUBLEBUFFER,
    PFD_TYPE_RGBA, p_bits,
    0, 0, 0, 0, 0, 0,
    0, 0, 0, 0, 0, 0, 0,
    16, 0, 0,
    PFD_MAIN_PLANE,
    0, 0, 0, 0
  };

  hDC = GetDC(hWnd);
  PixelFormat = ChoosePixelFormat(hDC, &pfd);
  SetPixelFormat(hDC, PixelFormat, &pfd);
  hRC = wglCreateContext(hDC);
  wglMakeCurrent(hDC, hRC);
  ShowWindow(hWnd, SW_SHOW);
  SetForegroundWindow(hWnd);
  SetFocus(hWnd);
  ReSizeGLScene(p_width, p_height);
  InitGL();
  return true;
}
```

The purpose of `CreateGLWindow` is to create a window with settings that allow it to work with OpenGL. The main tasks accomplished by this function are as follows:

- Set the window properties
- Register the application with Windows—`RegisterClass`
- Set up full screen mode if required—`ChangeDisplaySettings`
- Create the Window—`CreateWindowEx`
- Get a Windows device context—`GetDC`
- Set the OpenGL pixel format—`SetPixelFormat`
- Create an OpenGL rendering context—`wglCreateContext`
- Bind the Windows device context and OpenGL rendering context together—`wglMakeCurrent`
- Show the window—`ShowWindow`, `SetForegroundWindow(hWnd)`, and `SetFocus(hWnd)`
- Initialize the OpenGL Window—`ReSizeGLScene`, `InitGL`; create the `WinMain` function

The `WinMain` function is the entry point for the application. Add the following code:

```
int APIENTRY WinMain(_In_ HINSTANCE hInstance,
_In_opt_ HINSTANCE hPrevInstance,
_In_ LPTSTR    lpCmdLine,
_In_ int       nCmdShow)
{
  MSG msg;
  bool done = false;
  if (!CreateGLWindow("SpaceRacer3D", 800, 600, 16, false))
  {
    return false;
  }
  StartGame();
  int previousTime = glutGet(GLUT_ELAPSED_TIME);
  while (!done)
  {
    if (PeekMessage(&msg, NULL, 0, 0, PM_REMOVE))
    {
      if (msg.message == WM_QUIT)
      {
        done = true;
      }
      else
```

```
    {
      TranslateMessage(&msg);
      DispatchMessage(&msg);
    }
  }
  else
  {
    int currentTime = glutGet(GLUT_ELAPSED_TIME);
    float deltaTime = (float)(currentTime - previousTime) / 1000;
    previousTime = currentTime;
    GameLoop(deltaTime);
  }
}
EndGame();
return (int)msg.wParam;
}
```

It calls all of the other functions to initialize Windows, and OpenGL then starts the main message loop, which we hijack and adapt to be our game loop. As we explained all of this code in *Chapter 1, Building the Foundation* we won't do it again here.

Creating the Windows event handler

Finally, we have to have an event handler to receive events from Windows and process them. We created the forward declaration at the top of the code, and now we will actually implement the handler. Add the following code:

```
LRESULT CALLBACK WndProc(HWND hWnd, UINT message, WPARAM wParam,
LPARAM lParam)
{
  switch (message)
  {
    case WM_DESTROY:
    PostQuitMessage(0);
    break;
    case WM_SIZE:
    ReSizeGLScene(LOWORD(lParam), HIWORD(lParam));
    return 0;
    default:
    return DefWindowProc(hWnd, message, wParam, lParam);
  }
  return false;
}
```

This function will be called any time Windows sends an event to our program. We handle two events: WM_DESTROY and WM_SIZE:

- WM_DESTROY is triggered when the window is closed. When this happens we use PostQuitMessage to tell our main game loop that it is time to stop.

- WM_SIZE is triggered when the window is resized. When this happens, we call ReSizeGLScene.

The Game loop

We still need to add some stub functions for our game functions: StartGame, Update, Render, EndGame, and GameLoop. Add the following code before the WinMain function:

```
void StartGame()
{

}

void Update(const float p_deltaTime)
{
}

void Render()
{
  glClear(GL_COLOR_BUFFER_BIT | GL_DEPTH_BUFFER_BIT);
  glMatrixMode(GL_MODELVIEW);
  glLoadIdentity();
  DrawCube();
  SwapBuffers(hDC);
}

void EndGame()
{
}

void GameLoop(const float p_deltatTime)
{
  Update(p_deltatTime);
  Render();
}
```

These functions serve the same purpose that they did in RoboRacer2D. GameLoop is called from the Windows main loop, and in turn calls Update and Render. StartGame is called before the Windows main loop, and EndGame is called when the game ends.

The finale

If you run the game right now, you will see a nice black window. This is because we haven't told the program to draw anything yet! It seemed unfair to do all this work and get a black screen, so if you want to do a little extra work, add the following code just before the `StartGame` function:

```
void DrawCube()
{
  glClear(GL_COLOR_BUFFER_BIT | GL_DEPTH_BUFFER_BIT);
  glTranslatef(0.0f, 0.0f, -7.0f);
  glRotatef(fRotate, 1.0f, 1.0f, 1.0f);
  glBegin(GL_QUADS);
  glColor3f(0.0f, 1.0f, 0.0f);
  glVertex3f(1.0f, 1.0f, -1.0f); glVertex3f(-1.0f, 1.0f, -1.0f);
  glVertex3f(-1.0f, 1.0f, 1.0f); glVertex3f(1.0f, 1.0f, 1.0f);
  glColor3f(1.0f, 0.5f, 0.0f);
  glVertex3f(1.0f, -1.0f, 1.0f); glVertex3f(-1.0f, -1.0f, 1.0f);
  glVertex3f(-1.0f, -1.0f, -1.0f); glVertex3f(1.0f, -1.0f, -1.0f);
  glColor3f(1.0f, 0.0f, 0.0f);
  glVertex3f(1.0f, 1.0f, 1.0f); glVertex3f(-1.0f, 1.0f, 1.0f);
  glVertex3f(-1.0f, -1.0f, 1.0f); glVertex3f(1.0f, -1.0f, 1.0f);
  glColor3f(1.0f, 1.0f, 0.0f);
  glVertex3f(1.0f, -1.0f, -1.0f); glVertex3f(-1.0f, -1.0f, -1.0f);
  glVertex3f(-1.0f, 1.0f, -1.0f); glVertex3f(1.0f, 1.0f, -1.0f);
  glColor3f(0.0f, 0.0f, 1.0f);
  glVertex3f(-1.0f, 1.0f, 1.0f); glVertex3f(-1.0f, 1.0f, -1.0f);
  glVertex3f(-1.0f, -1.0f, -1.0f); glVertex3f(-1.0f, -1.0f, 1.0f);
  glColor3f(1.0f, 0.0f, 1.0f);
  glVertex3f(1.0f, 1.0f, -1.0f); glVertex3f(1.0f, 1.0f, 1.0f);
  glVertex3f(1.0f, -1.0f, 1.0f); glVertex3f(1.0f, -1.0f, -1.0f);
  glEnd();
  fRotate -= 0.05f;

}
```

Also, you need to make sure to declare the following global variable:

```
float frotate = 1.0f;
```

Now run the program, and you should see a colorful rotating cube. Don't worry about how this works yet—we will learn that in the next chapter.

Summary

In this chapter, we covered a lot of new material related to creating a 3D game. You learned how the game camera worked just like a video camera. Anything in the camera's frustum will be rendered to the screen. You also learned about the 3D coordinate system that is used to place objects in a 3D world. Finally, you learned about matrices and vectors, which form the underpinning of how 3D objects are manipulated.

Finally, we started with a blank project and walked through all of the code required to set up a 3D game that will use OpenGL to render. Remember, you will never have to memorize this code! But, it is important that you have a basic understanding of what purpose each line of code serves.

In the next chapter, you will learn to create and load 3D models from modeling program.

9
Super Models

In the previous chapter, you created a framework to render OpenGL in 3D. At the very end of that chapter, we added a block of code that rendered a cube. In this chapter, you will learn how to create 3D objects in Open GL, first using code, and then using a 3D modeling program. In this chapter, we will cover the following:

- **Graphics cards**: 3D graphics cards are basically small computers that are optimized to render objects in 3D. We will take a quick look at how a graphics card does what it does best.
- **Vertices**: 3D objects are drawn by plotting points and telling OpenGL to use these points to create an object that can be rendered on the screen.
- **Triangles**: Triangles are used to create all 3D objects. You will learn about the relationship between vertices and triangles and how they are used to create simple objects.
- **Modeling**: Once you understand how to create simple 3D objects using code, you will also understand that you are going to need a more effective tool if you ever want to create anything complicated. This is where 3D modeling software comes in and saves the day.
- Once you create a 3D model, you have to get the model into the game. We will create the code to load a 3D model into our game by reading the data that is created by the modeling software.

New Space

Until now, we have been working only in a two-dimensional space. This means that we were able create game objects with height and width. This works well because our computer screens are also two-dimensional. As we move into three-dimensional space, we need the ability to add another dimension to our objects: depth. As computer screens don't physically have a third dimension in which to display pixels, this is all accomplished by mathematical wizardry!

In *Chapter 8, Expanding Your Horizons* we discussed several methods that have been used (and are still used) to simulate three-dimensions in a two-dimensional display:

- Objects that are farther away can be made to appear smaller than objects that are close

- Objects that are farther away can be made to move more slowly than objects that are close

- Lines that are parallel can be drawn to converge toward the center as they are farther away

These three techniques have one major shortcoming: they all required the programmer to write code that makes each visual effect work. For example, the programmer has to make sure that objects that are receding from the player are constantly scaled down so that they become increasingly smaller.

In a true 3D game, the only thing that the programmer has to worry about is placing each object at the right coordinates in 3D space. A special graphics card takes care of performing all of the calculations to take care of size, speed, and parallax. This frees the programmer up from doing these calculations, but it actually adds a whole new set of requirements related to positing and rotating objects in three-dimensional space.

A computer in a computer

The thing about what it takes for your computer to process your game. The computer must receive input from the player, interpret that input, and then apply the results to the game. Once the input is completed, the computer must handle the physics of the game: objects must be moved, collisions must happen, and explosions must ensue. Once the computer has completed updating all of the objects in the game, it must then render these results to the screen. Finally, in order to be convincing, all of this must occur at least 30 times a second and often 60 times a second!

It is truly amazing that computers can process this much information that quickly. In fact, if it were truly up to the central processing unit of your computer to accomplish this, then it wouldn't be able to keep up.

The 3D graphics card solves this problem by taking care of the rendering process so that the main CPU of your computer doesn't have to. All your CPU has to do is deliver the data and the graphics card takes care of the rest, allowing the main CPU to continue processing other things.

A modern 3D graphics card is really an entire computer system that lives on a silicon card inside your main computer. The graphics card is a computer inside your computer! The graphics card has its own input, output, and its own processor known as the graphics processing unit, or GPU. It also contains its own memory, often up to 4 gigabytes or more.

The following diagram shows you the basic structure of a graphics card and how it processes information:

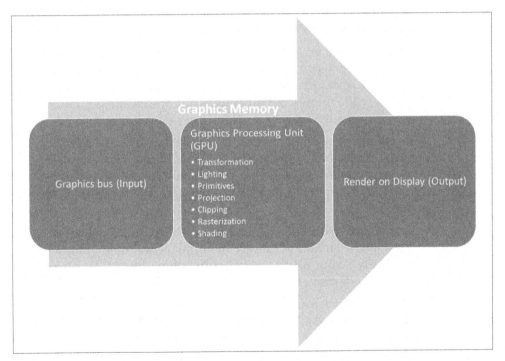

The preceding sequence that is depicted is known as the graphics pipeline. A detailed discussion of every step in the process is beyond the scope of our book, but it is good to have a basic understanding of the graphics pipeline, so here are the basics:

- **Graphics bus**: In computer lingo, a bus is just a way to move data. Think of a bus as a freeway: the more lanes you have on our freeway, the faster the traffic can move. Inside your computer, the traffic is bits of data, and most modern graphics cards have 64 lanes (known as a 64-bit bus), which allows up to 64-bits (or 8 bytes) of data to be moved simultaneously. The graphics bus receives its data directly from the CPU.

  - **Graphics Processing Unit**: The GPU does all the work, and as you can see, there is a lot of work to do.

  - **Transformation**: Each vertex, represented as a point in 3D space, must be properly positioned. There are several frames of reference to deal with. For example, local coordinates may describe how far a car's tires are from its body, while global coordinates describe how far the car is from the upcoming cliff. All of the data must be transformed into a single frame of reference.

  - **Lighting**: Each vertex must be lit. This means applying light and color to each vertex and interpolating the light and color intensity from one vertex to another. In the same way that the sun lights our world, while fluorescent tubes light our offices, the GPU uses lighting data to correctly light the world of your game.

  - **Primitives**: These are the simple objects that are used to build more complicated objects. Similarly to a virtual Lego set, the GPU constructs everything in your game using triangles, rectangles, circles, cube, spheres, cones, and cylinders. We will learn more about this later in the chapter.

  - **Projection**: Once the GPU has constructed a 3D model of the world, it must now create a 3D projection of the world onto 2D space (remember, your display only has two dimensions). This is similar to how the sun projects a 2D shadow of 3D objects.

  - **Clipping**: Once the 3D scene has been projected into 2D space, some vertices will be behind other vertices, and, therefore, can't actually be seen at this time. Clipping, or removing vertices that can't be seen, removes these vertices from the data, streamlining the entire process.

  - **Rasterization**: We now have a 2D model that mathematically represents the current image that must be displayed onto the screen. Rasterization is the process of converting this virtual image into actual pixels that must be displayed on the screen.

- ○ **Shading**: This final process determines the actual color that must be applied to each pixel on the screen to correctly display the model that has been created in the earlier phases. Code can even be written to manipulate the process to create special visual effects. Code that modifies the shading process in the graphics pipeline is called a shader.

- **Render**: Of course, the reason that we do all of this is so that we can display our game on the computer screen. The final output of the graphics pipeline is a representation of the current screen in the render buffer. Now, all the CPU has to do is swap the data in the render buffer to the actual screen buffer, and the result is the next frame in your game!

By the way, you will notice that behind the scenes (the big arrow in the preceding image) everything is supported by dedicated memory on the graphics card. All of the data is moved from the CPU to the memory of the graphics card, where it is manipulated and processed before being sent back to the CPU. This means that memory on the main computer doesn't have to be set aside to handle graphics processing.

> It is important to understand that the preceding diagram is a generic representation of the graphics pipeline. Specific hardware on various graphics cards may handle things differently, and the OpenGL and DirectX specifications are slightly different, but the preceding diagram is still the basic pipeline.

Drawing your weapons

It's time for us to learn how to draw things in OpenGL. Whether you are drawing your weapons, an alien spacecraft, or a blade of grass, it all starts by with very simple shapes that are combined to make more complex shapes.

Getting primitive

The most basic shapes that can be drawn in OpenGL are known as primitives. The primitives that can be drawn by OpenGL include:

- **Points**: As the name suggests, a point renders a single point and is defined by a single vertex.

- **Lines**: A line is rendered as a line drawn between two vertices.

- **Triangles**: A triangle is defined by three vertices and the three lines that pass from one vertex to the other.

- **Quads**: A quad is defined by four vertices and the four lines that pass from one vertex to the other. Technically, a quad is actually two triangles that have been joined together at the hypotenuse.

That's it, folks! Everything known to exist can be created from these four primitives. Extrapolating into 3D, there are these 3D primitives:

- A plane is a 2D extrusion of a line (okay, I know that a plane isn't really 3D!)
- A pyramid is a 3D representation of a quad and four triangles
- A cube is the 3D extrusion of a quad
- A sphere is a 3D construct based on a circle, which is created by lines (yes, lines, and the shorter each line, the more convincing the circle)
- A cylinder is a 3D extrusion of a circle

The objects in the preceding list aren't actually defined as OpenGL primitives. However, many 3D modeling programs refer to them as primitives because they are the simplest 3D objects to create.

Drawing primitives

In the previous chapter, we created a cube using the following code:

```
void DrawCube()
{
  glClear(GL_COLOR_BUFFER_BIT | GL_DEPTH_BUFFER_BIT);
  glTranslatef(0.0f, 0.0f, -7.0f);
  glRotatef(fRotate, 1.0f, 1.0f, 1.0f);
  glBegin(GL_QUADS);
  glColor3f(0.0f, 1.0f, 0.0f);
  glVertex3f(1.0f, 1.0f, -1.0f); glVertex3f(-1.0f, 1.0f, -1.0f);
  glVertex3f(-1.0f, 1.0f, 1.0f); glVertex3f(1.0f, 1.0f, 1.0f);
  glColor3f(1.0f, 0.5f, 0.0f);
  glVertex3f(1.0f, -1.0f, 1.0f); glVertex3f(-1.0f, -1.0f, 1.0f);
  glVertex3f(-1.0f, -1.0f, -1.0f); glVertex3f(1.0f, -1.0f, -1.0f);
  glColor3f(1.0f, 0.0f, 0.0f);
  glVertex3f(1.0f, 1.0f, 1.0f); glVertex3f(-1.0f, 1.0f, 1.0f);
  glVertex3f(-1.0f, -1.0f, 1.0f); glVertex3f(1.0f, -1.0f, 1.0f);
  glColor3f(1.0f, 1.0f, 0.0f);
  glVertex3f(1.0f, -1.0f, -1.0f); glVertex3f(-1.0f, -1.0f, -1.0f);
  glVertex3f(-1.0f, 1.0f, -1.0f); glVertex3f(1.0f, 1.0f, -1.0f);
  glColor3f(0.0f, 0.0f, 1.0f);
  glVertex3f(-1.0f, 1.0f, 1.0f); glVertex3f(-1.0f, 1.0f, -1.0f);
  glVertex3f(-1.0f, -1.0f, -1.0f); glVertex3f(-1.0f, -1.0f, 1.0f);
```

```
glColor3f(1.0f, 0.0f, 1.0f);
glVertex3f(1.0f, 1.0f, -1.0f); glVertex3f(1.0f, 1.0f, 1.0f);
glVertex3f(1.0f, -1.0f, 1.0f); glVertex3f(1.0f, -1.0f, -1.0f);
glEnd();
fRotate -= 0.05f;

}
```

Now, let's learn about how this code actually works:

1. Any time that we want to draw something in OpenGL, we first start by clearing the render buffer. In other words, every frame is drawn from scratch. The `glClear` function clears the buffer so that we can start drawing to it.

2. Before we start drawing objects, we want to tell OpenGL where to draw them. The `glTranslatef` command moves us to a certain point in 3D space from which we will start our drawing (actually, `glTranslatef` moves the camera, but the effect is the same).

3. If we want to rotate our object, then we provide that information with the `glRotatef` function. Recall that the cube in the previous chapter slowly rotated.

4. Just before we provide vertices to OpenGL, we need to tell OpenGL how to interpret these vertices. Are they single points? Lines? Triangles? In our case, we defined vertices for the six squares that will make the faces of our cube, so we specify `glBegin(GL_QUADS)` to let OpenGL know that we are going to be providing the vertices for each quad. There are several other possibilities that we will describe next.

5. In OpenGL, you specify the properties for each vertex just before you define the vertex. For example, we use the `glColor3f` function to define the color for the next set of vertices that we define. Each succeeding vertex will be drawn in this specified color until we change the color with another call to `glColor3f`.

6. Finally, we define each vertex for the quad. As a quad requires four vertices, the next four `glVertex3f` calls will define one quad. If you look closely at the code, you will notice that there are six groups of four vertex definitions (each preceded by a color definition), which all work together to create the six faces of our cube.

Now that you understand how OpenGL draws quads, let's expand your knowledge by covering the other types of primitives.

Making your point

There is only one kind of point primitive.

Gl_Points

The `glBegin(GL_POINTS)` function call tells OpenGL that each following vertex is to be rendered as a single point. Points can even have texture mapped onto them, and these are known as **point sprites**.

Points are actually generated as squares of pixels based on the size defined by the `GL_PROGRAM_POINT_SIZE` parameter of the `glEnable` function. The size defines the number of pixels that each side of the point takes up. The point's position is defined as the center of that square.

The point size must be greater than zero, or else an undefined behavior results. There is an implementation-defined range for point sizes, and the size given by either method is clamped to that range. Two additional OpenGL properties determine how points are rendered: `GL_POINT_SIZE_RANGE` (returns 2 floats), and `GL_POINT_SIZE_GRANULARITY`. This particular OpenGL implementation will clamp sizes to the nearest multiple of the granularity.

Getting in line

There are three kinds of line primitives, based on different interpretations the vertex list.

Gl_Lines

When you call `glBegin(GL_LINES)`, every pair of vertices is interpreted as a single line. Vertices 1 and 2 are considered one line. Vertices 3 and 4 are considered another line. If the user specifies an odd number of vertices, then the extra vertex is ignored.

Gl_Line_Strip

When you call `glBegin(GL_LINES)`, the first vertex defines the start of the first line. Each vertex thereafter defines the end of the previous line and the start of the next line. This has the effect of chaining the lines together up to the last vertex in the list. Thus, if you pass *n* vertices, you will get *n-1* lines. If the user only specifies only one vertex, the drawing command is ignored.

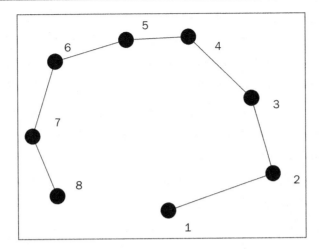

Gl_Line_Loop

The call `glBegin(GL_LINE_LOOP)` works almost exactly like line strips, except that the first and last vertices are joined as a line. Thus, you get n lines for *n* input vertices. If the user only specifies one vertex, the drawing command is ignored. The line between the first and last vertices happens after all of the previous lines in the sequence.

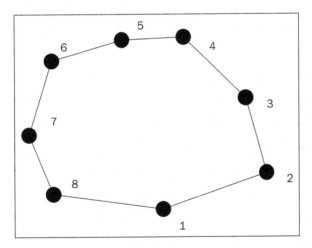

Triangulation

A triangle is a primitive formed by three vertices. There are three kinds of triangle primitives, based again on different interpretations of the vertex stream.

GI_Triangles

When you call `glBegin(GL_TRIANGLES)`, every three vertices define a triangle. Vertices 1, 2, and 3 form one triangle. Vertices 4, 5, and 6 form another triangle. If there are fewer than three vertices at the end of the list, they are ignored:

```
glBegin(GL_TRIANGLES);
   glVertex3f( 0.0f, 1.0f, 0.0f);
   glVertex3f(-1.0f,-1.0f, 0.0f);
   glVertex3f( 1.0f,-1.0f, 0.0f);
glEnd();
```

GI_Triangle_Strip

When you call `glBegin(GL_TRIANGLE_STRIP)`, the first three vertices create the first triangle. Thereafter, the next two vertices create the next triangle, creating a group of adjacent triangles. A vertex stream of n length will generate $n-2$ triangles:

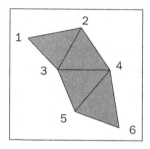

GI_Triangle_Fan

When you call `glBegin(GL_TRIANGLE_FAN)`, the first vertex defines the point from which all other triangles are defined. Thereafter, each group of two vertices define a new triangle with the same apex as the first one, forming a fan. A vertex stream of n length will generate $n-2$ triangles. Any leftover vertices will be ignored:

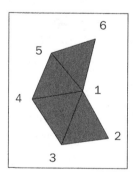

Being square

A quad is a quadrilateral, having four sides. Don't get confused and think that all quads are either squares or rectangles. Any shape with four sides is a quad. The four vertices are expected to be in the same plane and failure to do so can lead to undefined results. A quad is typically constructed as a pair of triangles, which can lead to artifacts (unanticipated glitches in the image).

Gl_Quads

When you call `glBegin(GL_QUADS)`, each set of four vertices defines a quad. Vertices 1 to 4 form one quad, while vertices 5 to 8 form another. The vertex list must be a number of vertices divisible by 4 to work:

```
glBegin(GL_QUADS);
   glVertex3f(-1.0f, 1.0f, 0.0f);
   glVertex3f( 1.0f, 1.0f, 0.0f);
   glVertex3f( 1.0f,-1.0f, 0.0f);
   glVertex3f(-1.0f,-1.0f, 0.0f);
glEnd();
```

Gl_Quad_Strip

Similarly to triangle strips, a quad strip uses adjacent edges to form the next quad. In the case of quads, the third and fourth vertices of one quad are used as the edge of the next quad. So, vertices 1 to 4 define the first quad, while 5 to 6 extend the next quad. A vertex list of *n* length will generate *(n - 2)/2* quads:

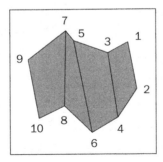

Saving face

All of the primitives that we discussed are created by creating multiple shapes that are glued together, more or less. OpenGL needs to know which face of a shape is facing the camera, and this is determined by the winding order. As you can't see both the front and back of a primitive, OpenGL uses facing to decide which side must be rendered.

In general, OpenGL takes care of the winding order so that all of the shapes in a particular list have consistent facing. If you, as a coder, try to take care of facing manually, you are actually second-guessing OpenGL.

Back to Egypt

As we have already demonstrated the code to draw a cube, let's try something even more interesting: a **pyramid**. A pyramid is constructed by four triangles with a square on the bottom. So, the simplest way to create a pyramid is to create four GL_TRIANGLE primitives and one GL_QUAD primitive:

```
int DrawGlPyramid(GLvoid)
{
glClear(GL_COLOR_BUFFER_BIT | GL_DEPTH_BUFFER_BIT);
glLoadIdentity();
glTranslatef(-1.5f,0.0f,-6.0f);
glBegin(GL_TRIANGLES);
glColor3f(1.0f,0.0f,0.0f);
glVertex3f( 0.0f, 1.0f, 0.0f);
glColor3f(0.0f,1.0f,0.0f);
glVertex3f(-1.0f,-1.0f, 1.0f);
glColor3f(0.0f,0.0f,1.0f);
glVertex3f( 1.0f,-1.0f, 1.0f);
glColor3f(1.0f,0.0f,0.0f);
glVertex3f( 0.0f, 1.0f, 0.0f);
glColor3f(0.0f,0.0f,1.0f);
glVertex3f( 1.0f,-1.0f, 1.0f);
glColor3f(0.0f,1.0f,0.0f);
glVertex3f( 1.0f,-1.0f, -1.0f);
glColor3f(1.0f,0.0f,0.0f);
glVertex3f( 0.0f, 1.0f, 0.0f);
glColor3f(0.0f,1.0f,0.0f);
glVertex3f( 1.0f,-1.0f, -1.0f);
glColor3f(0.0f,0.0f,1.0f);
glVertex3f(-1.0f,-1.0f, -1.0f);
glColor3f(1.0f,0.0f,0.0f);
glVertex3f( 0.0f, 1.0f, 0.0f);
glColor3f(0.0f,0.0f,1.0f);
glVertex3f(-1.0f,-1.0f,-1.0f);
glColor3f(0.0f,1.0f,0.0f);
glVertex3f(-1.0f,-1.0f, 1.0f);
glEnd();
}
```

A modeling career

When you consider the amount of code that is required to create even the most basic shapes, you might despair of ever coding a complicated 3D game! Fortunately, there are better tools available to create 3D objects. 3D modeling software allows a 3D modeler to create 3D object similar to how an artist uses drawing software to create 2D images.

The process of getting 3D objects into our game typically has three steps:

1. Creating the 3D object in a 3D modeling tool.
2. Exporting the model as a data file.
3. Loading the data file into our game.

Blending in

There are many popular tools that are used by professionals to create 3D models. Two of the most popular ones are 3D Max and Maya. However, these tools are also relatively expensive. It turns out that there is a very capable 3D modeling tool called **Blender** that is available for free. We will install Blender and then learn how to use it to create 3D models for our game.

Blender is a 3D modeling and animation suite that is perfect for beginners who want to try 3D modeling. Blender is open-source software created by Blender Organization, and it is available at no cost (although Blender Organization will be glad to accept your donations). Install Blender on your computer using the following steps:

1. Go to http://www.Blender.Org and hit *Enter*.
2. Click the **Download** link at the top of the page.
3. Download the files that are compatible with your computer. For my 64-bit Windows computer, I made the selection circled in the following screenshot:

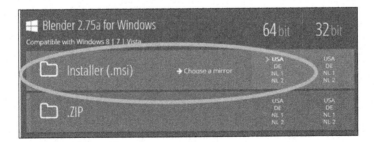

4. Once Blender is downloaded, run the installer program and accept all of the default values to install Blender on your computer.

Blender overview

Once you have installed Blender on your computer, open it up and you should see something like the following screen:

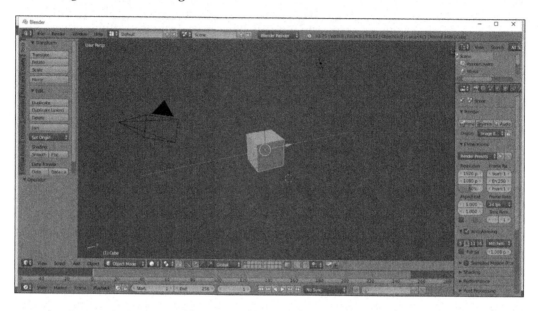

Don't let the complexity of the screen scare you. Blender has a lot of features that you will learn with time, and they have tried to put many of the features right at your fingertips (well, mouse tips). They have even created a model of a cube for you so that you can get started right away.

The middle of the screen is where the action takes place. This is the 3D view. The grid gives you a reference, but is not part of the model. In the preceding screenshot, the only model is the cube.

The panels surrounding the middle offer a host of options to create and manipulate your objects. We won't have time to cover most of these, but there are many tutorials available online.

Building your spaceship

Just like we did in the 2D portion of the book, we are going to build a simple 3D spaceship so that we can fly it around in our universe. As I am a programmer and not a modeler, it will be a ridiculously simple space ship. Let's build it out of a cylinder.

To build our space ship, we first want to get rid of the cube. Use your right mouse button to select the cube. You can tell that it is selected because it will have three arrows coming from it:

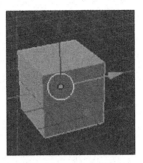

Now press the *Delete* key on your keyboard, and the cube will disappear.

 If you are like me, you will try and try to use the left mouse button to select objects. However, Blender uses the right mouse button to select objects!

You will probably notice two other objects in the 3D View:

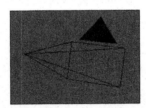

The object in the preceding image represents the camera. This is not a part of your game object, but rather it represents the angle of the camera as viewed from inside Blender. You can hide this by right-clicking on it and pressing *H*.

The object in the preceding image represents the light source. This is not a part of your game object, but rather it represents the light source that Blender is using. You can hide this by right-clicking on it and pressing *H*.

Now, let's create that cylinder. Locate the **Create** tab in the left panel and use your left mouse button to click on it:

Next, click on the cylinder button. Blender will create a cylinder in the 3D view:

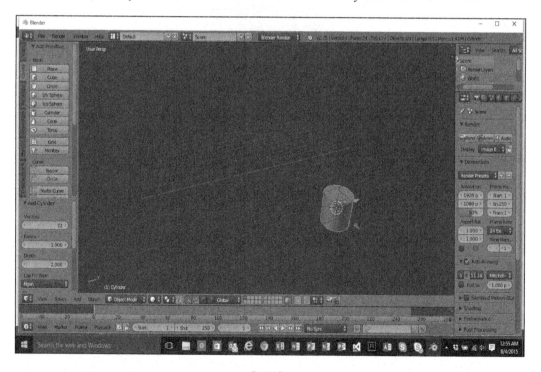

Notice the three arrows. These indicate that the cylinder is the selected object. The arrows are used to move, size, and rotate objects, but we won't be doing any of that today.

You should also notice a circle with a concentric dashed circle inside the cylinder. This indicates the origin of the object, which is the point around which the object will move, size, and rotate.

There are many more things that we would do if we were modeling a real object. As this is a coding book and not a modeling book, we won't do those things, but here are some ideas for future study:

- We could continue creating more and more objects and use them to build a much more complex spaceship
- We could use textures and materials to give our spaceship a skin

Exporting the object

In order to bring the spaceship into our game, we must first export the object into a data file that can be read into the game. There are many different formats that we could use, but for this game, we will use the `.obj` export type. To export the object, perform the following action:

1. Click the **File** command, then click **Export**.
2. Choose **Wavefront (.obj)** as the file type.
3. In the next screen, select the location for your export (preferably the location of your source code for the game) and name it `ship.obj`.

4. Click the **Export OBJ** button on the right-hand side of the screen.

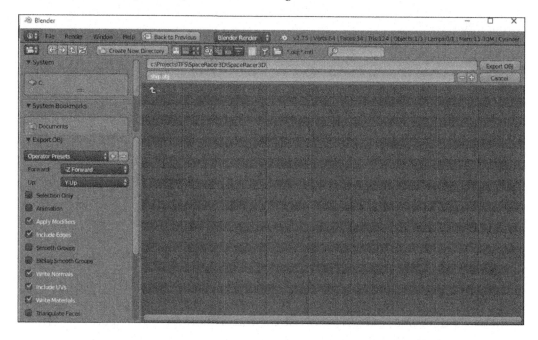

Congratulations! You are now one step away from bringing this object into your game.

Getting loaded

The `.obj` file is simply a text file that stores all of the vertices and other data that is used to render this object in OpenGL. The following screenshot shows the `ship.obj` file opened in Notepad:

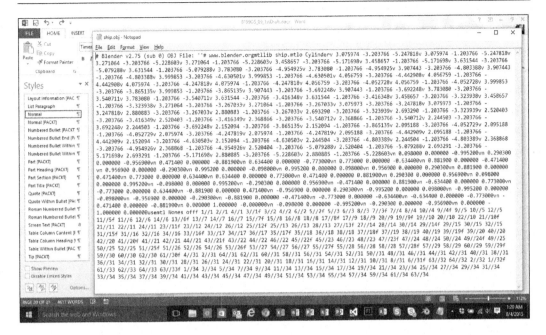

- #: This defines a comment
- v: This defines a vertex
- vt: This defines a texture coordinate
- vn: This defines a normal
- f: This defines a face

We will now write the code to load this data into our game. Open the SpaceRacer3D project into Visual Studio. Then add the following headers:

```
#include #include #include enum Primitive
{
 Triangles = 0,
 Quads = 1
};

struct Vec2
{
 Vec2()
 {
  x = 0.0f;
  y = 0.0f;
 }
 Vec2(const float p_x, const float p_y)
 {
```

```
   x = p_x;
   y = p_y;
  }

 float x;
 float y;
};

struct Vec3
{
 Vec3()
 {
  x = 0.0f;
  y = 0.0f;
  z = 0.0f;
 }
 Vec3(const float p_x, const float p_y, const float p_z)
 {
  x = p_x;
  y = p_y;
  z = p_z;
 }

 float x;
 float y;
 float z;
};

const bool LoadObj(
 const char * filepath,
 std::vectortemp_vertices;
 std::vectortemp_normals;
 FILE * file = fopen(filepath, "r");
 if (file == NULL)
 {
  return false;
 }
 bool finished = false;
 while (!finished)
 {
  char line[128];
  int check = fscanf(file, "%s", line);
  if (check == EOF)
  {
   finished = true;
  }
  else
```

```
{
  if (strcmp(line, "v") == 0)
  {
    Vec3 vertex;
    fscanf(file, "%f %f %f\n",  vertices.size(); i++)
{
 unsigned int vertexIndex = vertices[i];
 unsigned int normalIndex = normals[i];
 Vec3 vertex = temp_vertices[vertexIndex - 1];
 Vec3 normal = temp_normals[normalIndex - 1];
 o_vertices.push_back(vertex);
 o_normals.push_back(normal);
 }
 return true;
 }
```

Before you can compile the code you will need a to add a pre-processor definition. Open the project properties, and navigate to the C/C++ branch of the Configuration Properties. Add _CRT_SECURE_NO_WARNINGS to the Preprocessor Definitions.

Here is what the loader is doing:

The loader accepts for parameters (one input and three output):

- A filename.
- A pointer to an array of vertices.
- A pointer to an array of uvs.
- A pointer to an array of normal vectors.
- Three vectors (a type of array in C++) are created to hold the data that is parsed from the file. One to hold the vertices, one to hold the uvs, and one to hold the normals. A fourth vector is created to pair each vertex with a uv coordinate.
- Three temporary vectors are created to use as input buffers as the data is read.
- The fbx file is now read. The program looks for the flags that indicate what type of data is being read. For our purposes now, we are only concerned with the vertex data.
- When each piece of data is read, it is put into the appropriate vector.
- The vectors are returned so that they can be processed by the program.

Simple enough, eh? But, there's a lot of code because parsing is always fun! The most important data that is extracted from the model for our purposes is the array of vertices.

> We haven't discussed uvs and normal vectors because I don't want to this to be a whole book on modeling. Uvs are used to add textures to an object. as we didn't add any textures, we won't have uv data. Normal vectors tell OpenGL which side of an object is facing out. This data is used to properly render and light an object.

In the next chapter, we will use this loader to load our model into the game.

Summary

We covered a lot of ground in this chapter. You learned how to create 3D objects in code using OpenGL. At the same time, you learned that you don't really create 3D objects in code! Instead, real games use models that have been created in special 3D modeling software, such as Blender.

Even as a coder, it is useful to learn a little bit about using software, such as Blender, but you will eventually want to find artists and modelers who really know now to use these tools to their full extent. You can even find 3D models online and integrate them into your game.

To close things out, we learned how to load 3D models into our. Spend a few days playing around with Blender and see what you can come up with, and then on to the next chapter!

10
Expanding Space

Now that you know how to build your 3D world, it is time to do stuff! As we are building a space racing game, we need to be able to move our space ship around. We will also put some obstacles in the game so that we have something to race against. In this chapter, you will learn about the following topics:

- **Placing game objects**: We will take some 3D objects, load them into our game, and place them in 3D space.

- **Transformations**: We need to learn how to move in 3D. Moving in 2D was easy. In 3D, we have another dimension, and we will now also want to account for rotation as we move around.

- **Point of view**: We will learn how the point of view affects how we play the game. Do you want to be in the pilot's seat or just outside the ship?

- **Collisions**: We performed some collision detection in our 2D game. Collision detection in 3D is more complicated because we now have to consider all three spatial dimensions in our checks.

Creation 101

Our first task is to load our world. We need a few basic components. First, we need a universe. This universe will contain stars, asteroids, and our space ship. Open up SpaceRacer3D and let's get coding!

Preparing the project

Before we get going, we will need to move some code over from our 2D project. Copy the following files and settings from RoboRacer2D to SpaceRacer3D:

1. Copy `Input.cpp` and `Input.h` — we will use these classes to handle user input.

2. Copy `Sprite.cpp`, `Sprite.h`, `SOIL.h`, and `SOIL.lib` — we will use them to support the user interface in the next chapter. You may need to remove the line `#include "stdafx.h"` from `Sprite.cpp`.

3. Copy `fmodex.dll` — we need this for audio support.

4. Copy the settings from the project `Configuration Properties/C/C++/General/Additional Include Directories` setting — this is necessary to provide access to FMOD library:

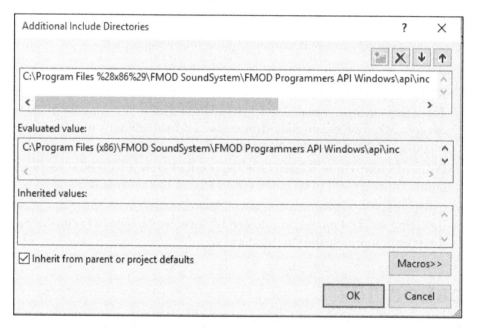

5. Copy the settings from the project `Configuration Properties/Linker/Input/ Additional Dependencies` setting — this is necessary to provide access to the OpenGL, FMOD, and SOIL libraries:

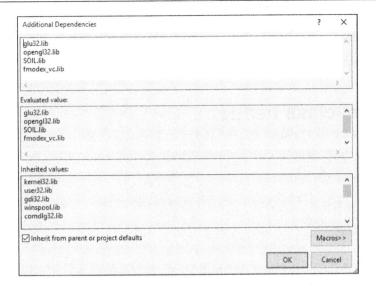

6. Copy the settings from the project Configuration Properties/Linker/ General/Additional Library Directories setting – this is also necessary to provide access to FMOD library:

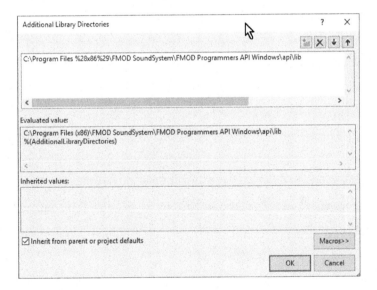

Loading game objects

In the previous chapter, we learned how to create 3D objects in Blender and export them as obj files. We then added code to our project to load the obj data. Now, we will use that code to load some models into our game.

We are going to load four models into our game: the space ship, and three asteroids. The idea will be to race through the asteroid field. As our loader holds the model data as three arrays (vertices, uvs, and normals), we will create a model class that defines these arrays and then use this class for each model that we want to load into the game.

The Model class header

Create a new class and header file named Model.cpp and Model.h, respectively. Open Model.h. First, let's get the header set up:

```
#pragma once
#include <stdlib.h>
#include <math.h>
#include "LoadObj.h"
#include "glut.h"
```

We need to use some constants defined in math.h, so we need to add a preprocessor directive. Add _USE_MATH_DEFINES to Configuration Properties/C/C++/ Preprocessor/Preprocessor Definitions. Also, notice that we include LoadObj.h because we will load the model from inside this class. Now, let's create the class:

```
class Model
{

  public:

  struct Color
  {
    Color()
    {
      r = 0.0f;
      g = 0.0f;
      b = 0.0f;
    }
    Color(const float p_r, const float p_g, const float p_b)
    {
      r = p_r;
      g = p_g;
      b = p_b;
    }
    float r;
    float g;
    float b;
  };
};
```

We will be using color a lot, so we are defining a struct to hold the r, g, and b values to make things more convenient. Now, for our methods we use the following code:

```
Model(const char* p_filepath, const Color p_color);
~Model();
void Update(const float p_deltaTime);
void Render();
void SetPosition(const float p_x, const float p_y, const float p_z);
void SetPosition(const Vec3 p_position);
const Vec3 GetPosition() const;
void SetHeading(const float p_x, const float p_y, const float p_z);
void SetHeading(const Vec3 p_heading);
const Vec3 GetHeading() const;
void SetColor(const float p_red, const float p_green, const float p_blue);
void SetColor(const Color p_color);
void SetBaseRotation(const float p_x, const float p_y, const float p_z);
void SetBaseRotation(const Vec3 p_rotation);
const Vec3 GetBaseRotation() const;
void SetHeadingRotation(const float p_x, const float p_y, const float p_z);
void SetHeadingRotation(const Vec3 p_rotation);
const Vec3 GetHeadingRotation() const;
void SetVelocity(const float p_velocity);
const float GetVelocity() const;
const bool IsShip();
void IsShip(const bool p_IsShip);
const bool IsVisible() const { return m_isVisible; };
void IsVisible(const bool p_isVisible) { m_isVisible = p_isVisible;
};
};
```

Here is a short description of each method:

- Model is the constructor. It takes a filename and a color. As our models are simple shapes, we will use color to give them some pizzazz.
- SetPosition and GetPosition manage the object's position in world space.
- SetHeading and GetHeading manage the direction the object is heading.
- SetColor and GetColor manage the objects color.
- SetBaseRotation and GetBaseRotation manage any local rotation applied to the object.
- SetHeadingRotation and GetHeadingRotation manage the orientation of the object in world space.
- SetVelocity and GetVelocity manage the speed of the object.

Now, for the variables, we use the following code:

```
m_vertices;
 std::vectorm_normals;
 Vec3 m_position;
 Vec3 m_heading;
 Vec3 m_baseRotation;
 Vec3 m_headingRotation;
 Color m_color;
 Primitive m_primitive;
 float m_velocity;

 bool m_isVisible;
 bool m_loaded;
 bool m_IsShip;

 float m_radius;
 bool m_collideable;
```

These are self-explanatory because they directly correspond to the methods described previously. This header is a good structure for everything that we will need to do to place objects in our world and move them around.

Implementing the Model class

Now let's implement the class. Open `Model.cpp` and let's get started. First, we implement the header, constructor, and destructor:

```
#include "Model.h"

Model::Model(const char* p_filepath, const Color p_color)
{
 m_filepath = p_filepath;
 m_loaded = LoadObj(m_filepath, m_vertices, m_normals, m_primitive);
 SetPosition(0.0f, 0.0f, 0.0f);
 SetHeading(0.0f, 0.0f, 0.0f);
 SetHeadingRotation(0.0f, 0.0f, 0.0f);
 SetBaseRotation(0.0f, 0.0f, 0.0f);
 IsShip(false);
 SetVelocity(0.0f);
 SetColor(p_color.r, p_color.g, p_color.b);
 SetRadius(1.0f);
 IsCollideable(true);
 IsVisible(true);
}
Model::~Model()
{
```

```
    m_vertices.clear();
    m_normals.clear();
}
```

The constructor sets everything up. Notice that we call `LoadObj` from the constructor to actually load the object into the class. The results will be stored into member arrays `m_vertices` and `m_normals`. `m_primitive` will hold an enum telling us whether this object is defined by quads or triangles. The remaining variables are set to default values. These can be defined at any time in the game by using the appropriate `accessor` method:

```
float Deg2Rad(const float p_degrees)
{
    return p_degrees * (M_PI / 180.0f);

}
```

`Deg2Rad` is a helper function that will convert degrees to radians. As we move the ship around, we keep track of the heading angle in degrees, but we often need to use radians in OpenGL functions:

```
void Model::Update(const float p_deltaTime)
{
  Vec3 targetRotation = GetHeadingRotation();
  Vec3 currentPosition = GetPosition();
  Vec3 targetPosition = GetPosition();

  float distance = m_velocity * p_deltaTime;
  Vec3 deltaPosition;

  deltaPosition.y = cos(Deg2Rad(targetRotation.z)) * distance;
  deltaPosition.x = -sin(Deg2Rad(targetRotation.z)) * distance;
  deltaPosition.z = sin(Deg2Rad(targetRotation.x)) * distance;

  targetPosition.x += deltaPosition.x;
  targetPosition.y += deltaPosition.y;
  targetPosition.z += deltaPosition.z;
  SetPosition(targetPosition);
}
```

The `Update` function updates the position of the object based on the object's velocity. Finally, we update `m_heading`, which will be used to orient the world camera during the render. Then update the object's position in world space:

```
void Model::Render()
{
  if (IsVisible())
  {
    glRotatef(-m_baseRotation.x, 1.0f, 0.0f, 0.0f);
```

```
        glRotatef(-m_baseRotation.y, 0.0f, 1.0f, 0.0f);
        glRotatef(-m_baseRotation.z, 0.0f, 0.0f, 1.0f);

        Vec3 targetRotation = GetHeadingRotation();
        Vec3 currentPosition = GetPosition();

      if (m_IsShip)
      {
        glPushMatrix();
        glLoadIdentity();
        glRotatef(targetRotation.x, 1.0f, 0.0f, 0.0f);
        glRotatef(targetRotation.y, 0.0f, 1.0f, 0.0f);
        glRotatef(targetRotation.z, 0.0f, 0.0f, 1.0f);
        GLfloat matrix[16];
        glGetFloatv(GL_MODELVIEW_MATRIX, matrix);
        glPopMatrix();
        glTranslatef(currentPosition.x, currentPosition.y,
currentPosition.z);
        glMultMatrixf(matrix);
      }

      switch (m_primitive)
      {
      case Primitive::Quads:
        glBegin(GL_QUADS);
        break;
      case Primitive::Triangles:
        glBegin(GL_TRIANGLES);
        break;
      }
      glColor3f(m_color.r, m_color.g, m_color.b);
      for (unsigned int i = 0; i < m_vertices.size(); i++)
      {
        if (m_IsShip)
        {
          glVertex3f(m_vertices[i].x, m_vertices[i].y, m_vertices[i].z);
        }
        else
        {
          glVertex3f(m_vertices[i].x + m_position.x, m_vertices[i].y + m_
position.y, m_vertices[i].z + m_position.z);
        }
      }
      glEnd();
    }
}
```

The Render function takes care of rendering this particular object. The setup for the world matrix will happen in the game code. Then each object in the game will be rendered.

Remember the camera? The camera is a virtual object that is used to view the scene. In our case, the camera is the ship. Wherever the ship goes, the camera will go. Whatever the ship points at, the camera will point at.

Now for the real mind-blower; OpenGL doesn't really have a camera. That is, there really isn't a camera that you move around in the scene. Instead, the camera is always located at coordinates **(0.0, 0.0, 0.0)**, or the world's origin. This means that our ship will always be located at the origin. Instead of moving the ship, we will actually move the other objects in the opposite direction. When we turn the ship, we will actually rotate the world in the opposite direction.

Now look at the code for the `Render` function:

- First, we use `glRotate` to rotate everything the object's base rotation. This comes in useful if we need to orient the object. For example, the cylinder that we modeled in the previous chapter is standing up, and it works better in the game lying on its side. You will see later that we apply a 90 degree rotation to the cylinder to achieve this.
- Next, we have to decide whether we are going to render quads or triangles. When Blender exports a model, it exports it as either quads or triangles. The loader figures out whether a model is defined as quads or triangles and stores the result in `m_primitive`. We then use that to determine whether this particular object must be rendered using triangles or quads.
- We use `glColor` to set the color of the object. At this point we haven't assigned any textures to our models, so color gives us a simple way to give each object a personality.

Now for the real work! We need to draw each vertex of the object in world space. To do this, we loop through each point in the vertices array, and we use `glVertex3f` to place each point.

The catch is this; the points in the vertices array are in local coordinates. If we drew every object using these points, then they would all be drawn at the origin. You will recall that we want to place each object in the game relative to the ship. So, we draw the ship at the origin, and we draw every other object in the game based on the position of the ship. We move the universe, not the ship.

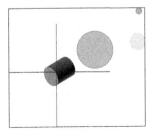

When the ship moves, the entire coordinate system moves with it. Actually, the coordinate system stays put and the entire universe moves past it!

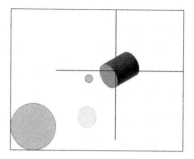

If we happen to be rendering the ship, we just draw it using its local coordinates and it is rendered at the origin. All of the other objects are drawn at a distance away from the ship based on the ships position.

Now, for the rest of the class implementation, use the following code:

```
void Model::SetPosition(const float p_x, const float p_y, const float
p_z)
{
  m_position.x = p_x;
  m_position.y = p_y;
  m_position.z = p_z;
}

void Model::SetPosition(const Vec3 p_position)
{
  m_position.x = p_position.x;
  m_position.y = p_position.y;
  m_position.z = p_position.z;
}

const Vec3 Model::GetPosition() const
{
  return m_position;
}
```

These methods set and retrieve the object's position. The position is changed based on the object's velocity in the Update method:

```
void Model::SetHeading(const float p_x, const float p_y, const float
p_z)
{
  m_heading.x = p_x;
  m_heading.y = p_y;
  m_heading.z = p_z;
}

void Model::SetHeading(const Vec3 p_heading)
{
  m_heading.x = p_heading.x;
  m_heading.y = p_heading.y;
  m_heading.z = p_heading.z;
}
const Vec3 Model::GetHeading() const
{
  return m_heading;
}
```

These methods set and retrieve the object's heading. The heading is changed based on the object's heading rotations in the Update method. Heading is the direction that the ship is headed in, and is used to rotate the world so that the ship appears to be heading in the correct direction:

```
void Model::SetColor(const float p_red, const float p_green, const
float p_blue)
{
  m_color.r = p_red;
  m_color.g = p_green;
  m_color.b = p_blue;
}

void Model::SetColor(const Color p_color)
{
  m_color.r = p_color.r;
  m_color.g = p_color.g;
  m_color.b = p_color.b;
}
```

These methods are used to manage the object's color:

```
void Model::SetVelocity(const float p_velocity)
{
  m_velocity = p_velocity;
}

const float Model::GetVelocity() const
{
  return m_velocity;
}
```

These methods are used to manage the object's velocity. The velocity is set in the game code during the input phase:

```
void Model::SetBaseRotation(const float p_x, const float p_y, const float p_z)
{
  m_baseRotation.x = p_x;
  m_baseRotation.y = p_y;
  m_baseRotation.z = p_z;
}

void Model::SetBaseRotation(const Vec3 p_rotation)
{
  m_baseRotation.x = p_rotation.x;
  m_baseRotation.y = p_rotation.y;
  m_baseRotation.z = p_rotation.z;
}

const Vec3 Model::GetBaseRotation() const
{
  return m_baseRotation;
}
```

These methods are used to manage the object's base rotation. The base rotation is used to rotate the object in local space:

```
void Model::SetHeadingRotation(const float p_x, const float p_y, const float p_z)
{
  m_headingRotation.x = p_x;
  m_headingRotation.y = p_y;
  m_headingRotation.z = p_z;
}
```

```
void Model::SetHeadingRotation(const Vec3 p_rotation)
{
  m_headingRotation.x = p_rotation.x;
  m_headingRotation.y = p_rotation.y;
  m_headingRotation.z = p_rotation.z;
}

const Vec3 Model::GetHeadingRotation() const
{
  return m_headingRotation;
}
```

These methods are used to manage the object's heading rotation. The heading rotation is used to rotate the world around the object so that the object appears to be heading in a particular direction. Only one object (the ship) will have a heading rotation. Another way to think about this is that the heading rotation is the rotation of the camera, which in our game is attached to the ship.

Modifying the game code

Now it's time to modify our game code so that it can load and manipulate game models. Open SpaceRacer3D.cpp.

We'll start by adding the appropriate headers. At the top of the code, modify the header definitions so that they look like the following code:

```
#include <windows.h>
#include "Model.h"
#include "Sprite.h"
#include "Input.h"
#include "glut.h"
```

Notice that we have added Model.h to load our models. We also included Sprite.h and Input.h from RoboRacer2D so that we can use those classes in our new game when necessary.

Now, we need to define some global variables to manage model loading. Just under any global variables that are already defined, add the following code:

```
Model* ship;
std::vector<Model*> asteroids;
```

These variables defined pointers to our game objects. As the ship is kind of special, we give it its own pointer. We want to be able to have an arbitrary number of asteroids; we set up a vector (a nice dynamic array) of pointers called asteroids.

Move down to the StartGame function, which we use to initialize all of our game models. Modify the StartGame function to look like the following code:

```
void StartGame()
{
//Ship
Model::Color c(0.0f, 0.0f, 1.0f);
ship = new Model("ship.obj", c);
Vec3 rotation(90.0f, 0.0f, 0.0f);
ship->SetBaseRotation(rotation);
ship->IsShip(true);
ship->SetVelocity(1.0f);

//Asteroid 1
c.r = 1.0f;
c.g = 0.0f;
c.b = 0.0f;
Model* asteroid = new Model("asteroid.obj", c);
Vec3 position(0.0f, 0.0f, -10.0f);
asteroid->SetPosition(position);
asteroids.push_back(asteroid);

//Asteroid 2
c.r = 0.0f;
c.g = 1.0f;
c.b = 0.0f;
asteroid = new Model("asteroid.obj", c);
position.x = 5.0f;
position.y = 0.0f;
position.z = -15.0f;
asteroid->SetPosition(position);
asteroids.push_back(asteroid);

//Asteroid 3
c.r = 0.0f;
```

```
c.g = 1.0f;
c.b = 1.0f;
asteroid = new Model("asteroid.obj", c);
position.x = 5.0f;
position.y = 5.0f;
position.z = -20.0f;
asteroid->SetPosition(position);
asteroids.push_back(asteroid);
}
```

We are going to create one object for the ship and three asteroids. For each object, we first define a color, then we create a new Model passing the filename of the object and the color. The Model class will load the object file exported from Blender.

Notice that we set the ship to be the camera with the IsCamera(true) call. We also attach the ship as the camera for every game object using the AttachCamera(ship) call.

We also set a position for each object. This will set the position in world space. This way we don't end up drawing every object at the origin!

Each asteroid is put in the asteroids array using the push.back method.

Now, we move to the Update function. Modify the Update function so that it looks like the following code:

```
void Update(const float p_deltaTime)
{

  ship->Update(p_deltaTime);

  for (unsigned int i = 0; i < asteroids.size(); i++)
  {
    asteroids[i]->Update(p_deltaTime);
  }
}
```

The update simply calls the Update method for every object in the game. As always, the update is based on the amount of time that has passed in the game, so we pass in p_deltaTime.

Now on to the Render function. Replace the existing code with the following code:

```
void Render()
{
 glClear(GL_COLOR_BUFFER_BIT | GL_DEPTH_BUFFER_BIT);
 glMatrixMode(GL_MODELVIEW);
 glLoadIdentity();

 for (unsigned int i = 0; i < asteroids.size(); i++)
 {
  asteroids[i]->Render();
 }
 ship->Render();
 SwapBuffers(hDC);
}
```

The rendering code is the real workhorse of the game. First, we set up the render call for this frame, then we call the Render method for each game object:

- GlClear: This clears the render buffer.
- GlMatrixMode: This sets the model to the model view. All translations and rotations are applied to the in the model view.
- glLoadIdentity(): This resets the matrix.
- Next, we call the Render method for each object in the game.
- Finally, we call SwapBuffers, which actually renders the scene to the screen.

Congratulations! If you run the game now, you should see the ship and the three asteroids off in the distance. As we set the velocity of the ship to 1.0, you should also see the ship slowly moving past the asteroids. However, we don't have any way to control the ship yet because we haven't implemented any input.

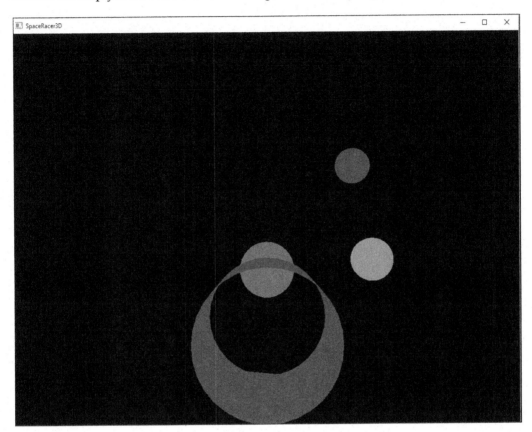

Taking control

We now have a framework to load and render game objects. But, we don't have any way to move our ship! The good news is that we already wrote an input class for RoboRacer2D, and we can reuse that code here.

Implementing input

Earlier in the chapter, I had you copy the Input class from RoboRacer2D into the source folder for SpaceRacer3D. Now, we have to simply wire it into our game code.

Open SpaceRacer3D. First, we need to include the input header. Add the following line of code to the headers:

```
#include "Input.h"
```

We also need to create a global pointer to manage the Input class. Add the following line just below the model pointers:

```
Input* m_input;
```

Next, we need to create an instance of the Input class. Add the following line of code to the top of the StartGame function:

```
m_input = new Input(hWnd);
```

Now, we have to create a function to handle our input. Add the following function just above the Update method:

```
void ProcessInput(const float p_deltaTime)
{
 Vec3 rotation;
 m_input->Update(p_deltaTime);
 Input::Command command = m_input->GetCommand();
 switch (command)
 {
 case Input::CM_STOP:
 {
  if (ship->GetVelocity() > 0.0f)
  {
   ship->SetVelocity(0.0f);
  }
  else
  {
   ship->SetVelocity(1.0f);
  }
 }
 break;
```

```
case Input::CM_DOWN:
{
 rotation = ship->GetHeadingRotation();
 rotation.x += -1.0f;
 if (rotation.x < 0.0f)
 {
  rotation.x = 359.0f;
 }
 if (rotation.x < 359.0f && rotation.x > 180.0f)
 {
  if (rotation.x < 315.0f)
  {
   rotation.x = 315.0f;
  }
 }
 ship->SetHeadingRotation(rotation);
}
break;
case Input::CM_UP:
{
 rotation = ship->GetHeadingRotation();
 rotation.x += 1.0f;
 if (rotation.x > 359.0f)
 {
  rotation.x = 0.0f;
 }
 if (rotation.x > 0.0f && rotation.x < 180.0f)
 {
  if (rotation.x > 45.0f)
  {
   rotation.x = 45.0f;
  }
 }
 ship->SetHeadingRotation(rotation);
}
break;
case Input::CM_LEFT:
{
 rotation = ship->GetHeadingRotation();
 rotation.z += 1.0f;
 if (rotation.z > 359.0f)
 {
  rotation.z = 0.0f;
 }
 if (rotation.z > 0.0f && rotation.z < 180.0f)
 {
  if (rotation.z > 45.0f)
  {
   rotation.z = 45.0f;
  }
```

```
    }
   ship->SetHeadingRotation(rotation);
  }
  break;
  case Input::CM_RIGHT:
  {
   rotation = ship->GetHeadingRotation();
   rotation.z += -1.0f;
   if (rotation.z < 0.0f)
   {
    rotation.z = 359.0f;
   }
   if (rotation.z < 359.0f && rotation.z > 180.0f)
   {
    if (rotation.z < 315.0f)
    {
     rotation.z = 315.0f;
    }
   }
   ship->SetHeadingRotation(rotation);
  }
  break;
  }
}
```

This code handles keyboard input. You will recall from RoboRacer2D that we mapped virtual commands to the following keys:

- CM_STOP: This is the spacebar. We use the spacebar as a toggle to both start and stop the ship. If the ship is stopped, pressing the spacebar sets the velocity. If the ship's velocity is greater than zero, then pressing the spacebar sets the velocity to zero.

- CM_UP: This is both the up arrow and the *W* key. Pressing either of these keys changes the heading rotation so that the ship moves up.

- CM_DOWN: This is both the down arrow and the *S* key. Pressing either of these keys changes the heading rotation so that the ship moves down.

- CM_LEFT: This is both the left arrow and the *A* key. Pressing either of these keys changes the heading rotation so that the ship moves left.

- CM_RIGHT: This is both the right arrow and the *D* key. Pressing either of these keys changes the heading rotation so that the ship moves up.

Every directional command works by retrieving the current heading angle and changing the appropriate component of the heading vector by one degree. The heading angle is used by each object's Update method to calculate a heading vector, which is used to point the camera in the Render method.

Finally, we need to call `HandleInput` from the games `Update` function. Add the following line of code to the top of the `Update` method, before the object update calls. We want to handle input first and then call each object's update method:

```
ProcessInput(p_deltaTime);
```

That's it! Pat yourself on the back and run the game. You can now use the keyboard to control the ship and navigate through your universe.

Asteroid slalom

It's now time to implement the final feature of this chapter. We are going to implement a slalom race with a twist. In a typical slalom, the point is to race around each obstacle without touching it. To keep things simple, we are going to race through each asteroid. If you successfully pass through each asteroid, you win the race.

Setting up collision detection

In order to determine whether you have passed through an asteroid, we have to implement some 3D collision detection. There are many types of collision detection, but we are going to keep it simple and implement spherical collision detection.

Spherical collision detection is a simple check to see whether the center of two 3D objects are within a certain distance of each other. As our asteroids are spheres, this will be a pretty accurate indication as to whether we have collided with one. The ship, however, is not a sphere, so this technique isn't perfect.

Let's start our collision detection coding by adding the appropriate methods to the `Model` class. Open `Model.h` and add the following methods:

```
const bool IsCollideable();
void IsCollideable(const bool collideable);
const bool CollidedWith(Model* target);
const Vec3 GetCenter() const;
void SetRadius(const float p_radius);
const float GetRadius() const;
```

Here is how we will use each method:

- `IsCollideable` is used to either get or set the `m_collideable` flag. Objects are set to collide by default. All of the objects in our game are set to collide so that we can detect if the ship has hit an asteroid. However, it is very common to have some objects in a game that you don't collide with. If you set `IsCollideable(false)`, then collision detection will be ignored.

- `CollidedWith` is the method that performs the actual collision detection.
- `GetCenter` is a helper function that calculates the center point of the object in world space.
- `SetRadius` and `GetRadius` are help functions to manage the collision radius for the object.

We also need to add two variables to track the radius and collision:

```
float m_radius;
bool m_collideable;
```

Now, open `Model.cpp` and add the following code to implement the collision methods.

First, we need to define the radius in the constructor. Add the following line of code to the constructor:

```
SetRadius(1.0f);
IsCollideable(true);
```

Now add the following methods:

```
const bool Model::IsCollideable()
{
  return m_collideable;
}

void Model::IsCollideable(const bool p_collideable)
{
  m_collideable = p_collideable;
}

const bool Model::CollidedWith(Model* p_target)
{
  if (p_target->IsCollideable() && this->IsCollideable())
  {
    const Vec3 p1 = this->GetCenter();
    const Vec3 p2 = p_sprite->GetCenter();

    float y = p2.y - p1.y;
    float x = p2.x - p1.x;
    float z = p2.z - p1.z;
    float d = x*x + y*y + z*z;

    float r1 = this->GetRadius() * this->GetRadius();
    float r2 = p_sprite->GetRadius() * p_sprite->GetRadius();
```

```
   if (d <= r1 + r2)
   {
     return true;
   }
  }
  return false;
}

const Vec3 Model::GetCenter() const
{
 Vec3 center;
 center = GetPosition();
 if (m_IsShip)
 {
  center.z = -m_position.y;
  center.x = m_position.x;
  center.y = m_position.z;
 }
 return center;
}

void Model::SetRadius(const float p_radius)
{
  m_radius = p_radius;
}

const float Model::GetRadius() const
{
  return m_radius;
}
```

- IsCollideable and the override are used to either get whether the object can be collided with or get the state of the collision flag.
- GetCenter returns the current position of the object. As we modeled all of our objects with the object origin at the center, returning the position also returns the center of the object. A more sophisticated algorithm would use the bounding size of the object to calculate the center.
- GetRadius and SetRadius manage the radius, which is required for the collision check code.
- CollidedWith is the method that performs all the work. After checking that both the current object and the target objects can collide, then the method performs the following actions:

  ○ Gets the center point of the two objects
  ○ Calculates the distance in 3D between the two centers

○   Checks to see whether the distance is less than the sum of the two radii. If so, the objects have collided:

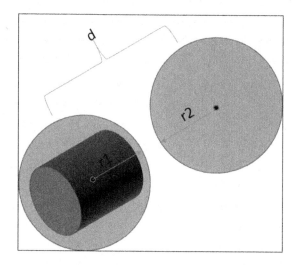

If you are astute, you will notice that this collision detection is very similar to the collision detection used in RoboRacer2D. We simply added the z dimension to the equations.

Turning on collision

Now, we will implement the collision code in our game. Open `SpaceRacer3D.cpp` and add the following function just before the `Update` function:

```
void CheckCollisions()
{
 bool collision = false;
 for (int i = 0; i < asteroids.size(); i++)
 {
  Model* item = asteroids[i];
  collision = ship->CollidedWith(item);
  if (collision)
  {
   item->IsCollideable(false);
   item->IsVisible(false);
   score++;
   asteroidsHit++;
  }
 }
}
```

This method performs the following actions:

- It defines a collision flag.
- It iterates through all of the asteroids.
- It checks to see whether the asteroid has collided with the ship.
- If the asteroid has collided with the ship, we set `IsCollideable` for the asteroid to `false`. This stops the collision from occurring multiple times as the ship passes through the asteroid. For our game, we only need to collide with each asteroid once, so this is sufficient.

We need to wire the collision into the `Update` function. Add the following line to the Update method just after the `HandleInput` call:

```
HandleCollisions();
```

That's it. We have now implemented basic collision detection!

Summary

We covered a lot of code in this chapter. You implemented a simple, yet effective framework to create and manage 3D objects in the game. This class included necessary features to load the model, position the model in 3D space, and check for collisions.

We also implemented input and collision detection in the game to create a modified slalom race, requiring you to navigate through each asteroid.

In the next chapter, we will implement a user interface and scoring system to make this a more complete game.

11
Heads Up

In this chapter, we will put some finishing touches on Space Racer 3D by adding some features that you would see in almost any game. Many of these features are similar to the finishing touches that we put on our Robo Racer 2D game, though there are some special considerations now that we are working in 3D. The topics that we will cover include the following:

- **2D in a 3D world**: So far, we learned how to render in 2D and how to render in 3D. However, there are special considerations to create 2D in a 3D world. As our user interface is typically created in 2D, we will learn how to mix the two types of rendering.

- **Creating a heads-up-display (HUD)**: It is very typical for first-person 3D games to have a continuous status showing information that is relevant to the game. We will learn how to create a basic heads-up-display or HUD.

- **More game state**: Just as we did in Robo Racer 2D, we will create a basic state manager to handle the various modes in our completed game.

- **Scoring**: We need a way to keep score in our game, and we need to set up the basic win and lose conditions.

- **Game over**: When the game is over, we'll give some credit with a 3D twist.

Mixing things up

Now that we are rendering in 3D, it isn't immediately obvious how we will render things in 2D. This is especially true of our user interface, which must be rendered on top of the 3D-scene and does not move or rotate with the rest of the world.

The trick to creating a 2D interface in a 3D world is to first render the 3D world, then switch modes in OpenGL, and then render the 2D content. The following image represents the 3D content that we need to render:

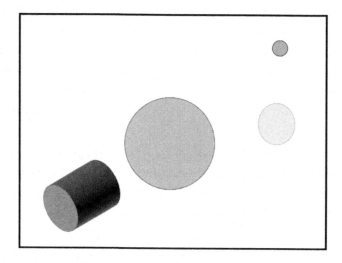

The next image represents the 2D text that we want to render:

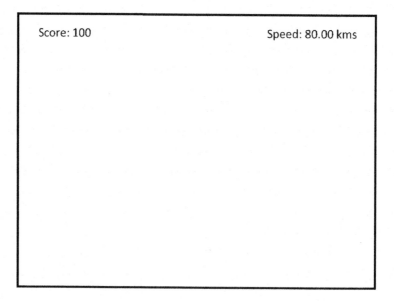

Score: 100   Speed: 80.00 kms

We want the final result to be the combination of the 3D and 2D content, as shown in the following figure:

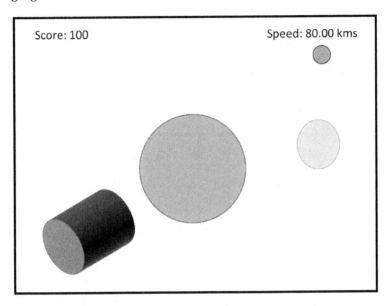

The saving state

State is a term that is used in many different ways in game programming. For example, we will create a state manager later in the chapter that will manage different states, or modes, in the game. Another way to define state is a set of conditions. For example, when we set things up to render in 3D, this is one set of conditions or state. When we set up things to render in 2D, this is another set of conditions or state.

The trick to being able to render in both 2D and 3D is to be able to set up one state, and then change to another state. OpenGL saves state in matrices. In order to change from one state to another, we need a way to save the current matrix, set up another matrix, and then return to the previous matrix once we are done.

Push and pop

OpenGL provides two methods to save the current state and then retrieve it later:

- `glPushMarix()`: This command saves the current state by placing it on the stack.
- `glPopMatrix()`: This command retrieves the previous state by pulling it off the stack.

A **stack** is a structure that allows you to put data on the top of it (a **push**), and then later retrieve the item from the top of it (a **pop**). A stack is useful when you want to save data in order, then later retrieve it in reverse order.

Let's say that we start with an initial set of conditions called **State A**:

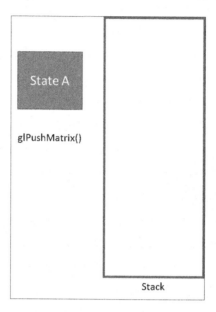

A call to `glPushMatrix()` will put **State A** on the stack:

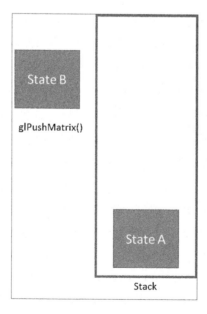

Next, we set up the conditions for **State B**. If we want to save this state, we issue another `glPushMatrix()` call:

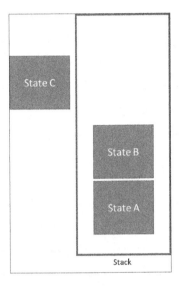

Now we have two items on the stack, and it should also be very clear why it is called a stack! We could then define **State C**. This sequence of steps can continue on as needed, creating a render state and then pushing it to the stack. In general, we want to unload the stack in the reverse order that we loaded it in. This is known as a **FILO** stack: first in, last out.

We take things off of the stack with the `glPopMatrix()` command:

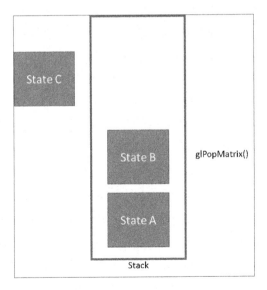

The result replaces **State C**, restoring the rendering settings to **State B**:

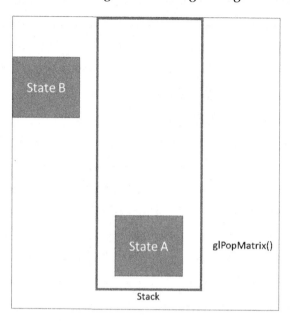

Another call to `glPopMatrix()` empties the stack and restores the rendering settings to **State A**:

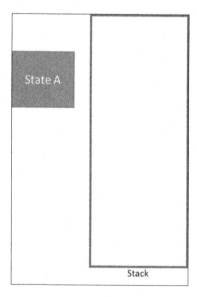

The model view allows 32 matrices to be put onto the stack. Each view has its own stack, so the projection view has a separate stack from the model view. Also, if you issue glPopMatrix and there is no matrix on the stack, you will receive an error. In other words, don't try to pop more than you have pushed!

> In order to best manage memory, you should always pop the states that you have pushed, even if you don't need to do anything with them. This frees up the memory that was being used to hold the data that was part of the state that you were saving.

Two state rendering

We are now going to set up our code to be able to render in both 3D and 2D. Open SpaceRacer3D.cpp. We are going to split up the rendering into two functions: Render3D, and Render2D. Then, we are going to call these from the main Render function. Let's start with Render3D. Add the following code just above the Render function (you can just cut it from the Render function):

```
void Render3D()
{
 if (gameState == GS_Running)
 {
  for (unsigned int i = 0; i < asteroids.size(); i++)
  {
   asteroids[i]->Render();
  }
  ship->Render();
 }
}
```

Next, we will create two support functions to turn 2D rendering on and off. The first will be Enable2D. Add the following function above the Render3D function:

```
void Enable2D()
{
  glColor3f(1.0f, 1.0f, 1.0f);
  glEnable(GL_TEXTURE_2D);

  glMatrixMode(GL_PROJECTION);
  glPushMatrix();
  glLoadIdentity();
  glOrtho(0, SCREEN_WIDTH, SCREEN_HEIGHT, 0, 0, 1);
```

```
    glMatrixMode(GL_MODELVIEW);
    glPushMatrix();
    glLoadIdentity();

    glPushAttrib(GL_DEPTH_BUFFER_BIT);
    glDisable(GL_DEPTH_TEST);
}
```

Enable2D performs the tasks that are necessary to change the rendering mode to 2D:

- The call to glColor3f sets the current drawing color to white. This takes some explanation. We will always render 3D first, then switch to 2D. If we didn't set the color to white, then all of the colors in the 2D content would be blended with the last color that was used by the 3D rendering. Setting the render color to white essentially clears the render color so that the 2D content will be rendered accurately. Setting the color to white doesn't actually mean everything will be drawn in white. It means that no additional coloring will be added to the objects that we render in 2D.

- The glEnable(GL_TEXTURE_2D) call is essential if you want to render 2D textures. If this were left out, then any 2D textures would not render correctly.

- The next four lines save the 3D projection matrix and set up the projection matrix to render in 2D. glPushMatrix pushes the current projection matrix to the stack. We then initialize the projection matrix with glLoadIdentity. Finally, we set up an orthographic projection with the call to glOrtho. Take a look at RoboRacer2D, and you will notice that it uses the same glOrtho call to set up 2D rendering!

- The next three lines save the 3D model view matrix and initialize it for our 2D drawing. glPushMatrix pushes the current model view matrix to the stack. We then initialize the model view matrix with the call to glLoadIdentity.

- Finally, we need to turn off checking on the depth buffer. The depth buffer check is only required for 3D rendering, and interferes with 2D rendering. glPushAttrib works just like glPushMatrix, except that it only pushes a single OpenGL attribute to the stack. In this case, we are pushing the current GL_DEPTH_BUFFER_BIT to the attribute stack, thus saving the current state of this bit from the previous 3D rendering. Next, we turn off depth checking with the glDisable call.

So, setting things up for 2D rendering involves four steps:

1. Reset the render color and enable 2D textures.
2. Save the 3D project matrix and set up the 2D projection matrix.
3. Save the 3D model view matrix and initialize the 2D model view matrix.
4. Save the 3D depth bit and turn off depth checking in 2D.

Now, we are ready to code the `Disable2D` function. Create this new function just below the `Enable2D` function that we just created:

```
void Disable2D()
{
  glPopAttrib();

  glMatrixMode(GL_PROJECTION);
  glPopMatrix();

  glMatrixMode(GL_MODELVIEW);
  glPopMatrix();

  glDisable(GL_TEXTURE_2D);
}
```

It shouldn't be too surprising that `Disable2D` performs actions in the reverse order that we performed them in `Enable2D`:

- First, we restore depth checking by calling `glPopAttrib()`, which takes the last attribute that was pushed to the attribute stack off the stack and restores that attribute in the current render state. This will restore depth checking to the state that it was in just before we started our 2D rendering.
- The next two lines restore the projection matrix to the 3D state it was in. Again, the call to `glPopMatrix` takes the item on the top of the stack and applies it to the current render state.
- The next two lines pop the model view matrix.
- The final line disables 2D textures.

Now, it is time to create our `Render2D` function. Add the following code just above the `Render3D` function:

```
void Render2D()
{
  Enable2D();
  // Future 2D rendering code here
  Disable2D();
}
```

The funny thing is that we don't have any 2D content to render yet! Later in the chapter, we will fill in the rest of the content of this function. The important thing to note here is that this function will take care of enabling 2D rendering with the call to `Enable2D`. Then the code will be added to render our 2D content. Finally, we will turn off 2D rendering with the call to `Disable2D`.

Now that we have all of the necessary supporting code to render in 2D and 3D, we will modify the `Render` function:

```
void Render()
{
  glClear(GL_COLOR_BUFFER_BIT | GL_DEPTH_BUFFER_BIT);
  glMatrixMode(GL_MODELVIEW);
  glLoadIdentity();
  Render3D();
  Render2D();
  SwapBuffers(hDC);
}
```

You will notice how simple this is now:

1. First, we clear the color buffer and reset the matrix. We always do this once before each frame of rendering.

2. Next, we render the 3D content.

3. Then we render the 2D content.

4. Finally, we swap the buffers, which renders all of our content to the screen.

If you run the game now, you should notice that nothing has changed. As we haven't created any 2D content to render, the 3D content will display just as it did before. Now we are ready add our 2D content. Along the way we will flesh out some additional features to make a more complete game.

A matter of state

Before we move on to actually rendering 2D items, we need to add a state machine to our game. Just as we did in RoboRacer2D, we need to be able to handle several different game states: displaying the splash screen, loading resources, displaying the main menu, running the game, pausing the game, and game over.

 Don't let the word **state** confuse you as it is used in several different ways in computer programming. We just finished a section on render state, learning how to push and pop this state from the OpenGL stacks. Now, we are talking about game state, which you can think of as the different modes that our game is in. A framework that handles different game states is known as a **state machine**.

Adding the state machine

Fortunately, we will be able to take some of the code directly from RoboRacer2D. Open up `RoboRacer2D.cpp`. You can do this from inside the SpaceRacer3D project by clicking **File**, then **Open**, and then browsing to `RoboRacer2D.cpp`. This will allow you to copy information from `RoboRacer2D.cpp` and paste it into SpaceRacer3D.

 Opening a file loads it into the current project, but it does not add the file to the current project. However, you want to be careful because if you make changes to the file and save them, the original source file will be modified.

Copy the `GameState` enum and then paste it at the top of `SpaceRacer3D.cpp` just after the header files:

```
enum GameState
{
    GS_Splash,
    GS_Loading,
    GS_Menu,
    GS_Credits,
    GS_Running,
    GS_NextLevel,
    GS_Paused,
    GS_GameOver,
};
```

We will be copying more code from `RoboRacer2D.cpp`, so go ahead and leave it open.

Next, we need to create a global game state variable. Add the following definition in the global variables section of `SpaceRacer3D.cpp`:

```
GameState gameState;
```

The `gameState` variable will store the current game state.

Getting ready for a splash

Just as we did in RoboRacer2D, we are going to start our game with a splash screen. The splash screen will be quickly loaded before any other resources, and it will be displayed for a few seconds before moving on to loading the game assets and starting the game.

Just under the definition for `gameState`, add the following lines:

```
float splashDisplayTimer;
float splashDisplayThreshold;
```

These two variables will handle the splash screen timing. Our splash screen is going to be one of the many 2D assets that we load into the game. Let's go ahead and define some variables for our 2D assets. Add the following lines of code to the global variables section of `SpaceRacer3D.cpp`:

```
Sprite* splashScreen;
Sprite* menuScreen;
Sprite* creditsScreen;
Sprite* playButton;
Sprite* creditsButton;
Sprite* exitButton;
Sprite* menuButton;
Sprite* gameOverScreen;
Sprite* replayButton;
```

You will notice that all of our 2D assets are being handled as Sprites, a class that we borrowed from RoboRacer2D.

While we are here, let's add the following two lines as well:

```
float uiTimer;
const float UI_THRESHOLD = 0.1f;
```

These two variables will be used to add a timing buffer to mouse clicks. Now, let's create a function to load the splash screen. Add the following function to `SpaceRacer3D.cpp` somewhere before the `StartGame` function:

```
void LoadSplash()
{
  gameState = GameState::GS_Splash;
  splashScreen = new Sprite(1);
  splashScreen->SetFrameSize(screenWidth, screenHeight);
  splashScreen->SetNumberOfFrames(1);
  splashScreen->AddTexture("resources/splash.png", false);
  splashScreen->IsActive(true);
  splashScreen->IsVisible(true);
  splashScreen->SetPosition(0.0f, 0.0f);
}
```

This code is exactly the same as the code from RoboRacer2D. In fact, feel free to copy and paste it directly from `RoboRacer2D.cpp`.

Remember: we set up our 2D orthographic viewport to exactly replicate the settings that we had in RoboRacer2D. This allows us to use the same exact code and positions for our 2D objects. Even better, it allows us to use the Sprite class from RoboRacer2D without changing any of the code.

> The LoadSplash function loads a file from the game resource folder called splash.png. You can download this file and all of the other 2D resources that are used in this chapter, from the book website. You should place all of them in a folder named resources under the same folder as the game source code. You also have to remember to add these resources to the **Resource Files** folder in the solution by right-clicking on **Resource Files**, then choosing **Add Existing Item**, then browsing to the resources folder and adding all of the items in that folder.

Next, we need to modify the StartGame function to load the splash screen. Move to the StartGame function add the following code:

```
LoadSplash();
uiTimer = 0.0f;
splashDisplayTimer = 0.0f;
splashDisplayThreshold = 5.0f;
```

The first thing that we do is call the LoadSplash function, which sets the game state to GS_Splash, and then loads the splash page. Next, we have to update and render the splash page. Move to the Update function and modify it so that it looks like this:

```
void Update(const float p_deltaTime)
{
 switch (gameState)
 {
 case GameState::GS_Splash:
 case GameState::GS_Loading:
 {
  splashScreen->Update(p_deltaTime);
 }
 break;
 case GameState::GS_Running:
 {
  inputManager->Update(p_deltaTime);
  ProcessInput(p_deltaTime);
  ship->Update(p_deltaTime);
  ship->SetVelocity(ship->GetVelocity() + ship->GetVelocity()*p_
deltaTime/10.0f);
  speed = ship->GetVelocity() * 1000;
  if (maximumSpeed < speed)
  {
   maximumSpeed = speed;
  }
```

```
     missionTime = missionTime + p_deltaTime * 100.0f;
     CheckCollisions();
     if (ship->GetPosition().z > 10.0f)
     {
      gameState = GS_GameOver;
      menuButton->IsActive(true);
      gameOverScreen->IsActive(true);
     }
    }
    break;
    case GameState::GS_GameOver:
    {
     gameOverScreen->Update(p_deltaTime);
     replayButton->IsActive(true);
     replayButton->Update(p_deltaTime);
     exitButton->IsActive(true);
     exitButton->Update(p_deltaTime);
     inputManager->Update(p_deltaTime);
     ProcessInput(p_deltaTime);
     ship->Update(p_deltaTime);
     CheckCollisions();
    }
    break;
    }
   }
```

The only real change is that we implemented part of the state machine. You will notice how we moved all of the code to run the game under the GS_Running game state case. Next, we added an update for the splash screen game state. We will eventually modify the Update function to handle all of the game states, but we have some more work to do yet.

Now, we are ready to render the splash screen. Move to the Render2D function and add the following line of code between the Enable2D and Disable2D calls:

```
     splashScreen->Render();
```

At this point, if you run the game, you will see a splash screen render. The game will not move beyond the splash screen because we haven't added the code to move on yet.

Creating the user interface

We are now ready to define our user interface, which will consist of 2D screens, text, and buttons. These will all work exactly as they did in RoboRacer2D. Look at the tip in the *Getting ready for a splash* section earlier in this chapter for a reminder of how to include prebuilt 2D resources in your project.

Defining the text system

The 2D text system is built by first creating a font framework, then creating functions to display text on the screen. Open `RoboRacer2D.cpp` and copy the following functions. Then paste them into `SpaceRacer3D.cpp`:

- `BuildFont`
- `KillFont`
- `DrawText`

We are going to add some new variables to handle the data that we want to display. Add the following lines of code to the global variables section of `SpaceRacer3D.cpp`:

```
int score;
int speed;
int missionTime;
int asteroidsHit;
int maximumSpeed;
```

These variables will hold the stats and scoring used by the game:

- `score`: This is the current game score
- `speed`: This is the current speed of the ship
- `missionTime`: This is the number of seconds that have elapsed since starting the mission
- `asteroidsHit`: This is the number of asteroids hit by the player
- `maximumSpeed`: This is the maximum speed obtained by the player

`Score`, `speed`, and `missionTime` will all be displayed on the heads-up-display (HUD) while the player is piloting the ship. `Score`, `asteroidsHit`, `missionTime`, and `maximumSpeed` will be displayed as stats at the end of the game.

Let's go to `StartGame` and initialize these variables:

```
score = 0;
speed = 1.0f;
maximumSpeed = 0;
asteroidsHit = 0;
missionTime = 0;
```

Now, let's create the functions to render these items on the screen. Add the following two functions to the game somewhere above the `Render2D` function:

```
void DrawUi()
{
  float startY = screenHeight - 50.0f;
  float x1 = 50.0f;
  float x2 = screenWidth / 2.0f - 50.0f;
  float x3 = screenWidth - 250.0f;

  char scoreText[50];
  char speedText[50];
  char missionTimeText[50];

  sprintf_s(scoreText, 50, "Score: %i", score);
  sprintf_s(speedText, 50, "Speed: %i", speed);
  sprintf_s(missionTimeText, 50, "Time: %f", missionTime / 100.0f);
  DrawText(scoreText, x1, startY, 0.0f, 1.0f, 0.0f);
  DrawText(speedText, x2, startY, 0.0f, 1.0f, 0.0f);
  DrawText(missionTimeText, x3, startY, 0.0f, 1.0f, 0.0f);

}

void DrawStats()
{
  float startX = screenWidth - screenWidth / 2.5f;
  float startY = 275.0f;
  float spaceY = 30.0f;

  char asteroidsHitText[50];
  char maximumSpeedText[50];
  char scoreText[50];
  char missionTimeText[50];
  sprintf_s(asteroidsHitText, 50, "Asteroids Hit: %i", asteroidsHit);
  sprintf_s(maximumSpeedText, 50, "Maximum Speed: %i", maximumSpeed);
  sprintf_s(scoreText, 50, "Score: %i", score);
  sprintf_s(missionTimeText, 50, "Time: %f", missionTime / 100.0f);
  DrawText(asteroidsHitText, startX, startY, 0.0f, 1.0f, 0.0f);
  DrawText(maximumSpeedText, startX, startY + spaceY, 0.0f, 1.0f,
0.0f);
  DrawText(scoreText, startX, startY + spaceY * 2.0f, 0.0f, 1.0f,
0.0f);
  DrawText(missionTimeText, startX, startY + spaceY * 3.0f, 0.0f, 1.0f,
0.0f);
}
void DrawCredits()
{
  float startX = screenWidth - screenWidth / 2.5f;
  float startY = 300.0f;
  float spaceY = 30.0f;
```

```
DrawText("Robert Madsen", startX, startY, 0.0f, 1.0f, 0.0f);
DrawText("Author", startX, startY + spaceY, 0.0f, 1.0f, 0.0f);
}
```

These functions work exactly like their corresponding functions in RoboRacer2D. First, we use `sprintf_s` to create a character string with the text that we want to display. Next, we use `glRasterPos2f` to set the render position in 2D. Then, we use `glCallLists` to actually render the font. In the `DrawCredits` function, we use the `DrawText` helper function to render the text.

Change `CheckCollisions` to look like the code below:

```
void CheckCollisions()
{
 bool collision = false;
 for (int i = 0; i < asteroids.size(); i++)
 {
  Model* item = asteroids[i];
  collision = ship->CollidedWith(item);
  if (collision)
  {
   item->IsCollideable(false);
   score++;
   asteroidsHit++;
  }
 }
}
```

This code updates the score and asteroid stats.

Defining textures

Now, it's time to load all of our textures. Add the following function to the game:

```
const bool LoadTextures()
{
 menuScreen = new Sprite(1);
 menuScreen->SetFrameSize(screenWidth, screenHeight);
 menuScreen->SetNumberOfFrames(1);
 menuScreen->AddTexture("resources/mainmenu.png", false);
 menuScreen->IsActive(true);
 menuScreen->IsVisible(true);
 menuScreen->SetPosition(0.0f, 0.0f);
 playButton = new Sprite(1);
 playButton->SetFrameSize(75.0f, 38.0f);
 playButton->SetNumberOfFrames(1);
```

```
playButton->SetPosition(690.0f, 300.0f);
playButton->AddTexture("resources/playButton.png");
playButton->IsVisible(true);
playButton->IsActive(false);
inputManager->AddUiElement(playButton);
creditsButton = new Sprite(1);
creditsButton->SetFrameSize(75.0f, 38.0f);
creditsButton->SetNumberOfFrames(1);
creditsButton->SetPosition(690.0f, 350.0f);
creditsButton->AddTexture("resources/creditsButton.png");
creditsButton->IsVisible(true);
creditsButton->IsActive(false);
inputManager->AddUiElement(creditsButton);
exitButton = new Sprite(1);
exitButton->SetFrameSize(75.0f, 38.0f);
exitButton->SetNumberOfFrames(1);
exitButton->SetPosition(690.0f, 500.0f);
exitButton->AddTexture("resources/exitButton.png");
exitButton->IsVisible(true);
exitButton->IsActive(false);
inputManager->AddUiElement(exitButton);
creditsScreen = new Sprite(1);
creditsScreen->SetFrameSize(screenWidth, screenHeight);
creditsScreen->SetNumberOfFrames(1);
creditsScreen->AddTexture("resources/credits.png", false);
creditsScreen->IsActive(true);
creditsScreen->IsVisible(true);
menuButton = new Sprite(1);
menuButton->SetFrameSize(75.0f, 38.0f);
menuButton->SetNumberOfFrames(1);
menuButton->SetPosition(690.0f, 400.0f);
menuButton->AddTexture("resources/menuButton.png");
menuButton->IsVisible(true);
menuButton->IsActive(false);
inputManager->AddUiElement(menuButton);
gameOverScreen = new Sprite(1);
gameOverScreen->SetFrameSize(screenWidth, screenHeight);
gameOverScreen->SetNumberOfFrames(1);
gameOverScreen->AddTexture("resources/gameover.png", false);
gameOverScreen->IsActive(true);
gameOverScreen->IsVisible(true);
replayButton = new Sprite(1);
replayButton->SetFrameSize(75.0f, 38.0f);
replayButton->SetNumberOfFrames(1);
```

```
replayButton->SetPosition(690.0f, 400.0f);
replayButton->AddTexture("resources/replayButton.png");
replayButton->IsVisible(true);
replayButton->IsActive(false);
inputManager->AddUiElement(replayButton);
return true;
}
```

There is nothing new here! We are simply loading all of our 2D assets into the game as sprites. Here are a few reminders as to how this works:

- Each sprite is loaded from a PNG file, specifying the number of frames. As none of these sprites are animated they all have one frame.
- We position each sprite with a 2D coordinate.
- We set the properties — visible means that it can be seen, and active means that it can be clicked on.
- If the object is intended to be a button, we add it to the UI system.

Wiring in render, update, and the game loop

Now that we have finally loaded all of our 2D assets, we are ready to finish the `Render2D` function:

```
void Render2D()
{
 Enable2D();
 switch (gameState)
 {
 case GameState::GS_Loading:
 {
  splashScreen->Render();
 }
 break;
 case GameState::GS_Menu:
 {
  menuScreen->Render();
  playButton->Render();
  creditsButton->Render();
  exitButton->Render();
 }
 break;
 case GameState::GS_Credits:
 {
  creditsScreen->Render();
  menuButton->Render();
  DrawCredits();
```

```
  }
  break;
case GameState::GS_Running:
  {
    DrawUi();
  }
  break;
case GameState::GS_Splash:
  {
    splashScreen->Render();
  }
  break;
case GameState::GS_GameOver:
  {
    gameOverScreen->Render();
    DrawStats();
    menuButton->Render();
  }
  break;
  }
  Disable2D();
}
```

Again, there is nothing here that you haven't seen already. We are simply implementing the full state engine.

We can also implement the full `ProcessInput` function now that we have buttons to click. Add the following lines to the `switch` statement:

```
case Input::Command::CM_UI:
  {
    if (playButton->IsClicked())
    {
      playButton->IsClicked(false);
      exitButton->IsActive(false);
      playButton->IsActive(false);
      creditsButton->IsActive(false);
      gameState = GameState::GS_Running;
    }
    if (creditsButton->IsClicked())
    {
      creditsButton->IsClicked(false);
      exitButton->IsActive(false);
      playButton->IsActive(false);
      creditsButton->IsActive(false);
      gameState = GameState::GS_Credits;
    }
```

```
if (menuButton->IsClicked())
{
 menuButton->IsClicked(false);
 exitButton->IsActive(true);
 playButton->IsActive(true);
 menuButton->IsActive(false);
 switch (gameState)
 {
 case GameState::GS_Credits:
 {
  gameState = GameState::GS_Menu;
 }
 break;
 case GameState::GS_GameOver:
 {
  StartGame();
 }
 break;
 }
}
if (exitButton->IsClicked())
{
 playButton->IsClicked(false);
 exitButton->IsActive(false);
 playButton->IsActive(false);
 creditsButton->IsActive(false);
 PostQuitMessage(0);
}
}
break;
}
```

Yep, we've seen all this before. If you recall, the Input class assigns a command enum to each button that can be clicked. This code simply processes the command, if there was any, and sets the state based on which button was just clicked.

We now implement the full Update function to handle our new state machine:

```
void Update(const float p_deltaTime)
{
 switch (gameState)
 {
 case GameState::GS_Splash:
 case GameState::GS_Loading:
 {
```

```
  splashScreen->Update(p_deltaTime);
  splashDisplayTimer += p_deltaTime;
  if (splashDisplayTimer > splashDisplayThreshold)
  {
   gameState = GameState::GS_Menu;
  }
 }
 break;
 case GameState::GS_Menu:
 {
  menuScreen->Update(p_deltaTime);
  playButton->IsActive(true);
  creditsButton->IsActive(true);
  exitButton->IsActive(true);
  playButton->Update(p_deltaTime);
  creditsButton->Update(p_deltaTime);
  exitButton->Update(p_deltaTime);
  inputManager->Update(p_deltaTime);
  ProcessInput(p_deltaTime);
 }
 break;
 case GameState::GS_Credits:
 {
  creditsScreen->Update(p_deltaTime);
  menuButton->IsActive(true);
  menuButton->Update(p_deltaTime);
  inputManager->Update(p_deltaTime);
  ProcessInput(p_deltaTime);
 }
 break;
 case GameState::GS_Running:
 {
  inputManager->Update(p_deltaTime);
  ProcessInput(p_deltaTime);
  ship->Update(p_deltaTime);
  ship->SetVelocity(ship->GetVelocity() + ship->GetVelocity()*p_
deltaTime/10.0f);
  speed = ship->GetVelocity() * 1000;
  if (maximumSpeed < speed)
  {
   maximumSpeed = speed;
  }
  missionTime = missionTime + p_deltaTime * 100.0f;
  CheckCollisions();
```

```
    if (ship->GetPosition().z > 10.0f)
    {
     gameState = GS_GameOver;
     menuButton->IsActive(true);
     gameOverScreen->IsActive(true);
    }
   }
   break;
   case GameState::GS_GameOver:
   {
    gameOverScreen->Update(p_deltaTime);
    replayButton->IsActive(true);
    replayButton->Update(p_deltaTime);
    exitButton->IsActive(true);
    exitButton->Update(p_deltaTime);
    inputManager->Update(p_deltaTime);
    ProcessInput(p_deltaTime);
   }
   break;
   }
  }
```

Finally, we need to modify the game loop so that it supports all of our new features. Move to the GameLoop function and modify it so that it looks like the following code:

```
  void GameLoop(const float p_deltatTime)
  {
   if (gameState == GameState::GS_Splash)
   {
    BuildFont();
    LoadTextures();
    gameState = GameState::GS_Loading;
   }
   Update(p_deltatTime);
   Render();
  }
```

As always, the game loop calls the Update and Render functions. We add a special case to handle the splash screen. If we are in the GS_Splash game state, we then load the rest of the resources for the game and change the game state to GS_Loading.

Note that several of the functions referenced previously haven't been created yet! We will add support for sound, fonts, and textures as we continue.

Summary

We covered a lot of code in this chapter. The main lesson in this chapter was learning how to render 2D and 3D at the same time. We then added code to load all of our 2D resources as sprites. We also added the ability to render text, and now we can see our score, stats, and credits.

We implemented that state machine for the game and wired that into the input, update, render, and game loop systems. This included creating states for a splash screen, loading resources, playing the game, and displaying various game screens.

You now have a complete 3D game. Sure, there is more that you can do with it. In the next and final chapter, we will learn a few new tricks, then the rest is up to you!

12
Conquer the Universe

Congratulations! You have come this far. If you are reading this chapter, then you have already created two games—a 2D game and a 3D game. Sure, they aren't going to sell and make you a million dollars, but you already completed more games than 90 percent of all people who try.

There is a lot more to learn, and there is no way that we can cover everything in a single book. This chapter will briefly cover a few more topics and hopefully give you at least enough information to experiment further after you are done with the book. In fact, we are going to set up a framework that will allow you to play, so we will call it the playground.

The topics that we will cover include the following:

- **The playground**: We will begin by setting up a template that you can use over and over again as you experiment with different features. This template will also be a good starting ground for any future games that you may want to create.

- **Texture mapping**: So far, we worked with color, not textures. It would be pretty difficult to make realistic games with only color. It turns out that we can put textures onto our models to make them more realistic. We will learn the basics of texture mapping on a simple 3D shape.

- **Lighting**: So far, we used the default lighting that was provided by OpenGL. Most of the time, we want more control over the lighting. We will discuss the various types of lighting and how they are used.

- **Skyboxes**: The game universe can't go on forever. We often use a device known as a skybox to surround our game world and make it look like it is larger than it really is. We will learn how to add a skybox to our space game.

- **Physics**: In the real world, objects bounce, fall, and do other things based on the laws of physics. We will discuss how objects interact with each other and the rest of the universe.

- **AI**: Many games have enemies or weapons seeking to destroy the player. These enemies are usually controlled by some form of **Artificial Intelligence (AI)**. We will discuss some simple forms of AI and learn how the game can control objects in the game.

- **Where to go from here**: Finally, I'll give you a few tips on how you can continue to improve your skills once you have completed this book. We'll talk about game engines and topics for additional study.

A fun framework

Now, it's time to create our playground. Before we start coding, let's decide on the basic features that we want to set up:

- Visual Studio project
- Windows environment
- OpenGL environment
- Game loop

That's all we are going to do for now. The idea is to set up a basic template that you can use to start any game or experimental project. We don't want to include too much in this basic framework, so we will leave out sound, input, sprite, and model loading for now. These can be added in as they are needed.

Setting up the Visual Studio project

Start a new blank project and name it FunWith3D. Make sure to add the correct libraries as we have done before in the project **Properties**, **Configuration Properties**, **Linker, Input, Additional Dependencies** property:

```
glu32.lib;opengl32.lib;SOIL.lib;
```

We are going to include the SOIL library because it is so useful to load images. You will want to copy the following files over from our SpaceRacer3D.cpp project folder:

- glut.h
- glut32.lib
- glut32.dll
- SOIL.h
- SOIL.lib

Add the following libraries to Properties, Configuration Properties, Input, and Additional Dependencies:

- `glut32.lib`
- `SOIL.lib`

Setting up the Windows environment

Create a new C++ file and name it `FunWith3D.cpp`. Then add the following code:

```
#include <windows.h>
#include <stdio.h>
#include "glut.h"
#include "SOIL.h"

const int screenWidth = 1024;
const int screenHeight = 768;

// Global Variables:
HINSTANCE hInstance = NULL;
HDC hDC = NULL;
HGLRC hRC = NULL;
HWND hWnd = NULL;

bool fullscreen = false;


// Forward declarations of functions included in this code module:
LRESULT CALLBACK WndProc(HWND, UINT, WPARAM, LPARAM);
```

Now, open `SpaceRacer3D.cpp` from the previous project and copy the following functions:

- `WinMain`
- `WndProc`

These are the header files and two functions that are required for Windows to do its stuff. All of this code has been explained in previous chapters, so I'm not going to re-explain it here. In fact, you could save yourself some typing and copy this code directly from our previous project.

Setting up the OpenGL environment

Now, it is time to set up OpenGL. Copy the following function from SpaceRacer3D and add them after the WndProc declaration:

- ReSizeGLScene
- InitGL
- KillGLWindow
- CreateGLWindow

Setting up the game loop

Now, we add the function that defines our game loop. Add these functions after the OpenGL code that you just added:

```
void StartGame()
{
}
void Update(const float p_deltaTime)
{
}

void Enable2D()
{
  glColor3f(1.0f, 1.0f, 1.0f);
  glEnable(GL_TEXTURE_2D);

  glMatrixMode(GL_PROJECTION);
  glPushMatrix();
  glLoadIdentity();
  glOrtho(0, screenWidth, screenHeight, 0, 0, 1);

  glMatrixMode(GL_MODELVIEW);
  glPushMatrix();
  glLoadIdentity();

  glPushAttrib(GL_DEPTH_BUFFER_BIT);
  glDisable(GL_DEPTH_TEST);
}

void Disable2D()
{
  glPopAttrib();

  glMatrixMode(GL_PROJECTION);
  glPopMatrix();
```

```
    glMatrixMode(GL_MODELVIEW);
    glPopMatrix();

    glDisable(GL_TEXTURE_2D);
}

void Render2D()
{
    Enable2D();
    //Add your 2D rendering here
    Disable2D();
}

void Render3D()
{
    //Add your 3D rendering here
}

void Render()
{
    glClear(GL_COLOR_BUFFER_BIT | GL_DEPTH_BUFFER_BIT);
    Render3D();
    Render2D();
    SwapBuffers(hDC);
}
void EndGame()
{
}

void GameLoop(const float p_deltatTime)
{
    Update(p_deltatTime);
    Render();
}
```

In order to be consistent with some other code that we have written, you need to add the following precompile directives in the project **Properties**, **Configuration Properties, C/C++, Preprocessor**, and **Preprocessor Definitions** property:

- _USE_MATH_DEFINES
- _CRT_SECURE_NO_WARNINGS

Congratulations! You now have a framework that you can use for any future projects and experiments. You have also just successfully reviewed the OpenGL and game code that we have been working with throughout the entire book.

You will notice that I also left the code in so that you will be able render in either 3D or 2D! All together, you now have a small yet effective start for your own game engine. I suggest that you save a copy of the folder containing this solution and project. Then, when you are ready to start a new project, you can simply copy the solution folder, give it another name, and you are ready to go. We are going to use this as the basis for any code that we write in this chapter.

> To save space and keep our little playground simple, I did not include some key features, such as input, sprites, models, and sound. If you feel that any of these are essential to your playground, then this will be your first exercise. In general, you will have to simply copy the relevant files and/or code into your project folder from the last version of SpaceRacer3D.

Texture mapping

Until now, all of our shapes and models used color, but a whole new world awaits us when we start applying textures to our models. Adding a 2D texture to a 3D model is known as **texture mapping**, or in some cases **texture wrapping**. Let's see what it takes to add a little texture to our 3D models. We are going to start with a simple cube.

First, use your favorite image editing software to create a 256 x 256 pixel square and give it some kind of texture. I will be using the following one:

Save this texture as a bitmap (BMP). We are going to use bitmaps, as opposed to PNGs, for texture mapping because the internal data structure of a bitmap happens to coincide with the data structure that is expected by OpenGL. In other words, it is easier!

I always create a folder called resources for my images. It is also a good idea to include these as resources in the Visual Studio project (right-click on the **Resources** folder in the **Solution Explorer** panel and choose **Add Existing...**, then navigate to the image).

Loading the texture

If you recall, we created a sprite class for our previous projects. We use the
AddTexture method of the Sprite class to make a call to the SOIL library to load
the image. We won't be using the Sprite class for these textures. The Sprite class
has a lot of methods and properties that don't apply to texturing 3D models, so
we are going to write our own texture loader for this use. Add the following code
somewhere above render functions:

```
void LoadTexture(const char* filepath, GLsizei height, GLsizei width,
unsigned int colordepth, GLuint &texture)
{
  unsigned char* data;
  FILE* file;

  file = fopen(filepath, "r");
  data = (unsigned char*)malloc(width * height * colordepth);
  fread(data, width * height * colordepth, 1, file);
  fclose(file);

  texture = SOIL_load_OGL_texture(filepath, SOIL_LOAD_AUTO, SOIL_
CREATE_NEW_ID, 0);
  glBindTexture(GL_TEXTURE_2D, texture);
  glTexImage2D(GL_TEXTURE_2D, 0, colordepth == 3 ? GL_RGB:GL_RGBA,
width, height, 0, colordepth == 3 ? GL_RGB:GL_RGBA, GL_UNSIGNED_BYTE,
data);
  glTexParameteri(GL_TEXTURE_2D, GL_TEXTURE_MIN_FILTER, GL_LINEAR);
  glTexParameteri(GL_TEXTURE_2D, GL_TEXTURE_MAG_FILTER, GL_LINEAR);
  free(data);
}
```

The purpose of LoadTexture is to load a texture into memory, and then set it up
to be a texture map for a 3D object. In order to accomplish this, we actually need to
load the texture twice. First, we directly open the file and read it as a binary file into
a buffer called data. We use the char datatype because we want to store the binary
data as unsigned integers and char does a really great job of this. So, our first few
lines of code:

- Define the data array
- Create a file handle
- Allocate memory for the data
- Read the file into the data buffer
- Close the file (but not the buffer)

Now, read the image a second time, though this time we use the SOIL library to read it as an OpenGL texture and use SOIL to load the texture and assign it to the OpenGL referenced by `texture`.

Then, we perform some fancy OpenGL operations on it to set it up as a model texture:

- `GL_BindTexture` simply tells OpenGL that we want this texture to be the current texture, to which we will apply the settings that follow.

- `glTexImage2D` tells OpenGL how to interpret the data that we have read in. We are telling OpenGL to treat the data as a 2D texture of the type RGB or RGBA (controlled by the `colordepth` parameter), and that the data is stored as unsigned integers (thus, the `char` data type).

- The next two functions, both calls to `glTexParameteri`, tell OpenGL how to handle the texture as it gets nearer to or farther away from the camera. They are both set up to use linear filtering to handle this level of detail.

- Finally, we close the data buffer as it is no longer needed.

We have set the `LoadTexture` function up so that you can call it for different textures based on your needs. In our case, we are first going to set up a handle to this texture. At the top of the code, add this line to the global variables section:

```
GLuint texMarble;
```

Next, we will place the call to load the texture in the `StartGame` function:

```
LoadTexture("resources/marble.bmp", 256, 256, 4, texMarble);
```

This call tells the program:

- The location of the file
- The width and height of the image
- The color depth of the image (in this case 4 = RGBA)
- The OpenGL texture handle

Rendering the cube

We are all set up now with a texture, but we need a model to texture. To keep things simple, we are going to use quads to create a cube and apply the marble texture to each face of the cube.

Just before we get started, we need to add three variables to track rotation. Add these lines to the global variables section:

```
float xrot = 1.0f;
float yrot = 1.0f;
float zrot = 1.0f;
```

Now, create the following function just below the `LoadTexture` function:

```
int DrawTexturedCube(GLvoid)
{
  glEnable(GL_TEXTURE_2D);

  glLoadIdentity();
  glTranslatef(0.0f, 0.0f, -5.0f);

  glRotatef(xrot, 1.0f, 0.0f, 0.0f);
  glRotatef(yrot, 0.0f, 1.0f, 0.0f);
  glRotatef(zrot, 0.0f, 0.0f, 1.0f);

  glBindTexture(GL_TEXTURE_2D, texMarble);

  glBegin(GL_QUADS);
  // Font Face
  glTexCoord2f(0.0f, 0.0f); glVertex3f(-1.0f, -1.0f, 1.0f);
  glTexCoord2f(1.0f, 0.0f); glVertex3f(1.0f, -1.0f, 1.0f);
  glTexCoord2f(1.0f, 1.0f); glVertex3f(1.0f, 1.0f, 1.0f);
  glTexCoord2f(0.0f, 1.0f); glVertex3f(-1.0f, 1.0f, 1.0f);
  // Back Face
  glTexCoord2f(1.0f, 0.0f); glVertex3f(-1.0f, -1.0f, -1.0f);
  glTexCoord2f(1.0f, 1.0f); glVertex3f(-1.0f, 1.0f, -1.0f);
  glTexCoord2f(0.0f, 1.0f); glVertex3f(1.0f, 1.0f, -1.0f);
  glTexCoord2f(0.0f, 0.0f); glVertex3f(1.0f, -1.0f, -1.0f);
  // Top Face
  glTexCoord2f(0.0f, 1.0f); glVertex3f(-1.0f, 1.0f, -1.0f);
  glTexCoord2f(0.0f, 0.0f); glVertex3f(-1.0f, 1.0f, 1.0f);
  glTexCoord2f(1.0f, 0.0f); glVertex3f(1.0f, 1.0f, 1.0f);
  glTexCoord2f(1.0f, 1.0f); glVertex3f(1.0f, 1.0f, -1.0f);
  // Bottom Face
  glTexCoord2f(1.0f, 1.0f); glVertex3f(-1.0f, -1.0f, -1.0f);
  glTexCoord2f(0.0f, 1.0f); glVertex3f(1.0f, -1.0f, -1.0f);
  glTexCoord2f(0.0f, 0.0f); glVertex3f(1.0f, -1.0f, 1.0f);
  glTexCoord2f(1.0f, 0.0f); glVertex3f(-1.0f, -1.0f, 1.0f);
  // Right face
  glTexCoord2f(1.0f, 0.0f); glVertex3f(1.0f, -1.0f, -1.0f);
```

```
glTexCoord2f(1.0f, 1.0f); glVertex3f(1.0f, 1.0f, -1.0f);
glTexCoord2f(0.0f, 1.0f); glVertex3f(1.0f, 1.0f, 1.0f);
glTexCoord2f(0.0f, 0.0f); glVertex3f(1.0f, -1.0f, 1.0f);
// Left Face
glTexCoord2f(0.0f, 0.0f); glVertex3f(-1.0f, -1.0f, -1.0f);
glTexCoord2f(1.0f, 0.0f); glVertex3f(-1.0f, -1.0f, 1.0f);
glTexCoord2f(1.0f, 1.0f); glVertex3f(-1.0f, 1.0f, 1.0f);
glTexCoord2f(0.0f, 1.0f); glVertex3f(-1.0f, 1.0f, -1.0f);
glEnd();

xrot += 0.01f;
yrot += 0.02f;
zrot += 0.03f;
return TRUE;
}
```

This code is very similar to the code that we used to draw a cube in a previous chapter. However, when we drew that cube, we applied color to each vertex. Now, we will apply our texture to each face. First, we set things up:

1. The first thing that we do is use glEnable(GL_TEXTURE_2D) to enable 2D textures. In our initial setup, we disabled 2D textures. If we did not enable them here, then our texture would not show up!

2. Next, we use glLoadIdentity() to initialize the current matrix.

3. We call glTranslatef(0.0f, 0.0f, -5.0f) to move the camera back (so that we will be outside the cube).

4. Three calls to glRotate3f will rotate the cube for us.

5. Then, we use glBindTexture(GL_TEXTURE_2D, texMarble) to inform OpenGL that for the next draw operations we will be using the texture referenced by texMarble.

With this setup completed, we are ready to get drawing:

1. We start with glBegin(GL_QUADS) to tell OpenGL that we will be drawing quads.

2. Now, each call comes in a pair. First a call to glTexCoord2f is followed by a call to glVertex3f. The call to glTexCoord2f tells OpenGL which part of the texture to put at the location specified by glVertex3f. In this way, we can map any point in the texture to any point in the quad. OpenGL takes care of figuring out which parts of the texture go between vertices.

3. When we are done drawing the cube, we issue the glEnd() command.

4. The last three lines update the rotation variables.

5. Finally, we have to make a call to `DrawTexturedCube` in the `Render3D` function:

```
DrawTexturedCube();
```

6. Run the program and see the cube in its textured glory!

Mapping operations

I owe you a little more explanation as to how texture mapping works. Take a look at these four lines of code from `DrawTexturedCube`:

```
glTexCoord2f(0.0f, 0.0f); glVertex3f(-1.0f, -1.0f, 1.0f);
glTexCoord2f(1.0f, 0.0f); glVertex3f(1.0f, -1.0f, 1.0f);
glTexCoord2f(1.0f, 1.0f); glVertex3f(1.0f, 1.0f, 1.0f);
glTexCoord2f(0.0f, 1.0f); glVertex3f(-1.0f, 1.0f, 1.0f);
```

These four lines define one quad. Each vertex consists of a texture coordinate (`glTexCoord2f`) and a vertex coordinate (`glVertex3f`). When OpenGL looks at a texture, here is what it sees:

No matter how big a texture is in pixels, in texture coordinates, the texture is exactly one unit wide and one unit tall. So, the first line of the preceding code tells OpenGL to take the point **(0,0)** of the texture (the upper-left corner) and map it to the next vertex that is defined (which is the upper-left hand corner of the quad, in this example). You will notice that the third line maps the coordinate **(1,1)** of the texture to the lower-right corner of the quad. In effect, we are stretching the texture across the face of the quad! However, OpenGL also adapts the mapping so that the texture doesn't look smeared, so this isn't exactly what happens. Instead, you will see some tiling in our case.

Let there be light!

Until this point, we haven't worried about lighting. In fact, we just assumed that light would be there so that we could see our images. OpenGL has a light setting that lights everything equally. This setting is turned on, by default, until we tell OpenGL that we would like to handle the lighting.

Imagine what our scene would look like if there was no lighting. In fact, this is going to happen to you some day. You will have everything set up and ready to roll, you'll run the program, and you'll get a big, black, nothing! What's wrong? You forgot to turn on the lights! Just as shown in the following image:

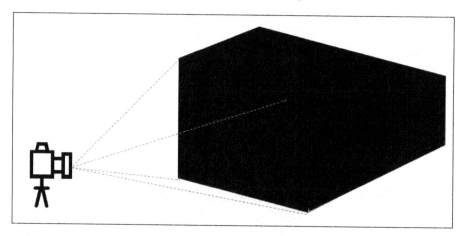

Just like real life, if you don't have a source of light, you aren't going to see anything. OpenGL has many types of lights. One common light is **ambient** light. Ambient light appears to come from all directions at the same time, similarly to how sunlight fills up a room.

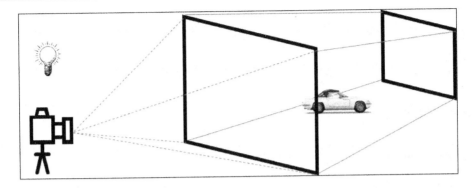

Lighting is very important in 3D games, and most games have multiple light sources to add realism to the game.

Defining a light source

Let's take over and define our own light source. Add the following lines of code to the top of the `DrawTexturedCube` function:

```
glEnable(GL_LIGHTING);
GLfloat ambientLight[] = { 0.0f, 0.0f, 1.0f, 1.0f };
glLightModelfv(GL_LIGHT_MODEL_AMBIENT, ambientLight);
glEnable(GL_COLOR_MATERIAL);
glColorMaterial(GL_FRONT, GL_AMBIENT);
```

Run the program, then come back to see what is happening:

- `glEnable(GL_LIGHTING)` tells OpenGL that we want to take control of the lighting now. Remember: once you enable lighting, it's up to you. In fact, if you enable lighting and don't define any lights, then you will get a completely black scene.

- Next, we define a color for our light. In this case, we are creating a blue light.

- Now we tell OpenGL what type of lighting we would like to use with `glLightModelfv`. In this case, we are turning on a blue, ambient light.

- Light has to have a material to reflect from. So, we use `glEnable(GL_COLOR_MATERIAL)` to tell OpenGL to use a material that will reflect color.

- The call to `glColorMaterial(GL_FRONT, GL_AMBIENT)` tells OpenGL that the front of this material should reflect light as if it was ambient light. Remember, ambient light comes from all directions.

Of course, you have already seen the result. Our cube is blue! Play around with different colors. We only have time to barely scratch the surface on lighting. You will also want to learn about diffuse lighting. Diffuse lights fade with distance. With a diffuse light, you not only set up the color, but you also place the light at a certain location.

The skybox

While space may be infinite, your computer isn't so there has to be a boundary somewhere. This boundary is called the skybox.

Imagine that our spaceship is flying through space! Space is big. While we may put some planets and asteroids in our universe to give the space ship something to interact with, we certainly won't model every star. Here is what our universe looks like:

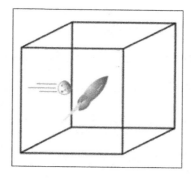

This is pretty empty, right? You probably already noticed this in our game, SpaceRacer3D. Of course, we could add some more objects of our own—more asteroids, add a bunch of stars—and in a real game, we would. But, there is always a limit to how many objects you can add to the game before you start having performance issues.

For the really distant objects, such as distant stars, we fake it by using 2D textures. For example, our game could use a texture of stars to imitate the stars and nebula in space, as shown in the following image:

Now, as a cube has six sides, what we really want is six textures. A typical skybox looks similar to the following image:

It doesn't take too much imagination to see how this texture can be wrapped around the cube and cover all size sides. This creates an image that covers all of the space encapsulated by the skybox and gives the illusion of being surrounded by stars and nebula, as shown in the following image:

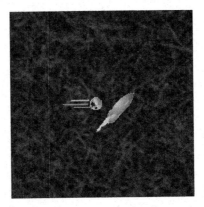

The following illustration shows the skybox in relation to the texture that will be applied to it from another perspective:

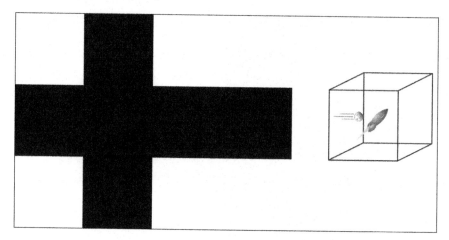

The cube containing the ship and asteroid represents the game world. The ship and asteroid are real objects in that world. The image on the left is a texture that contains the stars.

Now, imagine the star texture being wrapped around the cube, and there is your whole universe composed of the stars, the ship, and the asteroid. The star texture wrapped around the cube is the skybox.

Advanced topics

Unfortunately, for the last two topics, we only have time to give them an honorable mention. I included them because you are going to hear about these topics, and you need to know what these terms mean.

Game physics

Game physics are the rules that define how objects interact with other objects inside the game universe. For example, in SpaceRacer3D, the ship simply passes through the asteroids. However, there could be many other outcomes:

- The ship and asteroid could bounce off of each other (rebound)
- The ship could be sucked into the asteroid with the force increasing as the ship got closer (gravity)
- The asteroid could push against the ship the closer the ship got to it (reverse gravity)

Each of these effects would be programmed into the game. Each of these effects would also create a different kind of gameplay. An entire genre of games known as physics-based games simply define the laws of physics for a game universe and then let things interact to see what will happen.

AI

AI, or **artificial intelligence**, is another set of rules that defines how characters or objects that are controlled by the compute behave. AI is typically applied to enemies and other **Non-player Characters** (**NPCs**) to give them a life-like appearance in the game. Some examples of AI include:

- A mine that automatically detects that the enemy is close and blows up
- A homing missile that locks onto a space ship and draws closer no matter how the ship navigates
- An enemy character who detects that the player coming and hides behind a rock

AI is typically considered one of the most difficult areas of game programming. Some algorithms are quite easy (for example, the homing missile only needs the ships position to know how to track it), while others are very complex (for example, hiding behind a rock). Some games even provide an AI opponent for you to play against.

The future

You have, indeed, come a long way. If you are reading these words, and especially if you wrote all of the code along the way, then you have achieved a great accomplishment, but there is still so much to learn. I encourage you to find other books and never stop learning. The only thing that will stop you from becoming a great game programmer is you!

Summary

As always, we covered a lot of topics in this chapter. You learned how to map a texture onto an object, then you learned how to turn the lights on. You learned how a skybox can be used to make your world seem larger than it is. And you got just a taste of physics and AI, topics which could easily fill entire books on their own. Don't stop until you have got every piece of code in this book to work for you, and then start changing the code to different and amazing things.

Good luck!

Index

Symbols

2D, in 3D world
  interface, creating 268, 269
  pop 269-273
  push 269-273
  state, rendering 273-276
  state, saving 269
3D Coordinate Systems 194-196
3D game
  creating 202
  OpenGL files, retrieving 204
  project, creating 202, 203
  projects, linking to OpenGL libraries 204
3D model 194
3D object
  creating 231
  creating, with Blender 231
  exporting 235
  loading 236-239
  spaceship, building 232-235
3D space
  working on 220
_tWinMain function 11

A

alpha channel 48
ambient light 302
anatomy, _tmain function
  glutCreateWindow() function 24
  glutDisplayFunc() function 24
  glutInitWindowPosition() function 24
  glutInitWindowSize() function 24
  glutMainLoop() function 24
  initGL() function 24

  return 0 function 25
animation
  about 45
  background, scrolling 76, 77
  character movement, implementing 73
  delta time, calculating 74, 75
  delta time, using 73, 74
  implementing 71
  texture, flipping 75, 76
  update, adding to game loop 71
  Update function, implementing 71, 72
  Update function, implementing in
      Sprite class 72, 73
artificial intelligence (AI) 307
asteroid slalom
  collision detection, setting up 261-263
  collision, implementing 264, 265
  implementing 261
atlas
  about 45
  using 77
Audacity 170
audio
  about 168
  file formats 168, 169
  releasing 190
  sounds, creating 169, 170

B

Blender
  about 33, 231
  installing 231
  overview 232
  URL 231

boundary checking
about 106
anchor point, determining 106-109
background, defining 115, 116
collision rectangle, defining 110-112
embedding 113-115

C

callback function 82
camera
about 196
controlling 196
fixed camera, using 197
viewport 197, 198
Central Processing Unit (CPU) 14
circular collision detection
advantages 124, 125
coding 122-124
implementing 120
Pythagorean Theorem, using 121, 122
wiring 125, 126
cleanup, of resources
about 188
audio, releasing 190
fonts, releasing 190
input, releasing 189
sprites, releasing 188, 189
code
header files 23
main entry point 24
points, drawing 25, 26
update function 25
collideables
about 116
score, creating 116
spawn timer, setting 117-120
sprite, adding for pickup 117
column major order 201
composite 43
coordinate system 19
Cozendey
URL 170
credits screen
adding 151
betting back, to main menu 152, 153
creating 151, 152

D

delta time
calculating 74, 75
using 73
development environment
about 1, 2
project, starting with 6, 7
Visual Studio 3
DirectX
about 14
versus OpenGL 201
drawPoints function 25

E

embedding 109
EndGame function 13
event driven operating system 82

F

FILO stack 271
fixed camera
using 197
flipbook animation 46
flipping, texture 75, 76
FMOD
.dll files, accessing 172
about 171
channel priority 178, 179
header files, including 175, 176
initializing 177
linking, to library 172-175
URL 171
virtual channels 178
fonts
creating 154
font support, implementing 156, 157
releasing 190
text, drawing 155, 156
working with 154
framed animation 47
frames per second (fps) 9

G

game
  plotting 20
game engine 8
game level
  defining 159
  game, continuing 161, 162
  game progression, adding 158
  game stats, displaying 160, 161
  implementing 157
  next level screen, implementing 161
  score, displaying 157
game loop
  about 7
  setting up 294-296
GameLoop function 13
game objects, SpaceRacer3D
  loading 243
  Model class header, creating 244-246
  Model class, implementing 246-253
game over screen
  adding 162
  creating 163
  game, replaying 164, 165
game physics 306
game state
  defining 134
  input function 139
  new state, defining 139
  render function 139
  splash screen, loading 278, 280
  state machine 135
  state machine, adding 277
  state, planning 137, 138
  update function 139
game structure
  about 7, 8
  creating 9-11
  game loop 8
  initialization 8
  port of access 11
  shutdown 9
  Windows message loop 11-13
GIMP
  URL 47
glEnd() function 26

glPopMatrix() command 269
glPushMarix() command 269
GlueIt
  URL 60
GLUT files
  URL, for download 23
graphical user interface
  about 95
  button, creating 95
  buttons, adding 99, 100
  buttons, pushing 98, 99
  Input class, enhancing 95, 96
  UI element, checking 97
  UI elements, adding 96, 97
graphics bus
  about 222
  clipping 222
  Graphics Processing Unit 222
  lighting 222
  primitives 222
  projection 222
  rasterization 222
  shading 223
  transformation 222
graphics card
  processing 220-223
  structure 221
Graphics Processing Unit (GPU) 9, 14

H

header files, code
  glut.h 23
  stdafx.h 23
  windows.h 23

I

identity matrix 202
initGL function 23
input
  about 79, 80
  adding, to game loop 90
  implementing 82
  Input class, creating 86, 87
  Input class, implementing 89, 90
  keyboard input 80
  keyboard inputs, handling 85

message queue, handling 84, 85
mouse, handling 85
mouse, using 80
other inputs 81
processing 91-93
querying 88
releasing 189
Sprite class, modifying 94
touch 81
virtual key codes 87, 88
WndProc event listener, using 82-84
Integrated Development Environments (IDEs) 1

K

keyboard input 80

L

LAME
URL 171
left-hand coordinate system 196
lights
light source, defining 303
setting up 302, 303
line
Gl_Line_Loop 227
Gl_Lines 226
Gl_Line_Strip 226
lossless compression algorithm 48

M

matrix
about 199
identity matrix 202
vectors 199, 200
vectors, combining 200, 201
Maya 33
menu
adding 147
buttons, defining 148-151
creating 147, 148
mouse
using 80
music
adding 187

N

Non-player Characters (NPCs) 307
non-sprites
versus sprites 46

O

OpenGL
about 13, 14
adding, to project 15
coordinate system 20
DirectX 14
downloading 14
environment, setting up 294
files, retrieving 204
initializing 23
libraries, linking to projects 204
linking to 15-17
matrices 209
overview 13
URL 14
versus DirectX 201
OpenGL coordinate system
about 20
code, using 23
point, creating 21, 22
point, stretching 27, 28
program, running 26, 27
OpenGL window
creating 211-215
event handler, creating 215, 216
function, creating 207
game, executing 217
Game loop, adding 216
global variables, defining 206
header files, including 206
initializing 209, 210
removing 210, 211
setting up 205, 206
sizing 207-209
orthographic projection 208

P

parallax 193
perspective 192
perspective projection 208

pickups 116
playground
  creating 292
  game loop, setting up 294, 296
  OpenGL environment, setting up 294
  Visual Studio project, setting up 292, 293
  Windows environment, setting up 293
PNGs 47, 49
point
  creating 226
  Gl_Points 226
point sprites 226
pop
  using 269-273
powerups 116
primitives
  about 19, 29
  drawing 224, 225
  example 30-32
  geodesic dome 29, 30
  line 223, 226
  point 223
  point, creating 226
  quad 224, 229
  triangle 223, 227
  triangles, converting to models 32
project 15
push
  using 269-273
Pythagorean Theorem
  using 121, 122

Q

quad
  about 36, 229
  coding 37, 38
  Gl_Quads 229
  Gl_Quad_Strip 229

R

real 3D 193, 194
rectangular collision detection
  coding 130-132
  enemy, creating 127
  enemy, spawning 127-129
  implementing 127

wiring 132
rendering
  about 65, 223
  GetCurrentFrame function,
    implementing 70
  render, adding to game loop 65
  Render function, implementing 66
  Render function, implementing in
    Sprite class 67, 68
  UV mapping 69
rendering library 8
render process 8
right-hand coordinate system 196
row major order 201

S

score
  displaying 157, 158
Simple OpenGL Image Library (SOIL)
  about 49
  advantages 49
  image file, opening 51
  linking 50, 51
  SOIL header file, including 51
  URL 49
skybox
  defining 304-306
solution 15
sound effects
  adding 180
  need for 179
  setting up 180-182
  sounds, playing 182-184
  used, for UI feedback 185-187
SpaceRacer3D
  game code, modifying 253-256
  game code, reusing 258
  game objects, loading 243
  input, implementing 258-261
  loading 241
  project, preparing 242
splash screen
  adding 143
  creating 143
  defining 144, 145
  loading 278, 280

resources, loading 145, 147
sprites
  about 45
  creating 47
  flipbook animation 46
  framed animation 47
  frames, creating 58
  frames, saving 59
  loading 61-64
  loading, from individual textures 59
  PNGs 47-49
  releasing 188, 189
  sprite class, creating 52-58
  sprite sheet, creating 60
  sprite sheet, loading 61
  versus non-sprites 46
sprite sheet 45
stack 270
StartGame function 12
state machine
  about 135
  adding 277
  advantages 135-137
  implementing 139-143
state management
  about 100
  game, pausing 101-104
  state manager, creating 101

T

Texture Atlas Generator
  URL 77
texture mapping
  about 296
  cube, rendering 298-300
  performing 301, 302
  texture, loading 297, 298
textures
  about 19, 33
  flipping 75, 76
  loading 38, 39
  quad 36
  quad, coding 37, 38
  quad, creating 42
  reference (pivot point) 35, 36
  rendering 38

  used, for filling triangles 33-35
  wrapping 39-41
texture wrapping. *See* **texture mapping**
three dimension (3D)
  3D Coordinate Systems 194-196
  implementing 191, 192
  real 3D 193, 194
  simulating 192, 193
TinyXML
  URL 78
touch 81
transformations 201
translation matrix 200
triangle
  about 227
  Gl_Triangle_Fan 228
  Gl_Triangles 228
  Gl_Triangle_Strip 228

U

UI feedback
  sound effects, used 185-187
Unity Asset Store
  about 170
  URL 170
user interface
  creating 280
  GameLoop function, implementing 285-289
  Render function, implementing 285-289
  text system, defining 281-283
  textures, defining 283-285
  Update function, implementing 285-289
UV mapping 69

V

vanishing point 192
vectors
  about 199, 200
  combining 200, 201
velocity property 73
viewport 197, 198
virtual channels
  about 178
  priority 178, 179
virtual key codes 87, 88

Visual Studio
about 2, 3
code window 5
options 2
output window 6
project, setting up 292, 293
Solution Explorer panel 4
Standard Toolbar panel 4
start screen 3
URL 1
Visual Studio 2013 Express for Windows Desktop 2
Visual Studio Express 1

W

weapons
drawing 223
face, saving 229
primitives 223
pyramid, creating 230
Windows environment
setting up 293
Windows Message (WM) 83

Thank you for buying
OpenGL Game Development By Example

About Packt Publishing

Packt, pronounced 'packed', published its first book, *Mastering phpMyAdmin for Effective MySQL Management*, in April 2004, and subsequently continued to specialize in publishing highly focused books on specific technologies and solutions.

Our books and publications share the experiences of your fellow IT professionals in adapting and customizing today's systems, applications, and frameworks. Our solution-based books give you the knowledge and power to customize the software and technologies you're using to get the job done. Packt books are more specific and less general than the IT books you have seen in the past. Our unique business model allows us to bring you more focused information, giving you more of what you need to know, and less of what you don't.

Packt is a modern yet unique publishing company that focuses on producing quality, cutting-edge books for communities of developers, administrators, and newbies alike. For more information, please visit our website at www.packtpub.com.

About Packt Open Source

In 2010, Packt launched two new brands, Packt Open Source and Packt Enterprise, in order to continue its focus on specialization. This book is part of the Packt Open Source brand, home to books published on software built around open source licenses, and offering information to anybody from advanced developers to budding web designers. The Open Source brand also runs Packt's Open Source Royalty Scheme, by which Packt gives a royalty to each open source project about whose software a book is sold.

Writing for Packt

We welcome all inquiries from people who are interested in authoring. Book proposals should be sent to author@packtpub.com. If your book idea is still at an early stage and you would like to discuss it first before writing a formal book proposal, then please contact us; one of our commissioning editors will get in touch with you.

We're not just looking for published authors; if you have strong technical skills but no writing experience, our experienced editors can help you develop a writing career, or simply get some additional reward for your expertise.

OpenGL Development Cookbook

ISBN: 978-1-84969-504-6   Paperback: 326 pages

Over 40 recipes to help you learn, understand, and implement modern OpenGL in your applications

1. Explores current graphics programming techniques including GPU-based methods from the outlook of modern OpenGL 3.3.

2. Includes GPU-based volume rendering algorithms.

3. Discover how to employ GPU-based path and ray tracing.

4. Create 3D mesh formats and skeletal animation with GPU skinning.

Building Android Games with OpenGL ES [Video]

ISBN: 978-1-78328-613-3   Duration: 01:42 hours

A comprehensive course exploring the creation of beautiful games with OpenGL ES

1. Create captivating games through creating simple and effective codes in Java.

2. Develop a version of the classic game Breakout and see how to monetize it.

3. Step-by-step instructions and theoretical concepts describe each activity before you implement them.

Please check **www.PacktPub.com** for information on our titles

OpenGL 4 Shading Language Cookbook
Second Edition

ISBN: 978-1-78216-702-0   Paperback: 394 pages

Over 70 recipes demonstrating simple and advanced techniques for producing high-quality, real-time 3D graphics using OpenGL and GLSL 4.x

1. Discover simple and advanced techniques for leveraging modern OpenGL and GLSL.

2. Learn how to use the newest features of GLSL including compute shaders, geometry, and tessellation shaders.

3. Get to grips with a wide range of techniques for implementing shadows using shadow maps, shadow volumes, and more.

Learning Game Physics with Bullet Physics and OpenGL

ISBN: 978-1-78328-187-9   Paperback: 126 pages

Practical 3D physics simulation experience with modern feature-rich graphics and physics APIs

1. Create your own physics simulations and understand the various design concepts of modern games.

2. Build a real-time complete game application, implementing 3D graphics and physics entirely from scratch.

3. Learn the fundamental and advanced concepts of game programming using step-by-step instructions and examples.

CPSIA information can be obtained at www.ICGtesting.com
Printed in the USA
BVOW09s1028070316

439351BV00019B/318/P